D0962585

Praise for
Your Brand, The Next Media Company

"There's a difference between being a thought-leader and a do-leader. Thought leaders can tell you what you should be doing, but often have no practical, real-world experience translating thought into action. Do-leaders, on the other hand, are seasoned professionals who base their advice on what they've accomplished and failed at—a huge value add for any organization. Michael Brito, Senior Vice President of Social Business Strategy at Edelman Digital, is the epitome of a do-leader.

"In his book, *Your Brand, The Next Media Company*, he concisely breaks down one of the biggest challenges brands face today: developing, and more importantly living, their content strategy. By deftly tying team roles and responsibilities to the management of converged media programs, he takes a three-dimensional view of content strategy that's usually missed out on by leaders who push for ideals over ideas. And unlike some tell-all handbooks with little to offer besides tired to-do lists and recycled suggestions, he does it through intelligently-structured narrative that's peppered with applicable, pragmatic advice. *Your Brand, The Next Media Company* belongs on the bookshelf of every CMO."

—**Jascha Kaykas-Wolff**, Chief Marketing Officer, Mindjet

"Brito has written a practical and thoroughly engaging book for brands looking to effectively become a media company using a sustainable social business strategy. Whether early in the process or evolving your current approach, Brito's holistic view provides actionable insights to help you navigate both the internal and external challenges we all face. I recommend this book to anyone who wants their brand to remain relevant in a world where meaningful and authentic connections with social customers are now tables stakes!"

—**Amy Kavanaugh**, Vice President Public Affairs, Taco Bell (YUM Brands)

"Whether your business is selling widgets or services, success depends on thinking more in terms of delivering stories about those widgets or services and how people use them than about pumping out feature-rich fact sheets or ads. Your customers want to hear those stories, so find more ways to tell them! Reach out to your brand advocates and collaborate with them, and don't forget to include quality of engagement in your metrics for a better overall view of how you're doing. In other words, think like a publisher—you'll get better results. In his book *Your Brand, The Next Media Company*, Michael Brito walks you through this process and tells you how to get it done. A must-read for any marketer in this quickly evolving social world."

—**Ted Rubin**, Chief Social Marketing Officer, Collective Bias

"The future of digital media is alive and well, and it's you. In *Your Brand, The Next Media Company*, Michael Brito provides a clear roadmap for transforming your business into a more relevant, social, and meaningful media company. He has followed up a fantastic book on social business with a roadmap for transforming your company into an agile, ubiquitous, and relevant content machine; and he covers all bases from social business to content marketing to structuring your organization for success."

—**Lee Odden**, Founder and CEO of TopRank Online Marketing

"Every company is a media company, no matter your business model. I've been preaching this for over 7 years, and Michael Brito offers one of the most lucid and useful resources on the topic yet. Buy this book, you won't regret it."

—**Brian Clark**, CEO of Copyblogger Media

"Content Marketing is no longer just a concept, it's a way of business. Whether you are small business, nonprofit, or a large corporation, you need to read this book to learn the why and the how to setup your organization to become a media company. Michael Brito's experience and expertise are second to none, and he provides expansive and detailed approaches that are applicable to everyone."

—**Adam Hirsch**, Executive Vice President, Edelman Digital

"An incredibly accurate assessment of the social customer and the challenges we face today in garnering their attention. Brito captures the very essence of what it takes for brands to cultivate awareness and loyalty in today's saturated content marketplace. Packed with first-hand knowledge from tenured marketing and agency executives, this text is a must-read for anyone invested in tackling the content marketing space and making a true impact on the industry and, most importantly, the consumer."

—**Shafqat Islam**, Cofounder and CEO of NewsCred

"Yes, we are all media companies now…but so many brands don't know how to make this important transition. Take this book, read it, and put it under your pillow. This book will transform your marketing from 'also ran' to dominating your informational niche. Now is the time!"

—**Joe Pulizzi**, Founder, Content Marketing Institute

"Social media is causing a fundamental shift in the structure of business—both internally and externally. At this tumultuous time, *Your Brand, The Next Media Company* provides a clear map to guide your organization through the decisions you need to make NOW to ensure you stay relevant and evolve into a media company."

—**Josh March**, Cofounder and CEO of Conversocial

Your Brand, The Next Media Company

How a Social Business Strategy Enables Better Content, Smarter Marketing, and Deeper Customer Relationships

MICHAEL BRITO

800 East 96th Street,
Indianapolis, Indiana 46240 USA

Your Brand, The Next Media Company

Copyright © 2014 by Pearson Education

All rights reserved. No part of this book shall be reproduced, stored in a retrieval system, or transmitted by any means, electronic, mechanical, photocopying, recording, or otherwise, without written permission from the publisher. No patent liability is assumed with respect to the use of the information contained herein. Although every precaution has been taken in the preparation of this book, the publisher and author assume no responsibility for errors or omissions. Nor is any liability assumed for damages resulting from the use of the information contained herein.

ISBN-13: 978-0-7897-5161-4
ISBN-10: 0-7897-5161-5

Library of Congress Control Number: 2013945453

Printed in the United States of America

First Printing: October 2013

Trademarks

All terms mentioned in this book that are known to be trademarks or service marks have been appropriately capitalized. Que Publishing cannot attest to the accuracy of this information. Use of a term in this book should not be regarded as affecting the validity of any trademark or service mark.

Warning and Disclaimer

Every effort has been made to make this book as complete and as accurate as possible, but no warranty or fitness is implied. The information provided is on an "as is" basis. The author(s) and the publisher shall have neither liability nor responsibility to any person or entity with respect to any loss or damages arising from the information contained in this book.

Bulk Sales

Que Publishing offers excellent discounts on this book when ordered in quantity for bulk purchases or special sales. For more information, please contact

U.S. Corporate and Government Sales
1-800-382-3419
corpsales@pearsontechgroup.com

For sales outside of the U.S., please contact

International Sales
international@pearsoned.com

Editor-in-Chief
Greg Wiegand

Acquisitions Editor
Michelle Newcomb

Development Editor
Ginny Munroe

Managing Editor
Kristy Hart

Project Editor
Elaine Wiley

Copy Editor
Chrissy White

Senior Indexer
Cheryl Lenser

Proofreader
Kathy Ruiz

Technical Editor
Ariel Schwartz

Editorial Assistant
Cindy Teeters

Cover Designer
TJ Johnson

Cover Compositor
Alan Clements

Senior Compositor
Gloria Schurick

Que Biz-Tech Editorial Board
Michael Brito
Jason Falls
Rebecca Lieb
Simon Salt
Peter Shankman

TABLE OF CONTENTS

SECTION 2: SETTING THE STAGE FOR SOCIAL BUSINESS TRANSFORMATION

3 Establishing a Centralized "Editorial" Social Business Center of Excellence

4 Empowering Employees, Customers, and Partners to Feed the Content Engine

Foreword

The diet for media consumption by your customers is ferocious.

Are you properly feeding them before your competitor does?

Newsfeeds, inboxes, streams, and apps mean that people take in lots of information in a rapid pace. Unfortunately, most corporations have yet to catch up with this trend, as they slowly move forward with static websites, lengthy white papers, and tiring press releases.

Consumption preferences aren't the only thing that's changed, as people themselves are media engines, creating content to connect to their trusted peers and confidants. Together, the market is talking to itself, but many companies are unable to keep up.

Companies must change. They must become like media brands, and become publishers, content creators, and newsrooms themselves. To do this isn't easy, you need a purpose, a plan, a process, and the right people.

This is why this book, *Your Brand, The Next Media Company* matters.

Because you must develop the right content, improve your marketing, engage your customer relationships in a deeper way, in their terms. Michael's book answers why and how by illustrating the changes in the space, provides pragmatic advice by advising on change management, process/workflow creation, and technology.

What makes Michael credible? I've worked with Michael when he was my client at Intel. Together, we partnered on a study to measure the social behaviors of its customers, when I was an industry analyst at Forrester research.

Not only was Michael a practice leader from one of the top media brands in the world, he was an educator, as I've seen him speak at Stanford, address audiences at events, and be a community leader in the Silicon Valley space.

Today, Michael brings together market thought leadership, but tightly winds it with pragmatic insights from working with his own clients at Edelman, and shares his viewpoints on his own website, the Social Business Blog, Britopian. I consider Michael a friend, a respected peer, and an industry leader.

So get out there, read this book, earmark important pages, highlight key sections, and activate Your Brand to become a media company.

Let's feed our customers with the media they desire.

Jeremiah Owyang
Industry Analyst

About the Author

Michael Brito is a Senior Vice President of Social Business Strategy at Edelman Digital. He provides strategic counsel to several of Edelman's top global accounts and is responsible for delivering social business and content strategy, community management operations and also helps his clients scale social programs globally. Previously, Michael worked for major brands in Silicon Valley including Hewlett Packard, Yahoo!, and Intel Corporation working in various marketing, social media, and community management roles.

He is a frequent speaker at several industry conferences as well as a guest lecturer at various universities including UC Berkeley, the University of San Francisco, Stanford University, Syracuse University, Golden Gate University, and Saint Mary's College of California. He is also an Adjunct Professor at San Jose State University and UC Berkeley and teaches social business and strategic social media to undergraduate and graduate students.

Michael has a Bachelor of Arts in Business degree from Saint Mary's College and a Master of Science, Integrated Marketing Communications degree from Golden Gate University. He proudly served eight years in the United States Marine Corps. Michael is also the author of *Smart Business, Social Business: A Playbook For Social Media In Your Organization*, which was released in July 2011.

Dedication

This book is dedicated to the three most important people in my life—my wife, Kathy, and two daughters, Milan and Savvy. Kathy, thank you for supporting me all these years. I couldn't do what I do without your love, support, and encouragement. Milan, you will always be my princess, the air I breathe. Your smile brings joy and warmth to my heart. Savvy, my next book will be one that we do together. Thank you for always wanting to sit on my lap, climb on my back, and snuggle with me on the couch. I cherish those moments. Thank you all for loving me and making all the bad guys go away.

Acknowledgments

First, I want to thank my mentor Jeremiah Owyang for writing the Foreword of this book. I have learned a lot from you over the years and I am grateful for your friendship.

I also want to thank several of the vendors that helped me with various chapters specifically, Sprinklr, Social Flow, Jive, Spredfast, Expion, Compendium, GaggleAMP, Napkin Labs, Kapost, Outbrain, Skyword, Tickr, Tracx, Newscred, HootSuite, Contently, Mutual Mind, One Spot, and InPowered. There are too many of you personally to name but I really do appreciate your support. You know who you are!

A special thank you to Joe Chernov, Ann Handley, Jascha Kaykas-Wolff, Sean McGinnis, Michael Brenner, Sandra Zoratti, Jeff Elder, Danny Brown, Carla Johnson, and Dave Kerpen for your help and contributions to various portions of the book.

Lastly, I want to thank the special people who spent time reviewing my book and suffered reading through all the documentation that I had sent along. I am very humbled and grateful for each of you:

- Jascha Kaykas-Wolff, Chief Marketing Officer, Mindjet

- Pete Cashmore, CEO, Mashable

- Elisa Steele, Chief Marketing Officer, Skype (Microsoft)

- Amy Kavanaugh, Vice President Public Affairs, Taco Bell (YUM Brands)

- Shafqat Islam, CEO, NewsCred

- Brian Clark, CEO, Copyblogger Media

- Ted Rubin, Chief Social Marketing Officer, Collective Bias

- Ann Handley, Chief Content Officer, MarketingProfs

- Lee Odden, Author of *Optimize* and CEO, TopRank

- Mei Lee, Vice President, Digital Marketing, Conde Nast

- Adam Hirsch, Senior Vice President, Edelman Digital

- Kinsey Schofield, TV Personality, Journalist

- Joe Pulizzi, Founder, Content Marketing Institute

- Joshua March, CEO, ConverSocial

Thank you again for your gift of kind words.

We Want to Hear from You!

As the reader of this book, *you* are our most important critic and commentator. We value your opinion and want to know what we're doing right, what we could do better, what areas you'd like to see us publish in, and any other words of wisdom you're willing to pass our way.

We welcome your comments. You can email or write to let us know what you did or didn't like about this book—as well as what we can do to make our books better.

Please note that we cannot help you with technical problems related to the topic of this book.

When you write, please be sure to include this book's title and author as well as your name and email address. We will carefully review your comments and share them with the author and editors who worked on the book.

Email: feedback@quepublishing.com

Mail: Que Publishing
ATTN: Reader Feedback
800 East 96th Street
Indianapolis, IN 46240 USA

Reader Services

Visit our website and register this book at quepublishing.com/register for convenient access to any updates, downloads, or errata that might be available for this book.

Why This Book Matters Right Now and for the Next Several Years!

Tweetable Moment: *Everyone is influential and through everyday conversations we influence others down the purchase funnel.*
—#nextmediaco

About a year ago, I bought a special gift for my six-year-old daughter Savvy for her birthday. His name is Bailey, and he is a Teacup Yorkie. He was the cutest puppy ever, and we have taught him how to sit, shake, lie down, and roll over. He's well-behaved and super spoiled, and he has certainly become a major part of our family. If you and I are friends on Facebook, Twitter, or Instagram, you already know this.

In the summer of 2012, we were planning a trip to Arizona to see my mom and sisters. My first thought was Bailey. Do we take him with us? Do we leave him in a kennel or find him a babysitter? I wasn't about to leave my newly adopted son with a stranger, and unfortunately we didn't have anyone to watch him for a few days. I decided that he would join us, but I wasn't sure which airline was dog friendly. After all, he was our first family pet.

So I hit up Google as I normally do in situations like this.

My first search query was something like "airlines that treat dogs safely," but nothing of value came up. After about five minutes of searching, I came across an article that horrified me. The article, "More Pets Died on Delta Flights in 2011, but Why?" was straight from Yahoo!:

> More pets died on Delta flights in 2011 than on any other airline, a government report reveals.
>
> The report, issued each year by the U.S. Department of Transportation, shows that 19 of the 35 air travel–related pet deaths in 2011 took place in the baggage holds of Delta planes, up from 16 in 2010. Five pets were also injured on Delta in the same year, more than on any other airline.

After reading the full article, it was obvious that the pets' owners may have been as much to blame as the airline. But still, the only thing that stuck was that 19 of 35 air travel–related deaths happened on Delta Airlines in 2011, which was also up from 16 in 2010. So I did what a normal social media user would do and solicited feedback from my online community; I also tweeted the article and mentioned Delta a few times. Several of my friends then had some misgivings about giving their future business to Delta without clarification or explanation about this report. One friend even sent me a private note afterward and told me about his personal horror story with the airline.

So I booked our family trip with Southwest.

I can't be certain there wasn't some technology glitch, but no one from Delta ever responded—not a word from marketing, customer service, or management—all silent.

The point here is that everyone is influential despite your Klout score or how many friends, fans, or followers you have. Me, you, people who use Twitter and Facebook or don't use Twitter and Facebook, online and offline. Through everyday, random and organic conversations, we influence others to buy certain products or services or to not buy certain products or services. And these conversations are based on our personal experiences that we have with a brand on a given day. We either influence others or are being influenced by others—it's the world we live in today. Even if someone from Delta responded and said that they were taking measures to prevent situations like this in the future, it doesn't necessarily mean I would have changed my mind, although I certainly would have taken it into consideration.

We are not only influential, but we are also busy. There is a content and media surplus in the marketplace and most consumers have an attention deficit.

Every day, consumers are so inundated with media, social connections, status and relationship updates, event invites, tweets, retweets, mentions, direct messages,

+1s, likes, loves, texts, emails, alerts, and other random noise that we purposely create filters so that we only consume the content that is relevant to us at a specific moment in time. And the fact that we must hear, see, or interact with a message three to five times before we acquiesce to it becomes extremely problematic, especially for those who work in brand or marketing communications.

So for you to reach the dynamic and unpredictable nature of consumers today, you must begin to *think, communicate, and market your products differently.* Traditional marketing tactics alone cannot effectively reach consumers. A 30-second television spot during the Super Bowl is nice, but it's not going to turn around a failing brand—neither will a clever tweet during the half-time show. Aggressive social media marketing won't work either. You must have a fully integrated content marketing plan or be what I call "brand omnipresent," which means delivering value across the entire online ecosystem to fully change consumer behavior or brand perception. To do this, a consistent value message must exist across every form of content application, and all forms of media—paid, social, owned, or earned—must tell a similar story.

Unfortunately, this is much easier said than done.

Content is the number one challenge for brands today. The ability to tell a compelling and integrated brand story across the Web requires a significant amount of internal planning, cross-team collaboration, and coordination among different marketing teams in various geographies, and processes and workflows must be in place to optimize the content supply chain—content ideation, creation, approval, distribution, and optimization. This book gives a detailed approach to overcome many of these obstacles, allowing your brand to fully transform into a media company.

Why I Wrote This Book

My first book, *Smart Business, Social Business: A Playbook for Social Media in Your Organization* was released in July 2011. I started writing the book in the summer of 2010, and back then the term "social business" itself was still fairly new. Most of the conversations in the space were between pundits arguing about its definition—and rightfully so. Unfortunately, many of these arguments are still happening today. Some believe that it should be called social enterprise or social organization because the term "social business" already exists and means something completely different. Nobel Peace Prize winner Professor Muhammad Yunus first coined the term *social business* and defines it like this (Wikipedia):

> Social business is a cause-driven business. In a social business, the investors or owners can gradually recoup the money invested, but cannot take any dividend beyond that point. The purpose of the

investment is purely to achieve one or more social objectives through the operation of the company, since no personal gain is desired by the investors. The company must cover all costs and make revenue, but at the same time achieve the social objective.

As much as Professor Muhammad's definition is important to our world today, I define social business strategy as the following:

A social business strategy is a documented plan of action that helps evolve and transform the thinking of an organization, bridging internal and external social initiatives resulting in collaborative connections, a more social organization and shared value for all stakeholders (customers, partners, and employees).

Regardless of how you define social business, it's hard to argue that organizations today must change if they want to stay relevant and competitive. I have seen business change and have lived through its ups and downs for many years. *Smart Business, Social Business* was my eyewitness account of living through these changes while working for large brands such as Hewlett Packard, Yahoo!, and Intel. In the book, I plead the case that all business, large and small, must evolve into a social business just for the sake of being a social business.

Where I got it wrong is I didn't continue the story.

Becoming a social business for the sake of "becoming a social business" is only half the battle. Enterprise collaboration for the sake of enterprise collaboration might be a good idea, but how will it benefit content or better customer relationships? And deploying internal communities using software platforms like IBM or Jive just because your competitors are doing so is a waste of time, money, and resources.

There must be positive business outcomes.

There needs to be a reason why.

There has to be a strategic initiative as to why you want to change your business— one that makes smart business sense.

Even before my first book was released, I often talked about the need for companies to socialize their internal business models and communication strategies. But the question I often got was "Why?" Why is it important for my business to deploy internal communities, tear down silos, coordinate go-to-market plans, or get my rear-end out of my cubicle and have a conversation with my colleagues down the hall? These are all good questions, and this book is full of answers. Becoming a social business with no vision for where it's going to take you is like investing thousands of dollars building your first home from the ground up and never moving in to live in it and enjoy it.

I look at social business strategy as an enabler. Let me explain.

I am a marketing guy by trade, so many of the challenges I help my clients with are the ones that help them improve the way they communicate externally and internally. Sometimes it's about operationalizing a content marketing strategy. Other times, it's about building processes and workflows that can help scale social media globally. And many times, it's fixing disjointed content and community management practices.

In other words, to fix many of these challenges, you need a social business strategy that can stand the test of time and one that enables better content, smarter marketing, integrated communities, and more effective customer relationships. And that's exactly what this book is about—enablement. It's about tackling a real-world marketing problem and using a social business strategy to solve it. Figure I.1 illustrates how deploying a social business strategy enables external marketing initiatives.

SOCIAL BUSINESS FRAMEWORK

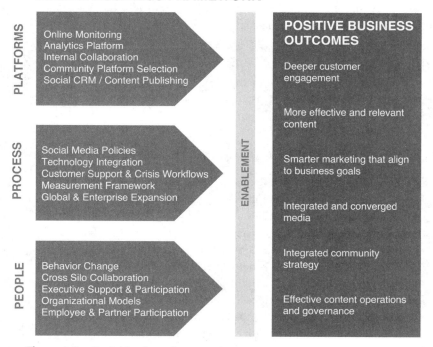

Figure I.1   *Social business framework*

So what is this real-world business problem?

It's actually pretty simple. Your brand needs to start thinking, acting, and operating like a media company. And the reason why is right in plain sight. There is a content surplus in the marketplace today, and consumers have attention deficit. Their daily lives are dynamic and unpredictable and all consumers are influential. For you to reach them with your brand message, you need to manufacture an environment where you are creating, curating, and aggregating relevant content—at the right time, in the right channel, and to the right customer. And your brand story must be consistent everywhere. Unfortunately, it's not like we can turn on the "media company" button and change operations and behavior overnight. It requires a change in attitude, behavior, and thinking coupled with processes and governance models, as well as technology that can facilitate the transformation.

Richard Edelman, Chief Executive Officer and President of Edelman Public Relations has said for a few years now that "every company is a media company." Sadly, some companies don't know it, resist the change, or have no clue on how to fully transform their businesses into media companies. This book will help enable your brand, whether large or small, to leverage the frameworks, practices, and strategies of social business to fully transform your brand into an operational content marketing machine. Or better yet, a media company.

But before you continue reading, it's important for you to get a baseline understanding of the definition of a media company.

In the book *Content Rules*, co-author Ann Handley (Chief Content Officer at MarketingProfs) defines a media company as the following: "A media company is any business that publishes useful material to attract and build a certain audience."

During a conversation on Facebook, she elaborated further:

> **"A media company is any business that publishes useful material to attract and build a certain audience."**

> It used to be that you needed significant resources to do that, but in a digital and social world, every business (and every one of us) has a new ability (and opportunity!) to be a media company far more cheaply and easily. Of course, I'm talking about tactics—every one of us now has the ability to use media tactics (publishing, building an audience). The key difference between a traditional media company (where I started my career) and a new media company is the revenue stream. The former makes its money from advertising; the latter makes its money from product or service sales. In other cases, though, the quality of the content and the audience are key.

Here is a different perspective from Shafqat Islam, the CEO of NewsCred:

> Media companies have historically been defined by their aptitude to create and deliver content, responsible for all elements of the content stack. The creation and distribution of content has always been underwritten by advertising—selling audience to marketers. However, in

today's world, the definition is changing since the creation and
distribution of content is no longer limited to traditional publishers.
Brand marketers are no longer just buying audience. They are the ones
who are participating in the conversation by creating and distributing
content to their audience directly. As such, in today's world, brands are
starting to become media companies, challenging the positions traditionally occupied by magazines and newspapers.

Although these are great definitions, it's important to understand that traditional
media companies such as Gannett, Time Warner, *New York Times*, and more
recent "New Media" companies such as Mashable, AOL with the acquisition of
Huffington Post, Techcrunch, and even Google are in the business of creating,
displaying, or bringing content to a given audience. For the most part, they don't
necessarily sell a tangible product or service. So when thinking about transitioning
your brand into a media company, you must consider it from a communications
and content perspective. Core business objectives such as selling products and
increasing market share, revenue, margins, and stock price should always remain
front and center.

As mentioned earlier, this book is about using a social business strategy to
transform your brand into a media company. Notice in Figure I.2 that the black
portions illustrate a social business strategy and how it enables various initiatives
that will help operationalize various elements of your content strategy. When all
of these are achieved and optimized, your brand will reach media company
transformation.

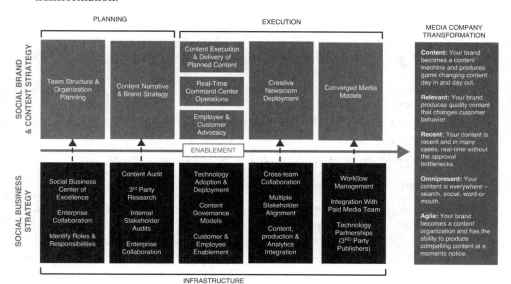

Figure I.2   *Social business strategy enables the transformation from brand to media
company.*

How This Book Is Organized

This book consists of eleven chapters, which are divided among three sections. The following are the titles and brief overviews of the sections and chapters for your reference. Though not comprehensive, these short descriptions give you a good idea of what each chapter is all about.

Section 1: Understanding the External and Internal Landscape

This section is all about understanding the external marketplace, how your customers interact with media content, and how your business must change to adapt, stay competitive, and blow your competitors out of the water. This section will not only give you a complete view of your target consumers, but it will also help you understand the fundamentals of a social business strategy that is needed to take your brand and transform it into a media company.

Chapter 1: Understanding the Social Customer and the Chaotic World We Live In

Chapter 1 is about the social customer. It highlights several case studies and reports that give you a firm understanding of how difficult it is to reach customers with the right content, at the right time, and in the right channel. This chapter also discusses the growing influence of social customers as well as the external factors causing this shift and challenge in marketing today.

Chapter 2: Defining Social Business Strategy and Planning

Chapter 2 is about defining social business strategy. Essentially, this chapter condenses the entire content of *Smart Business, Social Business* into one chapter and introduces new thinking, implementation strategies, and models.

Section 2: Setting the Stage for Social Business Transformation

Section 2 focuses on building your social media strategy infrastructure and foundation so that as you focus on your operations internally, you can prepare for your transformation externally. This section gives you a step-by-step plan of attack to help you build your Centralized "Editorial" Center of Excellence (CoE) and shows you how this team integrates within other business groups within your company.

Additionally, I show you how to create an atmosphere of listening and help you identify assets within your company—employees and customers—who love your product.

Chapter 3: Establishing a Centralized "Editorial" Social Business Center of Excellence

Chapter 3 builds on the foundation of Section 1 and kicks off Section 2. This chapter discusses, in practical terms, the need to create a centralized editorial team that is responsible for driving change within the organization. In many cases today, it is often referred to as a Social Business CoE. This chapter goes into detail about how you must build controls, processes, and workflows that facilitate collaboration among teams, partners, and even customers.

Chapter 4: Empowering Employees, Customers, and Partners to Feed the Content Engine

Chapter 4 is about enabling employees, customers, and channel partners within your supply chain to help you feed the content engine day in and day out. This chapter also gives you a systematic approach on how to build a brand advocacy program for your business, taking into consideration its infrastructure, the content plan, how you engage with your advocates, and the need to establish Key Performance Indicators (KPIs) that determine the success of the program and technology considerations.

Chapter 5: Building Your Social Business Command Center

Today, many command center operations are deployed to manage "reactive" customer support issues and/or crisis communications. Chapter 5 discusses how you can leverage a command center to monitor for trends happening in the news cycle and capitalize on real-time content creation. This chapter also gives step-by-step instructions on how to launch command centers and highlights several vendors in the space that offer off-the-shelf command center solutions.

Chapter 6: Understanding the Challenges of Content Marketing

Chapter 6 highlights a few brands that have taken content marketing to the next level. This chapter also examines several content marketing reports that have been released over the last two years and analyzes the similarities and differences of each. One of the goals of this chapter is to have you look beyond the content marketing buzzword and begin to think of your brand like a media company.

Section 3: Developing Your Content Strategy

This final section helps you formulate what you are going to say and how you are going to say it. Media companies are content machines. They have the right structures in place, aligned teams, a robust editorial process, and they execute the distribution of their content flawlessly. Your brand must follow this model, and this section shows you how to do it.

Chapter 7: Defining Your Brand Story and Content Narrative

Chapter 7 is about helping you define your brand story. You learn how to move beyond just the "brand message" and take into consideration several other inputs that will help you craft a unique story and create game changing content. As complex as this might seem, you learn how to simplify your content narrative similar to a children's storybook so that it's easily digestible for your target consumers.

Chapter 8: Building Your Content Channel Strategy

After you have defined your story, you then have to decide how and where you want to tell it. Chapter 8 chapter gives you several models and frameworks for you to decide how you want to drive your channel strategy, providing detailed examples of how to categorize your content by theme and channel.

Chapter 9: The Role of Converged Media in Your Content Strategy

Chapter 9 discusses the topic of how the customer journey between devices, channels, and media has become increasingly complex and how new forms of technology are only making it more so. You learn how to configure your strategy so that all channels work in concert, enabling brands to reach customers exactly where, how, and when they want, regardless of the channel or device.

Chapter 10: How Content Governance Will Facilitate Media Company Transformation

This chapter defines content governance as a strategic imperative when deploying an enterprise-wide content strategy for the purposes of establishing accountability, auditing content engagements, managing risk and setting permissions. Every person, whether employee or customer, has a specific role and/or responsibility when it comes to creating content, approving content, and distributing content. Chapter 10 also showcases "proactive" content workflows for planned and unplanned content and highlights "reactive" workflows as well.

Chapter 11: Structuring Your Teams to Become a Content-Driven Organization

Chapter 11 begins with a quick lesson in change management; mainly because change management initiatives are important to help you transition your brand into a media company. There isn't a right way or wrong way to structure your content teams. Every company is different, and culture, leadership, and business objectives vary and are often dynamic. This chapter showcases different models that you can adopt as you begin to structure your teams efficiently for content creation, approval, and distribution.

I hope you enjoy reading the book as much as I enjoyed writing it.

Understanding the External and Internal Landscape

This section of the book is about understanding the external marketplace—how your customers interact with media content and how your business can change to adapt, stay competitive, and blow your competitors out of the water.

Before making any dramatic changes to your business, you must first do a complete analysis of the external and internal factors your business faces. It's wise that you get a complete, 360-degree view of the customer ecosystem and understand the factors that affect your customers' behaviors. Multiple screens and devices, mass amounts of content, media, and marketing messages command their attention every day. Also, many consumers have CADD (Customer Attention Deficit Disorder), meaning they can't pay attention to any one thing at a given time. They are multitasking and consuming mass amounts of content on multiple devices with unpredictable behavior patterns.

Internally, it's important to understand how a social business strategy can help your organization change the way you think, act, operate, and communicate when it comes to social media, content marketing, and general communication principles. This section not only gives you a complete view of your target consumers, but it also helps you understand the fundamentals of a social business strategy, which is needed to take your brand and transform it into a media company.

Chapter 1: Understanding the Social Customer and the Chaotic World We Live In

There is a content and media surplus in the market today. And, most consumers suffer from attention deficit. This chapter describes the unpredictable nature of customers and how difficult it is for brands to reach them with targeted and relevant content:

- We Live in a Multi-Screen Economy
- CADD (Content Attention Deficit Disorder) Is Among Us
- Relevance Is the Key to Content Consumption
- The Customer Journey Is Dynamic

- Customers Are Influential
- Business Objectives Stay the Same Despite the Changes Externally
- Vendor Spotlight—Social Flow

Chapter 2: Defining Social Business Strategy and Planning

For any change to happen in your company, you will need a calculated plan that can facilitate change effectively. This chapter gives a comprehensive overview of social business strategy and how it can be implemented to facilitate the transition from brand to media company:

- The Social Media "Bright and Shiny" Object
- Social Media Has Caused Internal Business Challenges
- The Three Pillars of Social Business: People, Process, and Platforms
- The Social Business Value Creation Model
- The Differences Between a Social Brand and a Social Business
- Vendor Spotlight—Sprinklr

1

Understanding the Social Customer and the Chaotic World We Live In

Tweetable Moment: *Ninety percent of all media consumption, or 4.4 hours a day, happens across phones, tablets, computers, and TVs.* —#nextmediaco

I wake up every day about 6:00 a.m. The first thing I do to start my day is check all the notifications on my phone. I open up the Hootsuite app, refresh it, and check my @mentions, retweets, and direct messages. I also check for any new followers. I then go to Facebook and check if anyone commented on, liked, or shared any of my content. I check my feed, and at times I go on a liking frenzy of my own. Instagram is next, and I normally check to see who friended me and liked and/or commented on any photos in my stream. Sometimes I spend a few minutes liking and commenting on others' photos as well. LinkedIn is usually the last social network I check, specifically to see who has been stalking my profile followed by LinkedIn Today. Texts, emails, and phone messages are usually done later in the morning.

I then head downstairs, turn on the TV, make my breakfast, and read the latest news on Pulse from my iPad Mini while eating oatmeal and glancing up at the morning news on television. I usually share interesting news on Facebook, Twitter, or both if I have time. After breakfast, life is a little more routine—wake up the kids, make them breakfast and lunch, and then get them out the door and off to school.

When I get to work, my online behavior is rarely ever routine. Between meetings and sometimes during, I randomly check my networks or Google things I need to know and tweet along the way. Each day is different, dynamic, and very unpredictable. It's very difficult, even for me, to determine my next move or what content I will consume next.

Sound familiar?

It should because many consumers (of which you're one too) behave in a very similar fashion and it's only going to get worse. The amount of content, media, and overall marketing messages will only grow. It's inevitable and we can thank technology innovation, the multitude of devices, and a healthy economy for that. And our attention spans will always remain constant, which is why we filter out noise and only consume content and media that are important to us at a very specific moment in time. I won't spend more than a chapter trying to convince you that the world we live in today is like no other and that reaching consumers is difficult to do. I think you already know that. It's probably one reason you bought this book.

But as you read on and prepare to transform your brand into a media company, there are several factors you should consider as it relates to today's fast-paced, dynamic, and unpredictable marketplace:

- We live in a multi-screen economy.
- CADD (Customer Attention Deficit Disorder) is among us.
- Relevance is key to content consumption.
- The customer journey is dynamic.
- Customers are influential.

This chapter takes a closer look at these factors.

We Live in a Multi-Screen Economy

In 2012, Google, in partnership with market analysts Ipsos and Sterling Brands, released a study titled, "The New Multi-screen World: Understanding Cross-Platform Consumer Behavior." The report stated that 90% of consumers move between multiple devices to accomplish a specific task, whether it's on smartphones, PCs, tablets, or the television. That means 9 out of 10 people have more than one device for consuming content and even more media. In its most simplest terms to convey the difference between content and media is that content is information (that is, tweets, status updates, and so on) carried by or transmitted by a specific media (device, social network, or application.)

The study revealed that although a lot of market attention is being focused on smartphone usage, this device isn't used for media consumption as much as the others: 17 minutes per interaction, compared to 30 minutes on tablets, 39 minutes on PCs, and 43 minutes watching television. Figure 1.1 shows a breakdown of usage across each device.

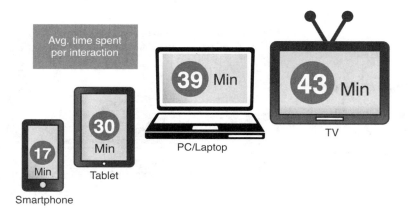

Figure 1.1   *Interaction time for the four primary media devices on which consumers spend their time*

However, though smartphones have the shortest usage times, they are often used as a starting point for consumers when they begin specific tasks. Google calls it *sequential screening* or *device usage. Simultaneous screening* is multiple device usage at the same time either for a related or unrelated activity.

More specifically, the study found that 9 out of 10 consumers use multiple screens sequentially, so starting a specific task such as searching for a product or service, booking a flight online, or managing personal finances doesn't just happen on one device. In fact, 98% of the consumers surveyed move between multiple devices to finish the tasks they started earlier in the day.

In the world of simultaneous device usage, the study found that television is no longer front and center commanding our undivided attention, with 77% watching the tube while using other devices to perform random tasks. In many cases consumers use their smartphones or tablets to search for something they just watched during a television show or check emails during the commercial. Sounds a lot like my behavior if you ask me. Figure 1.2 illustrates the differences between sequential and simultaneous device usage models.

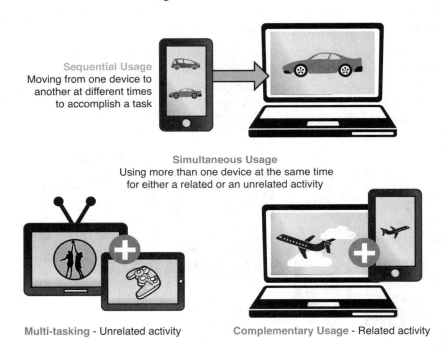

Sequential Usage
Moving from one device to another at different times to accomplish a task

Simultaneous Usage
Using more than one device at the same time for either a related or an unrelated activity

Multi-tasking - Unrelated activity

Complementary Usage - Related activity

Figure 1.2   *There are two modes of multi-screen usage—sequential and simultaneous.*

So what does this study mean for you and your brand? As you create content, whether it be videos, photography, infographics, or simply the development of a website's user interface, you must take into consideration the number of devices, screens, and operating systems in the marketplace and optimize for each one. This is a huge shift even from just a few years ago when you only had to worry about different screen resolutions on computer displays.

Additionally, given the dynamic nature of consumers' device usage, you must also ensure that there is a level of consistency in the way you tell your brand story. All successful brands have an amazing story to tell. From the brand identity, to the website and blog, to the Facebook page and the content you share on it, each piece of content needs to contribute a chapter to that story. Successful stories allow customers to connect with you emotionally. When that connection is made, those customers are more

All successful brands have an amazing story to tell.

likely to choose your brand over the one that doesn't have a story to tell or has one that's disjointed, boring, or doesn't align to their interests. It's much like dating. Wouldn't you would rather go out on a date with someone who is amazing, inspiring, and tells good stories rather than someone with no personality or interesting story?

TOMS and Zappos are two brands that have amazing stories. In TOMS' case, most consumers know that for every pair of shoes purchased, a pair is donated to a child in need. When they sell a pair of eyewear, part of the profit is used to save or restore the eyesight for people in third-world countries. That's their story, and they stick to it everywhere they have presence online. Customers feel good when they purchase a pair of TOMS shoes and they tell others about it too.

The Zappos story is all about the culture of customer service and delivering happiness to each of their 24+ million customers. It's not only a great story, but it's simple to communicate to others, which Zappos does extremely well. It's also true. If you ever have an issue with a Zappos product and tweet about it, an army of Zappos employees will respond to you and ask how they can help.

Finally, you must also ensure that search engine visibility is a focal point of your mobile content strategy. What's the point of optimizing content for various screens and devices if it's not even discoverable in search? Lee Odden, author of *Optimize: How to Attract and Engage More Customers by Integrating SEO, Social Media, and Content Marketing*, states in his book that any and all content on the Internet can be searched, so any and all content that brands create can be optimized. Lee makes an excellent point here if you think about push versus pull marketing. When someone goes to Google, they are usually on a mission to find information. And you are doing yourself a disservice if your content is absent from the search results.

Because mobile content consumption is the gateway into search, social media, and all other forms of media, it must be central to your content strategy.

CADD (Customer Attention Deficit Disorder) Is Among Us

My daughter Milan turned 11 in September 2012. She decided to have a sleepover at our house with 10 of her girlfriends from school to celebrate. Halfway through the night, I noticed that it was awfully quiet downstairs in the living room—no talking, no laughing, no giggling—behavior that was common during sleepovers when I was a kid. I figured they were watching a movie because the volume on the television was unbearably loud. When I went to downstairs to see why they were so quiet, I noticed something interesting. With the TV flicking in the foreground, each of the 10 girls was looking down at her iPod Touch, playing games and texting at the same time. It's the world we live in. It's CADD.

The "New Multi-Screen World" Google study clearly illustrates that CADD is among us. The mere fact that consumers have more than one device paints a solid picture of this scenario. Figure 1.3 gives a clear illustration of how consumers are multitasking on each of those devices.

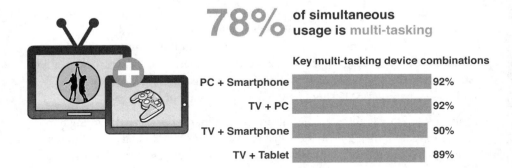

78% of simultaneous usage is multi-tasking

Key multi-tasking device combinations

PC + Smartphone	92%
TV + PC	92%
TV + Smartphone	90%
TV + Tablet	89%

Figure 1.3 *Consumers perform different activities at the same time.*

I have five devices myself, so I am certainly talking about yours truly here. We can blame the multitude of devices, all the marketing messages, coffee, or a combination of all three for our collective attention deficit, but the key takeaway here is that you are competing with more than just clutter and noise. For example, if you are a brand manager for Ford, you should be more concerned with the billions and billions of status updates, tweets, likes, and shares than what GM is doing in the social media space.

The content and media surplus and an attention deficit in the world today means that the content you create must be relevant.

Relevance Is the Key to Content Consumption

Consumers want relevance. I want relevance. We all want relevance. We are inundated daily with content and media that we just don't care about, and it's the sole reason why we create relevance filters.

Several years ago when I was planning to refinance my home, I remember driving down Highway 101 and seeing billboard after billboard after billboard of financial companies advertising their interest rates. I heard radio advertisements, read status updates, overheard conversations in the office, and even noticed display ads from Quicken Loans all over the Web. You might have experienced something similar when you were in the market to buy a new car or camera and noticed all the relevant advertisements that commanded your attention. The funny thing is that the very minute after I refinanced my home, each and every one of those brand messages went away. But they didn't really go away. They just weren't relevant to me anymore. My filters went back up, and I moved on.

Relevance is understanding what your customers are interested in and determining what you want to say that adds value to that interest and conversation. The difficulty is creating a content strategy that considers what's important to your customers and at the same time is relevant to your brand message. For example, if you work for a jewelry manufacturing company, I don't foresee cereal as being a part of your content strategy. It's just not relevant to your brand or interesting to your customers. Fashion, on the other hand, could be more relevant since jewelry and fashion can be considered synonymous in some cases; and you may actually have license to talk about it. What you will have to do is create editorial principles that define how flexible you want to be with your content based on what your brand is comfortable talking about and what it's not comfortable talking about. In Chapter 7, "Defining Your Brand Story and Content Narrative," I will give you a step-by-step plan of action on how to create a game-changing content strategy—one that can truly change your customer's behavior in a positive way.

The good news is that it's not that difficult to identify what's important to your fans within your communities. You probably already have a demographic profile that gives you the basics, so that's a start. I am sure you have done some research using focus groups or surveys as well. And Facebook Insights does give additional information if you need it. But there are other things you can do to get more information about your customers' interest graph. Many tools are available today in the marketplace such as Demographics Pro (http://www.demographicspro.com/), Simply Measured (http://simplymeasured.com), and Wisdom App (https://www.facebook.com/appcenter/wisdomapp) that can give you a complete breakdown of what other content, pages, and brands your fans also care about and use—basically a complete analysis of your customers' interest graph.

One of my favorite tools in the market is Keyhole.co (formerly Visibli). Their claim is that over 90% of any brand's audience doesn't talk about the brand, so their focus is on what *else* a brand's audience is talking about. Using their analytics toolset, you can get some serious intelligence about your audience on Twitter, specifically what types of content they share among themselves, which topics they care about most, which websites they share from, and other valuable insights. They provide three levels of intelligence:

- **Follower Intelligence**: This can give you detailed insights into your specific audience, including what your followers are interested in, which stories they are sharing and talking about most, which domains they share content from, who among them is the most influential or engaged, as well as who influences them.

- **Competitor Intelligence**: This is the same data as Follower Intelligence but gives insight into the followers of competitive brands, to help with competitor audience targeting.
- **Influencer Intelligence**: This provides insights into what industry influencers are talking about, including which stories from within an industry are influencers most interested in, and which websites most of these stories are sourced from.

Keyhole also shows you the percentage of followers who are interested in certain categories such as science, technology, health and beauty, news and politics, movies and TV, music, sports and recreation, entertainment, books, food and drink, and shopping. Most importantly, it identifies where your audience over-/under-indexes against the industry and competitor audiences, so you know where to focus most of your energy.

For content and social marketers, Keyhole also identifies the top stories and topics that your audience is talking about in real-time, so that brands can act as true media companies and participate in the conversations that matter to their followers *right now*. These insights are valuable and give you more of a complete analysis of who your customers are and what they care about most.

For example, doing a quick analysis of Nike's Twitter account, the results show that 31% of their community is interested in Sports & Recreation (obviously), 19% is interested in Health, and 10% in Fashion & Style. However, when we compare Nike's audience to Reebok's audience, we learn that Nike's audience over-indexes in Sports & Recreation, but under-indexes in Health and Fashion & Style. This implies that while Nike's audience might be more active in traditional sports, Reebok's audience is more interested in healthy living, as well as apparel—great information to know when deciding how to best engage this audience and building your content strategy.

Nike's audience also has a tendency of sharing Fashion & Style (that is, apparel) content from many well-known websites, such as Complex.com and DimeMag.com. However, for highest efficiency, we may want to know where Nike's audience over-indexes compared to the rest of the world. From that perspective, the best website to target this audience on is TheShoeGame.com. They're also comparatively heavy users of ChallengeLoop.com.

Platforms like Keyhole.co give you the ability to tailor your content and make it more relevant to your followers' interests. All your customers want from your brand is stellar products or services, value, and relevance—and if you can't deliver that, your competition will.

The Customer Journey Is Dynamic

We have already looked at the challenges of living in a multi-screen economy. We have also determined that many of us suffer from CADD and that all we want is content relevance. Those two factors alone make it difficult to reach consumers. So here is another factor to consider: We live in a noisy and dynamic world filled with media and messages, and we are inundated with content. If you don't believe me, here are a few 2012 Facebook stats for you to digest before you read on (source: AllFacebook.com):

- Monthly active users on Facebook total 850 million.
- There are 250 million photos uploaded every day.
- Twenty percent of all page views on the Web are on Facebook.
- There are 425 million mobile users.

Twitter is seeing exponential growth and usage as well (source: Lab42.com):

- There are over 465 million Twitter accounts.
- Seventy-five million tweets are sent out per day.
- One million accounts are added to Twitter every day.
- The top three countries on Twitter are the United States at 107 million, Brazil at 33 million, and Japan at nearly 30 million.

I won't bore you with more data, but we can't forget the growth of networks such as LinkedIn, Google+, Instagram, and Pinterest. It's no wonder we filter out the noise and only consume the content that is relevant to us at a very specific moment in time. There is just way too much going on in the world—too much content, too much media, and too much of everything. Figure 1.4 illustrates a day in the life of one of your customers and the amount of noise that surrounds him or her.

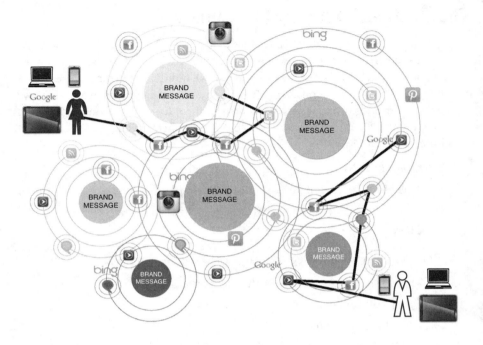

Figure 1.4 *The customer journey is dynamic.*

In my last book, *Smart Business, Social Business*, I wrote at length about the Edelman Trust Barometer, which is the largest exploration of trust, to date, and the largest survey of its kind. For 2013, Edelman surveyed more than 31,000 respondents in 26 markets around the world and measured their trust in institutions, industries, and leaders. One finding in the survey is that individuals need to hear, read, and see things three to five times before they start to believe it, which has been a consistent data point every year. So if your company is launching a new product or service, your customers need to hear it or read about it at multiple touch points. The same is true if you are launching an awareness campaign that's trying to reposition your brand in the marketplace. So as I mentioned earlier in this chapter, your story must be consistent and tell a very similar story in every tweet, news article, status update, promoted post, search, and so on.

In fact, what's interesting about the Google study mentioned earlier in this chapter is that search behavior links both sequential and simultaneous usage across multiple devices. In other words, we tend to use search as our gateway into specific content that we are looking for and in some cases perform similar searches on a different device. This makes your paid search and search engine optimization (SEO) strategies even that more critical. For example, and as illustrated in Figure 1.5, a high percentage of respondents claimed to have used search after performing various online tasks—a prior search, browsing the Internet, shopping online, or watching a video. The question you have to ask yourself is whether or not consumers will find your content when performing their search activities.

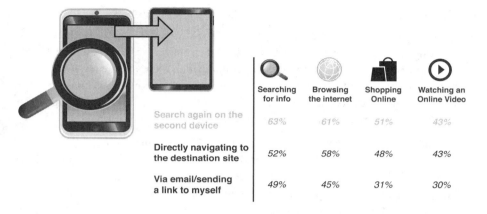

	Searching for info	Browsing the internet	Shopping Online	Watching an Online Video
Search again on the second device	63%	61%	51%	43%
Directly navigating to the destination site	52%	58%	48%	43%
Via email/sending a link to myself	49%	45%	31%	30%

Figure 1.5 *Consumers rely on search to move between devices.*

- Paid media (display ads, search, promoted posts, and sponsored stories)
- Earned media (influencer and advocate outreach programs and events)
- Owned media (Twitter, Facebook, YouTube, and blogs)

Chapter 9, "The Role of Converged Media in Your Content Strategy," covers the various forms of media in great detail.

Customers Are Influential

How many times have you posted a status update about a negative experience you had with a brand? Perhaps it was a situation with your cable company, a restaurant, or maybe an airline. On the other hand, how many times have you read a status update from one of your friends about their positive experience with a brand? It could have also been a Yelp Review or product review on Amazon. Did that influence your decision to buy, or do you just ignore it? I see this type of behavior every single day in the social networks that I spend time in. If someone isn't ranting about a certain brand they hate, they are praising the brands they love. So in most cases, you are influencing others based on the experiences you share about brands. Or, you are being influenced by others based on the experiences they share with you directly or after reading an online review. I have been on both sides of the field and am glad to say that I trust the opinions of the people in my community and hope they trust me.

Influence is a hot topic these days especially with the emergence of influencer scoring systems such as Klout, Kred, Peer Index, and Tweetlevel (an Edelman product). Andrew Grill, CEO of Kred, told me in an interview for this book that influencers don't have to be celebrities; they can be anyone who people look up to and trust who has a respected opinion about any topic in a community.

I agree with Andrew, and the reality is that all of your customers are influential regardless of how many friends, fans, or followers they have. No, they probably don't obsess over their Klout scores or get mad when their scores go down, but they are definitely influencing others to buy your products and, in some cases, to not buy your products. And they are doing this through organic and everyday conversations they are having with their friends, both online and offline.

To highlight a study that proves this point, the Cone Online Influence Trend Tracker, released in 2011, is somewhat dated but shows some interesting trends in customer behavior as it relates to influence. Figure 1.6 shows that 85% of consumers go online to research products before deciding to make a purchase. What's interesting is that they do this research after someone has given them a recommendation. They want additional validation before they make the purchase.

Cone Online Influence Trend Tracker

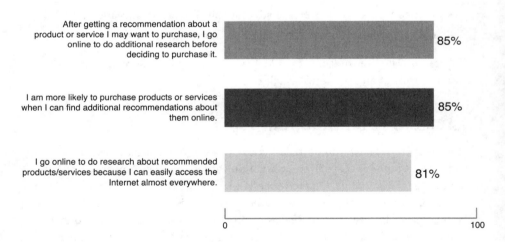

Figure 1.6   *Eight-five percent of consumers verify products and services online before purchasing.*

Figure 1.7 shows that four out of five consumers have changed their minds about purchasing a product based solely on negative information they found online from other customers. This is up from just 68% of consumers who said the same thing in 2010.

The good news is that positive information about products and services has a similar effect on consumer decision making, with 87% of consumers agreeing that a favorable review has confirmed their decision to purchase. However, the survey suggests that negative information is gaining traction and is now just as powerful in tipping the scales against a recommended purchase.

This happened to me in the summer of 2012, as you learned in the Introduction of the book. It's a great example of what I'm talking about here. After I heard some negative information about a specific airline, I did some additional research and found the very telling report from the U.S. Department of Transportation about the large number of pet deaths and injuries on that airline. So do you think I booked travel with them? No.

Cone Online Influence Trend Tracker

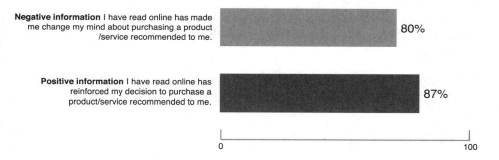

Figure 1.7   *Negative information is just as powerful as positive.*

The net-net of this is data is that customers' opinions matter a great deal in the digital ecosystem. And whether they know it or not, they are aiding and influencing other customers in seeking out products and services as well as guiding them down the purchase funnel simply through organic conversations about their experiences.

Business Objectives Stay the Same Despite the Changes Externally

I have covered a lot of information in this chapter as it relates to the external marketplace—media, marketing, customers, and influence. And when you try to couple it together and make some sense of it all, it can certainly get discouraging. Unfortunately, the market doesn't stop changing when we get discouraged. To steal a popular slogan from the U.S. Marines, you need to *improvise, adapt, and overcome*—and be prepared to pivot your business operations quickly. Otherwise you and your brand will quickly become irrelevant.

Despite the changes that you need to adapt to externally, your business objectives will always remain the same internally. Your revenue goals will never go away. You still have to sell products despite the market conditions or economic state. The pressure of cutting operational and marketing costs and increasing margins will continue to drive business decisions. And though you might not have direct control over stock price, market share, or mind share, you still could be held accountable. The good news is that this book provides you with a roadmap that will help you adapt your thinking while operationalizing your content marketing strategy.

> There is a content surplus in the marketplace today, and consumers suffer from attention deficit. What is your brand doing to stand out?

There is a content surplus in the marketplace today, and consumers suffer from attention deficit. What is your brand doing to stand out?

Vendor Spotlight—Social Flow

Earlier in this chapter, I talked about the need for you to create relevant content to reach consumers with CADD. The challenge here is what might be relevant today might not be relevant tomorrow. And to complicate it a little further, what might be relevant an hour ago might not be relevant right now. Attention is finite, and you don't have a lot of time to get your message in front of the masses. SocialFlow addresses this issue head on.

The best way to describe SocialFlow is that it's a content publishing and ad platform that uses real-time analytics and a predictive algorithm to publish content at the time when customers are paying attention. They have two core products, Cadence and Crescendo.

As depicted in Figure 1.8, Cadence uses predictive analytics to determine the value of your content within the social graph. In real time, Cadence determines when a specific audience is available, paying attention and what relevant topics they are most likely to engage with based on what they are currently discussing.

It then automatically publishes your content when the audience is paying attention. SocialFlow then ties these messages back into business goals by measuring the conversion rate of each message, such as clicks to a website as measured by a web analytics platform like Adobe SiteCatalyst or Google Analytics.

Figure 1.8   *Cadence helps optimize content in real time.*

SocialFlow's Crescendo product, also referred to as their Attention Buying Platform, uses proprietary technology to optimize "interest targeting" based on real-time conversations pulled in from the social graph, rather than using traditional demographic filters. As seen in Figure 1.9, the platform then optimizes the acquisition of custom audiences, sponsored actions, sponsored stories, promoted posts, and mobile app installs all while tracking very specific conversions. In a nutshell, the platform is smart enough to bid on the right keywords for Facebook ads that reflect what their most engaged fans are talking about and sharing at that precise moment. So instead of buying against larger buckets of expensive keywords, Crescendo can buy key terms that are being discussed in real time and for less money.

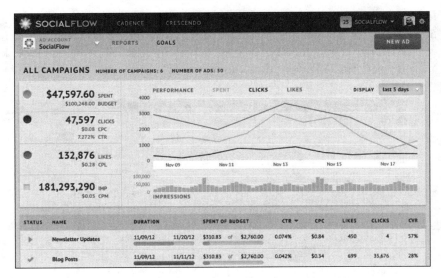

Figure 1.9 *Crescendo informs ad-buying decisions and maximizes returns using real-time trending data.*

Crescendo and Cadence naturally complement each other and highlight how paid and earned media can be integrated and can work together effectively. By building up a large community, you can tap into their conversations to learn how to target similar consumers outside of your own media. And ultimately, if the content is relevant and timely, it can turn a consumer into a fan and a fan into an advocate.

In addition to its core products, Cadence and Crescendo, SocialFlow also analyzes social signals and identifies when marketing dollars should be spent on Promoted Tweets, Promoted Posts, and Sponsored Stories, extending the reach of relevant content and coordinating marketing efforts on Twitter and Facebook.

Defining Social Business Strategy and Planning

Tweetable Moment: *A social business strategy delivers better content, smarter marketing, and more effective customer relationships.*
—#nextmediaco

As you read through the rest of these chapters and ulti-mately finish this book, it's important to get a firm under-standing of what social business means and how it can be implemented in your company. Whether you work for small firm or large enterprise, many of the frameworks and models can be easily adapted to fit your business needs. You should realize, though, that deploying a social business strategy is never the same in any two companies even if they are similar in size or sell competing products. There are too many variables at stake when considering this business transformation. Leadership, culture, infor-mation systems, and employee behavior vary. They also change and evolve frequently as leadership, managers, and employees cycle in and out of a company.

The transformation from brand to a media company does not happen overnight. In fact, the foundation of this transformation revolves around the behaviors of your organization. Being able to identify the opportunity, scope out a plan, influence change, and ultimately achieve support from the executives in your company is a process that can take anywhere between 24 to 36 months in some cases. A social business strategy helps deliver this change systemically and with precision. But before I jump into dissecting social business strategy, let's first discuss how the business world got here in the first place.

Figure 2.1 illustrates a timeline of how social business is becoming top-of-mind today. Back in 1995 when Al Gore supposedly invented the Internet, customers have been gaining influence. With the rise of user-generated content, technology innovation, and the ability for anyone with Internet access and/or a mobile phone to publish forms of media, it's no wonder companies jumped into social media headfirst. These dates can certainly be argued, but in 2003, companies began to create social media channels to engage with these influential customers. Finally in 2008, companies realized and experienced all of the challenges that social media had created, both internally and externally—hence the rise of *social business* (see Figure 2.1).

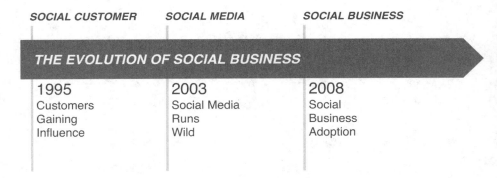

Figure 2.1   *The rise of social business strategy is a natural result of the growing influence of customers.*

The Social Media "Bright and Shiny" Object

How many times have you heard someone say, "Brands just need to join the conversation," or "There are conversations happening about your brand, and you need to engage!" Maybe you don't hear these rumblings much anymore but three to five years ago, these questions and topics plagued blog post headlines everywhere. I was guilty too. I found one of my blog posts that dated back to 2007 titled, "Social Media Speaks Volumes, but Are You Listening?" that solidifies my point:

> As I mentioned many times before, consumers are tired of being marketed to. They are fed up with the millions and millions of marketing messages that are thrown in their faces and computer monitors everyday. And even when these messages are coming from a third party (*Cnet, Techrunch, NY Times*), there is still no guarantee as to the authenticity of the messages.
>
> And as I continue to repeat myself again and again, consumers are talking. They are having conversations online and offline about brands. They are sharing their experiences with each other; and they are either praising your brand or tearing it apart like a pit bull. And it's almost a guarantee that if it's the latter, they are telling more than one person about it. This is the kind of viral marketing that you don't really want to be viral.

Additionally, there were and still are social media so-called experts who like to play "Monday morning quarterback" and call out large brands and media companies for the mistakes they make in social media. Unfortunately, many of these gurus have never worked for a brand and don't understand the complexities of working for a large organization. In most cases, it's not like these companies are devising a master plan to deceive the world; they just mess up every now and then.

As the hype of social media continued to gain traction, the majority of brands gave in and finally joined the conversation. Some did it well, and others not so well, but it had to happen. They were pressured into it by the external market, bloggers, influencers, their customers, agencies, and even internal marketing teams who wanted to seize the opportunity and jump head first into social media. Understandably, then, they made mistakes, and the subtle conversation suddenly went from, "Brands need to join the conversation," to, "Brands need to be more open and authentic," almost overnight.

In the early days, British Airways got slammed on the Internet for being on Twitter for a few months and only updating their account seven or so times. As did Toyota when they had a product recall but failed to inform their Twitter followers about it. But more recently, the criticism has become a lot more complex for a good reason.

In 2012, Kenneth Cole, a well-known apparel manufacturer and retailer in New York, tried to take advantage of the trending hashtag and tweeted the following during a crisis in Egypt where many people had lost their lives:

> Millions are in uproar in #Cairo. Rumor is they heard our new spring collection is now available online at http://bit.ly/KCairo -KC

What makes this story even more disheartening is that the tweet came directly from Kenneth Cole himself, the CEO and founder of the brand. Fortunately, it took him only a day or two to write an apology on their Facebook page after deleting the tweet.

Another well-known brand, KitchenAid made a similar mistake when an employee used the @KitchenAidUSA account and tweeted something inappropriate about President Barack Obama's recently deceased grandmother during the 2012 presidential debate:

> Obamas gma even knew it was going 2 b bad! 'She died 3 days b4 he became president' Wow!—#nbcpolitics

KitchenAid recanted the statement quickly, with head of the marketing issuing a sincere apology on the company's Facebook page, but the damage was already done.

These are just two examples of well-known brands that made mistakes using social media. The visibility of these mistakes was external, but the root cause had to do with lack of internal planning and content governance. And, unfortunately, situations like this still happen today, and it's because companies fail to think strategically about the potential implications of jumping head first into social media without plans, processes, and controls that can prevent predicaments like these. In addition to these challenges they face externally, social media has caused a multitude of internal challenges as well.

Social Media Has Caused Internal Business Challenges

If you work for a medium to large-sized company, many of these challenges might be familiar to you. I have personally lived through several of them myself:

- Employees' inappropriate use of social media
- Internal confusion about roles and responsibilities
- Inconsistent social media measurement practices
- Outdated crisis communication models
- Expanding social media programs globally without proper planning
- Disjointed content and community management practices
- The daunting task of technology selection and adoption
- Nonexistent content governance models

Employees' Inappropriate Use of Social Media

This one hits close to home for me because I have been in trouble a few times in my career for tweeting something I shouldn't have. I guess I have a certain side of me that's a bit rebellious.

If you Google "fired for using Facebook" or "fired for using Twitter," you will find several examples of employees who were fired for the things they said or did in social media. In some cases, inappropriate photos were posted on Instagram or Facebook. In other cases it was questionable or offensive tweets, status updates, comments on others' wall posts, or blog posts. And it's not always an intern or junior employee who didn't know better.

Adam Smith, former CFO of the medical supplies manufacturer Vante, recorded a video of himself bullying a Chick-fil-A drive-thru employee in Tucson and posted it on YouTube. This was in response to Chick-fil-A's CEO Dan Cathy making anti-gay comments on a national syndicated radio show, which also spurred hundreds of protests in cities where Chick-fil-A conducts business. He was fired.

Francesca's, a women's clothing retailer based in Houston announced that it was firing CFO Gene Morphis for tweeting inappropriately about confidential business matters. The official announcement said that he had "improperly communicated company information through social media."

Having a social business strategy in place ensures that there are social media policies and guidelines for your company and that employees are trained on how to use social media professionally even when using their personal platforms.

Internal Confusion About Roles and Responsibilities

When I speak at a conference, I usually ask the audience where they think the social media job function should report into. I give them two options: public relations or marketing. The crowd is usually split right down the middle with some hesitant to answer because they probably aren't sure.

If I were to ask you the same question, how would you answer? I am sure it would depend on where you report into today. The truth is, you are not alone. Many companies today aren't sure how to organize their teams or how to identify and assign roles and responsibilities around social media. This is causing distress among teams and hurting employee morale. It's also causing teams who want to own social media to go out and create their own communities and social media initiatives without integrating with other, internal teams. This results in disjointed content and inconsistent storytelling.

A social business strategy helps you identify roles and responsibilities so that all stakeholders collaborate and integrate their marketing strategies. In some cases, it also helps you or your leadership design new teams and reporting functions.

Inconsistent Social Media Measurement Practices

Two things are happening today. Either no one is measuring social media marketing initiatives or everyone is measuring it differently. In either case, this is a huge problem. Imagine the CMO of a very large company with several product lines walks into your office and asks you how many people you reached or engaged with within your communities over the last six months, collectively and by product line. Can you pull that data right away? Probably not—and that's the reality for many companies today.

A social business strategy not only helps you determine what to measure, but it also helps you ensure that all of your stakeholders have a seat at the table when creating your measurement framework.

Outdated Crisis Communication Models

You probably already have a crisis communications plan tucked away somewhere on your laptop or in an email somewhere. And chances are you haven't had to use it lately if that's the case. The challenge today with crisis communications is that information is now in real-time with gigabytes of tweets, status updates, and photo uploads moving across the Web every minute. And most companies don't function or report in real-time, much less are prepared to respond to a critical issue in real-time either.

A social business strategy can be used to create a proactive crisis communication plan, complete with process and escalation workflows, so that corporate communication's team and employees can be prepared for any crisis that might plague your business.

Expanding Social Media Programs Globally Without Proper Planning

Social media expansion into new markets isn't easy, especially when you consider the differences in language and nuances that make another culture different from yours. Unfortunately, this isn't preventing some teams to go off and create regional social media channels without first understanding the risks and implications of doing so. Nor are they considering the need for local community management, content creation, and integration with corporate or other regions as well as consistent measurement practices. This, in turn, is causing disjointed content and community management practices.

A social business strategy can help you build governance models so controls are in place that prevent disparate teams from going rogue and creating new social media channels without proper planning.

Disjointed Content and Community Management Practices

This is one of the biggest problems for companies today—content and community management. A 2012 study from the Altimeter Group—one of the leading and most credible analyst firms on social business—released a study, "A Strategy for Managing Social Media Proliferation," and found that companies have an average of 178 social media channels. See Figure 2.2 for a breakdown of each social channel.

Platform	Average Number of Accounts
Twitter	39.2
Blog	31.9
LinkedIn	28.8
Message Boards/Communities	23.4
YouTube	9.4
Foursquare	6.3
All others	5.3
Flickr	3.8
SUM	178

Figure 2.2   *An Altimeter study found that companies have an average of 178 social media accounts.*

The mere fact that all these channels exist is concerning to me for a few reasons. Content is finite. With 178 channels, it's almost impossible to keep content alive, fresh and engaging, not to mention that 95% of these channels were probably created from internal silos and have dying communities. This is because they were probably created for short-term campaigns or product launches. Second, you will learn in Chapter 6, "Understanding the Challenges of Content Marketing," that it's not easy to create compelling content so even if the community was still somewhat alive, most likely the content is mediocre at best.

Not only can a social business strategy prevent situations like this, but it can also help drive a content strategy that's consistent, tells a good story, and is integrated across every media channel—paid, earned, and owned media.

The Daunting Task of Technology Selection and Adoption

Do a search in Google for "social media vendors," and you will see pages and pages of vendors in the search results. The space is crowded with vendors offering social CRM (Customer Relationship Management), content publishing, analytics, and online monitoring services. This makes selecting the right vendor a daunting task. And after the technology itself is deployed, it's even more difficult to drive user adoption in the organization.

A social business strategy helps you match your brand's technology requirements with vendors that have the right technical capabilities. It also helps drive adoption through specific collaborative and creative engagement models.

Nonexistent Content Governance Models

In some companies, content governance models just don't exist. Although they are not the sexiest of social business initiatives and often go unnoticed, establishing governance within your company is probably the most important and strategic initiative you could plan for. Undoubtedly, you have experienced some chaos in your organization. Perhaps it was some of challenges already listed in this section. If not yet, you will eventually in the near future. And, if you decide to ignore it or put it on the back burner, you could end up managing and then consolidating 178 social media channels and possibly terminating a few employees for inappropriate tweets along the way. Here a few examples of what governance can mean for you:

- Social media policies
- Processes that help determine whether to create a new social media channel or use an existing channel
- Password management for branded social media channels
- Processes for approving content before it goes live

HMV is a British retail chain and is the largest of its kind in the United Kingdom and Canada. In February 2012, it faced mutiny as disgruntled employees took over the the Twitter account to express their anger and frustration for being fired. These employees essentially "live tweeted" their own termination and shared the experience with HMV's 61,000+ followers. Having a governance policy in place could have prevented this from happening.

With all these challenges happening both internally and externally, you need to implement a social business strategy to help minimize risk and streamline internal communication, kickstarting the transformation into a media company.

The Three Pillars of Social Business: People, Process, and Platforms

It is difficult to understand all the issues of social business. It gets even more complicated when everyone's definition of social business is different. So before continuing, let's go back to its definition from the Introduction of this book:

> A social business strategy is a documented plan of action that helps evolve and transform the thinking of an organization bridging internal and external social initiatives resulting in collaborative connections, a more social organization, and shared value for all stakeholders (customers, partners, and employees).

At the core of this business transformation are the people of the organization (leadership, executives, change agents, and so on) as illustrated in Figure 2.3. For true change to happen in your organization, all stakeholders must embrace this change first. Your behaviors, the way you work and the way you communicate and influence others all play a crucial role in this transformation process.

Change is imitated, and it's based on actions. It's like a manager who preaches work/life balance and yet sends emails at 1:00 a.m. and expects responses by 8:00 a.m. A balanced lifestyle will never happen unless the manager changes his or her own behavior first. Once that happens, others will "imitate" and follow suit. Taking it back to this context, if you want to drive social business adoption within your organization, you must, in turn, become social and begin to build social behaviors into your everyday workflow and job routine.

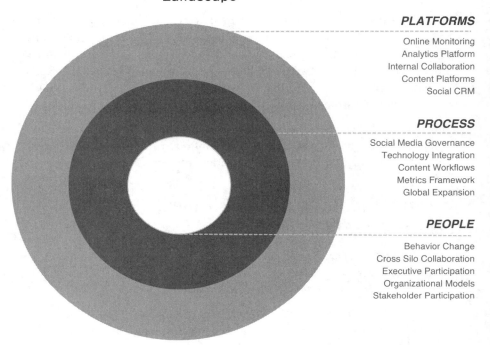

PLATFORMS

Online Monitoring
Analytics Platform
Internal Collaboration
Content Platforms
Social CRM

PROCESS

Social Media Governance
Technology Integration
Content Workflows
Metrics Framework
Global Expansion

PEOPLE

Behavior Change
Cross Silo Collaboration
Executive Participation
Organizational Models
Stakeholder Participation

Figure 2.3   *The three pillars of a social business strategy are people, process, and platforms.*

In addition to behavior change, this pillar also involves team dynamics and orga-nizational structure. The easiest way to explain it is that you need to build your teams in a way that allows you to scale your content operations internally. This might mean that you create a centralized editorial team to manage all social media initiatives or a decentralized team that has more autonomy and freedom to try new things and innovate. It also involves an employee strategy that empowers, trains, and enables your employees and colleagues to engage with customers externally.

The second pillar is process or workflow. Most internal processes will vary and be different based on the organizational challenges you must solve and the general company culture. The constant, which will be similar in most companies, is the establishment of social media policies that will help shape employee behavior on the social Web. Other processes to consider are controls for other teams that want to expand social media into new markets or channels; processes that will deter-mine how/when new branded social media channels will be created as well as the "content supply chain." This process will be the most critical as you think about transitioning your brand to a media company. The content supply chain is a set of processes that govern content ideation, creation, approval, distribution, and opti-mization of content.

The last pillar is platform or technology. After behavior change has manifested and you have documented the processes and controls, the last thing to think about is technology. Certainly, you might already have technology solutions in use, and that's fine. In this case you have to work backwards and attempt to fill in the gaps. As mentioned earlier in the chapter, the social media vendor space is extremely crowded. There are social CRM vendors (SalesForce, Nimble, InsideView, SpredFast, Sprinklr), content publishing vendors (Kapost, Compendium, Relaborate, Cadence9, Contently, Skyword), online monitoring vendors (Radian6, Adobe Social, Sysomos, PeopleBrowsr, Tracx, Netbase), brand advocate platforms (Dynamic Signal, Zuberance, Fancorps, Influitive, Extole, Napkin Labs) and finally, community platforms for internal/external collaboration (Jive, Lithium, Yammer, Social Cast, Igloo, and IBM Connections). Yikes! And, this is just a small sample of vendors to choose from.

The list can potentially continue forever, but as you can see, there are several software vendors to consider, so it's important that you plan accordingly and collaborate with IT to build a scalable road map for technology implementation and user adoption.

Now that you understand the different pillars of social business, let's take a look at the social business value creation model.

The Social Business Value Creation Model

Social business strategy isn't a theory, buzzword, or the "next big thing." It's simply a natural business evolution. It's why companies like Accenture, Deloitte, KPMG, and others have been in business and profitable for several decades. They help companies change behavior, improve processes, and expand into new markets because of the dynamic nature of business. And many of these traditional management-consulting firms are now expanding their service offerings to include "social" (fill in the blank) because companies are now faced with new and improved challenges as we just discussed earlier in this chapter. The sole focus of social business isn't just about making business more social because it's the "thing to do" or to collaborate for the sake of collaboration; there must be value creation. And value can mean just about anything depending on the goals of your organization. It can refer to

- Increase in revenue
- Decrease in calls in the call center (cost savings)
- Increase in employee morale
- Employee retention and hiring top talent
- Cost savings by improving internal business processes
- Product (and process) innovation

To my demise of being ridiculed by my colleagues who are "anti-marketing," when I consider social business, I have to consider the brand, content, and customer experience as well. All three of these elements must co-create value to its stakeholders. Consider the Social Business Value Creation Model in Figure 2.4.

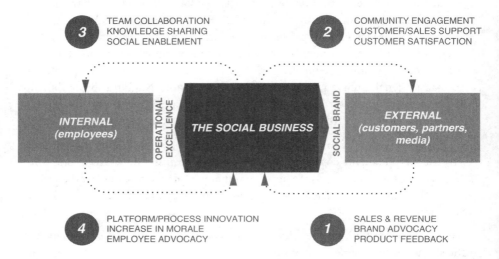

Figure 2.4 *A social business strategy must provide value to all stakeholders.*

The model looks complicated, but it's quite easy to understand. Let's start with the area marked number 1.

Customers provide value to your brand in a variety of different ways. The most obvious is through sales. The more they buy from you, the higher your revenue will be. This is value. They also provide value by indirectly selling your products to others, which is a form or brand advocacy (that is, when they aid and influence their friends down the purchase funnel through organic conversations)—definite value creation. And whether you solicit it or not, in some cases they will give you feedback about how to improve your products or services. Sometimes the ideas will be good, and other times they won't. This completes a one-way value exchange from the customer to the brand.

To complete the value chain and moving on to number 2, your brand provides value back to the customer simply through two-way dialog or general community engagement. The good news is that many customers don't need incentives to talk about you or with you. They just want to know you are listening. And even then, some customers just have a natural affinity toward your brand and will talk about you regardless if there's an absence of engagement. Having an amazing product or service definitely helps too.

While saying "thank you" or retweeting your customer's content creates just a small percentage of value, there is a lot more to it. You must be prepared to solve your customers' problems quickly and efficiently. Doing so not only provides customer value but also drives brand advocacy. The 2012 State of Social Customer Service Report showed that 71% of customers that get their problems solved quickly and efficiently are more likely to recommend that brand to others. In some cases, you might have to provide sales support if the opportunity presents itself.

As we transition to internal elements of the value chain, it's important to emphasize that there should be a core team that is responsible for driving all of these work streams, both internally and externally. In the next chapter, I discuss this concept, referred to as a Centralized "Editorial" Social Business Center of Excellence, in more detail.

A social business strategy creates value internally by enabling the brand to scale through content governance, process creation, and technology enablement. In looking more deeply at number 3, value is created when structures and workflows are put in place that allow for team collaboration and knowledge sharing, whether it be various marketing, product or country marketing teams. Employees and teams feel a sense of empowerment and ownership when they are a part of an initiative that delivers significant value to the organization and brand. They will naturally own it.

Also there is a high degree of value when teams and employees are able to increase their own social proficiency. This is done through technology and training.

To close the loop on the Social Business Value Exchange Model, employees and teams deliver value back to the business in a variety of different ways. First is through product and process innovation. A few years ago, I was at a marketing conference for grocery executives. I was talking with a VP of Marketing for a well-known grocery retailer, and he was telling me that his business was growing and expanding really fast. So rather than opening up additional stores, he wanted to first see if he could optimize the checkout process, so he had hired a Six Sigma Black Belt to try and eliminate the waste. It makes sense, right? He just wanted to get customers through the checkout line faster. The first thing I asked him was if he involved the cashiers in this initiative. After all, they do live through the process day in and day out and help customers eight hours a day. He scratched his head and said that it was a really great idea. Not sure if it ever happened.

The point is that when teams come together to solve a specific business goal or challenge, great ideas are born. If you are an Amazon Prime member, you can thank an employee. Prime came to life in late 2004, the result of a years-long search at Amazon for a scalable loyalty program. An Amazon software engineer named Charlie Ward first suggested the idea of a free shipping service via a suggestion box feature on Amazon's intranet. And rumor has it that Amazon Prime accounts for 20% of Amazon's overall revenue. Not a bad idea if you ask me.

Empowering employees is a huge opportunity in value creation. Employees of a company are trusted as external spokespersons when consumers seek information about a company's product and services. They are even more credible than the CEO, according to the 2013 Edelman Trust Barometer. However, empowerment is not actionable. Simply creating a training program, telling employees to join Twitter and engage with customers won't work. A social business strategy, if done right, will enable and mobilize employee advocacy and brand journalism through technology, process, content enablement, and ongoing best practice sharing.

The Differences Between a Social Brand and a Social Business

A social brand and a social business are completely different yet exactly the same. However, there is still some confusion in the marketplace about the difference between the two. First, you have to understand what being a social brand actually means.

A *social brand* is any company, product, or individual that uses social technologies to communicate with customers, their partners and constituencies, or the general public. It's a very basic definition, but going back to the value exchange model, it's essentially numbers 1 and 2. It's the way a brand communicates externally, whether they do a good job or bad one.

I defined a social business strategy earlier in the chapter. Again, it is a documented plan of action that helps evolve and transform the thinking of an organization bridging internal and external social initiatives resulting in collaborative connections, a more social organization, and shared value for all stakeholders (customers, partners, and employees).

So in other words, having a social business strategy enables better content, smarter marketing, and more effective customer relationships. Figure 2.5, created by the Managing Director of Edelman Digital in Chicago, David Armano, shows the relationship between a social brand and social business and how each must work together to produce business results.

Figure 2.5   *The social brand and social business must be in alignment to see business results.*

The following is an example that will help bring clarity to the differences between a social brand and a true social business.

John is irritated because he dialed in to a customer support department and was put on hold for 30 minutes. No one ever answered his call. He goes to the brand's Facebook page and leaves a comment expressing his anger. No response. He then @mentions the brand directly on Twitter. No response. So he writes a blog post criticizing the heck out of the brand and shares it all over the social Web. Still, no response.

In most organizations, a corporate Twitter account is owned and managed by someone in the Public Relations or Marketing department. And because of the organizational silos that still plague businesses today, these teams probably aren't talking with their colleagues in customer support. So here's a situation where a social brand is being unresponsive and angering customers because the escalation processes don't exist and there is an absence of internal communication and collaboration.

Now, let's take a different angle. Assume the marketing or PR person did escalate John's tweet or Facebook comment to customer support, which then took care of his issue. He's happy now and he's telling others. And then the same thing happens with Mary, Chris, Steve, and several other customers. And the customer support team realizes that it needs to shift internally to address all of these online inquiries. Progress, for sure. Happy customers are always a good thing to have.

But a social business strategy goes above and beyond addressing isolated customer support issues. It takes that customer feedback (because its people are communicating and working together internally) and fixes the root cause of the problem, whatever it is.

Another quick example that has been cited in hundreds of case studies and blog posts is when companies create products with their customers, giving birth to innovation. Take the Starbucks' Splashstick as an example—the little green stirrer that also prevents the spillage of hot coffee. The Splashstick was a suggestion from a community member in the MyStarbucksIdea community website. In co-creating a product with its community, Starbucks changed the coffee-drinking experience for millions of customers and solved a vexing business problem of hot coffee spillage.

Of course, I'm oversimplifying the issue because situations like these take time, a commitment to change, processes, and the establishment of governance models. But, Starbucks is a good example of an organization reaping the benefits of social brand and social business alignment. First, they are using social technologies to communicate externally with their customers. They communicate publicly with their partners (employees who work in retail stores) using Facebook (https://www.facebook.com/starbuckspartners). And, lastly, they are taking the collective feedback from the community and innovating their products or service and solving customer support issues quickly and efficiently—all characteristics of a successful social business.

So to recap, here is why a social brand and social business are completely different:

- A social brand focuses on external communications.
- A social business focuses on building collaborative business models that enable external communications and marketing.
- A social brand is primarily about engagement with customers.
- A social business empowers and enables employees to communicate externally with customers.
- A social brand is owned by marketing.
- A social business should be owned by the entire organization.
- A social brand is measured by clicks, impressions, reach, Likes, comments, retweets, and so on.
- A social business is measured by a change of behaviors—specifically when social behaviors become a part of employees' daily workflow.

One way in which social brands and businesses are the same is that they serve the same purpose and underlying goal, which is creating value for all stakeholders—customers, partners, and employees. Customers create value by offering insights and opinions (both good and bad) about his or her brand experience. The social brand creates value with the customer by listening, engaging, and solving problems and then sharing feedback and insights internally. And finally, the social business creates value for customers by listening to the collective feedback of the community and innovating its products, services, policies, and processes—thus, creating the full cycle of value creation.

Vendor Spotlight—Sprinklr

Sprinklr is an enterprise-grade social media management infrastructure provider, sometimes referred to as a Social Media Management System (SMMS) or Social CRM. At a basic level, the platform enables you to post content to multiple social media channels, monitor brand-related conversations, and engage in two-way dialog with customers. It also helps you analyze and engage with disparate audiences; build, manage, and deploy social apps; and perform extensive reporting and analytics. Although Sprinklr's platform is certainly robust and does a lot to support enterprise capabilities, I focus on three key areas that I feel are the most important: engagement, governance, and analytics.

Sprinklr's engagement platform allows you to publish simultaneously to multiple Twitter accounts, Facebook pages, Wordpress blogs, and YouTube Channels—even Weibo, RenRen, and QQ. This functionality alone will save you a lot of time not having to repost the same material multiple times. The platform has built-in Participation, Spam, and Influencer Indices that tell you which of your friends, fans, and followers are the most active and most relevant within your communities. Additionally, the system allows you to search, filter, and analyze audience members or create rules to automatically tag, profile, and prioritize them for you, taking advantage of its built-in Natural Language Processing technology to determine the sentiment of each conversation and provide a score for each message.

Figure 2.6 is a screenshot of Sprinklr's engagement dashboard, which allows for community managers and/or customer support agents to drill down on the community activity.

Figure 2.6   *Sprinklr's engagement dashboard*

Sprinklr also gives you the capability to build Social Applications and deploy them—with varying degrees of permission and governance—to regional and local areas. The Social App Suite allows you to build polls, contests, surveys, and more. One of the more powerful uses is for social customer service application, reducing time-to-resolution and improving customer satisfaction for large brands such as Target Canada. Essentially, the application lives within Facebook, but it's connected to an existing database of answers to give customers the ability to ask specific questions or search through the knowledgebase to find answers. On the back end after a customer asks a question, support agents or community managers are notified and can either answer the question directly or escalate it to someone who can, all through the Sprinklr platform.

As described earlier in the chapter, governance is a huge challenge for brands today and this is where Sprinklr really excels. The platform allows you to create custom workflows and controls that determine who in the organization can post content, respond to content, approve and edit content, add new channels, configure permissions, and run reports. This is essential in media company operations. It also comes in handy if you work in a decentralized organization where there are multiple stakeholders using social media to engage with customers. The system allows administrators to monitor the activity of all users; it also allows moderators to monitor the activity of customized groups of users and social network accounts. Sprinklr provides reporting widgets to add to its Reporting Dashboards (covering logins, actions, and so on) by user, groups of users, accounts, and so on. It also provides an audit trail visible on each message actioned against in some way (for example, moved to a queue or replied to) in the system. Finally, Sprinklr provides a centralized calendar that will help you get a view of the content planning process, which is essential as you prepare your brand to transition into a media company.

Having a lot of amazing data is worthless unless you can distill it into action-able insights and takeaways. Sprinklr's reporting engine offers you the ability to sort, analyze, and present data across one channel, multiple channels, functions, and also at the brand level. It reports on engagement (Likes, comments, shares, retweets), share of voice, community growth and attrition, and also provides oper-ational reporting details, such as average response time, time-in-queue, and others. There are 300 predefined native reporting widgets. Figure 2.7 shows one view of Sprinklr's current reporting dashboard.

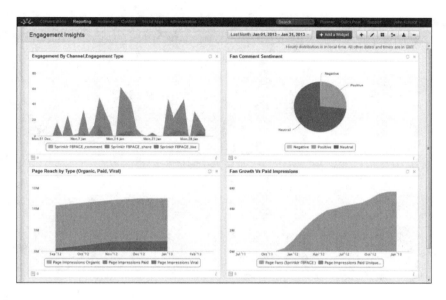

Figure 2.7   *Sprinklr's analytics and reporting dashboard*

SECTION II

Setting the Stage for Social Business Transformation

This section is about building the infrastructure and foundation so that as you focus on your content operations internally, you can prepare for your transformation externally.

The first step in this type of change management initiative is to build a centralized editorial team, often referred to as a Social Business Center of Excellence (CoE). This section gives you a step-by-step plan of attack to help you build your CoE and show you how this team should integrate with other groups within your company.

All media companies have one great asset—several hundred journalists and freelance writers who are creating content day in and day out. Most brands also have a similar asset—employees and customers who love the products, the company, and the brand. It's imperative that you empower "brand advocacy" and enable internal advocates (employees) and external advocates (customers) to help you feed the content engine daily, help tell your brand story from a trusted source, and influence others.

Additionally, it's important that you build an infrastructure of listening. Most companies today are launching Social Business Command Centers that allow them to listen and engage online whenever someone mentions the brand. Command centers can be used one of two ways. First, and the most common way, is from a reactive standpoint, responding to customer inquiries and managing crises. Others are using command centers to spot trends that might be relevant to the brand and then creating real-time marketing content to capitalize on the news cycle. If you are a fan of NFL Football, you might remember what Oreo did during the halftime show of Super Bowl XLVII. As a 49er fan, unfortunately, I missed it.

Chapter 3: Establishing a Centralized "Editorial" Social Business Center of Excellence

This chapter describes the first step of transitioning your brand to a media company, which is to establish a centralized team that will drive content operations and other forms of governance within your company:

- A Lesson from Tesla Motors
- Building Your Social Business Center of Excellence (CoE)
- The Responsibilities of a Center of Excellence
- The Organizational DNA and Team Dynamics
- Considerations for Building a Social Business Center of Excellence
- How the Center of Excellence Integrates into Your Organization
- Vendor Spotlight—Jive

Chapter 4: Empowering Employees, Customers, and Partners to Feed the Content Engine

Consumers trust each other and "people like themselves" more so than they trust people like you, me, or marketers. This chapter is all about mobilizing your brand stakeholders (employees, partners, and customers) to serve as brand journalists and content contributors that can generate game-changing content and help tell your brand story from a trusted voice:

- An Overview of Employee Advocacy
- Advocacy, Trust, and Credibility Are Synonymous
- An Overview of Customer Advocacy
- How to Scale and Plan an Enterprise Advocacy Program
- GaggleAMP Helps Scale Employee Advocacy
- Napkin Labs Helps Scale Customer Advocacy
- Pure Channel Apps and the Channel Partner Content Opportunity
- Vendor Spotlight—Expion

Chapter 5: Building Your Social Business Command Center

Listening to customers is important. Listening to customers and then taking action is game-changing. This chapter is about becoming a listening organization that uses technology to respond to brand mentions and conversations; as well to leverage trending topics for real-time content marketing purposes:

- The Strategic Importance of a Social Business Command Center
- The Social Business Command Center Framework
- How to Build a Social Business Command Center

- Social Business Command Centers in Action
- The New Form of Command Center Operations: Real-Time Marketing
- Vendor Spotlight: HootSuite, Mutual Mind, PeopleBrowsr, Tickr, and Tracx

Chapter 6: Understanding the Challenges of Content Marketing

While content marketing is the new buzzword today, most companies struggle with creating meaningful content. This chapter provides an overview of the challenges of content marketing taking into consideration both quantitative and qualitative data and then drives home the importance of thinking about content more strategically:

- Examples of Brands Taking Content Marketing to the Next Level
- Content Marketing Challenges: What the Experts Say
- Content Marketing Challenges: What Does the Data Show?
- Moving Past the Content Marketing Buzzword
- Vendor Spotlight—Kapost

Establishing a Centralized "Editorial" Social Business Center of Excellence

Tweetable Moment: *Every company is a media company whether they accept it or not. Embrace it like @TeslaMotors did.—#nextmediaco*

Every company is a media company. This is what Tom Foremski, publisher of tech blog Silicon Valley Watcher, has been saying for years now, probably since 2005 or so. And although I agree in concept, I also agree that most public relations and marketing people, and some lazy media companies still "meddle and produce corporate marketing speak" as Tom wrote in a blog post in 2012. They still don't get it.

So maybe every company isn't a media company quite yet. Maybe it's an unforeseen opportunity that many companies have yet to realize. Perhaps saying that every company needs to evolve into a media company is more accurate.

Richard Edelman, CEO of Edelman Public Relations, has also been saying this for quite some time. Most recently in his 6:00 a.m. blog post, titled "Our Time To Lead," he argues that PR must take the lead in this evolution and that every company "should" be a media company and generate content that can be shared across the online ecosystem. Although every company "should" make this transition, most don't realize it, resist it, or have no clue on how to make it happen.

So you may be asking yourself, "Why a media company?"

Following are five characteristics of media companies you must adopt for your brand if you expect to make an impact, break through the noise, and reach consumers with game-changing content.

- **Storytelling:** Media companies tell stories. Conde' Nast has a diverse narrative told through their media properties from fashion and travel to sports and weddings. Traditional news organizations also tell stories, although their narrative is current or breaking news. Some news outlets have tried to up-level their narrative by using anecdotes like "Fair & Balanced" to differentiate themselves from their competition.

- **Content:** Media companies are content machines with an "always on" mentality. It doesn't matter what time of day it is or what the hour; media companies distribute content all the time. For example, the *New York Times* publishes 1,500+ articles per day (including those from AP, Reuters, and so on) and 200 to 400 blog posts.

- **Relevance:** Media companies provide relevant content all the time to someone, somewhere. They aren't in the business of providing content that's a few days or weeks old, unless they are holding off on a story to get more detailed information. The content is recent and, in many cases, real-time.

- **Ubiquity:** Media companies are everywhere. They dominate the search engine results and their content is shared daily across social media channels. They produce videos and advertise, and even their journalists have started building their own personal brands, which also feed the content engine day in and day out.

- **Agility:** Media companies move quickly. They have subject matter experts and contributing writers who are prepared to write about any topic at any time. They also employ creative teams that can produce visual content at a moment's notice. They aren't held captive by approvals from a brand team or lawyers. They are content organizations and move quickly. They have workflows that facilitate the entire content supply chain (ideation, creation, approval, distribution, and integration).

There is a content surplus in the marketplace today, and consumers have attention deficit. For you to reach them with a relevant message, you need to build a content organization where you are creating relevant content—at the right time (sometimes in real time), in the right channel, and to the right customer.

Once you begin the transition and leverage the characteristics mentioned above (storytelling, content, relevance, ubiquity, agility), you can not only create proactive, relevant, and real-time content to reach consumers; but you can also respond to criticism quickly and change brand perception.

Tesla, an electric car manufacturing company, certainly has characteristics of a media company and didn't back down after the *New York Times* wrote a negative article about their Model S vehicle.

A Lesson from Tesla Motors

In February 2013, *New York Times* reporter John Broder wrote a negative review about his experience driving the Tesla Model S electric vehicle. His article, "Stalled Out on Tesla's Electric Highway" essentially made accusations that Tesla did not deliver on their brand promise, specifically around car performance and battery life.

His article documented a trip he took from Washington, D.C. to Connecticut in the Model S, which has an EPA rated range of 265 miles per charge. Tesla had installed two sets of high-speed charging stations, one in Newark, New Jersey, and one in Milford, Connecticut, which are about 200 miles apart, to service all of the commuters who travel between Washington and Boston.

Broder tested this route on a 30-degree day. What's interesting is that cold temperatures are known to negatively affect the performance of the type of lithium-ion batteries used in the Model S vehicle. Broder wrote in detail how the estimated range dropped faster than the miles being covered, forcing him at one point to "set the cruise control at 54 mph and turn the climate control system to low to conserve energy." It certainly didn't help Tesla that Broder also posted a photo of the Model S being hoisted onto the back of tow truck because he didn't have enough battery life to get him to the next charging station.

An unfavorable article in the *New York Times* isn't going to make or break a company, but it sure did have an impact. A few weeks after the article was posted, Elon Musk, CEO of Tesla Motors, went on record to say that the negative review and bad press may have reduced the company's value by $100 million. Speaking on *Bloomberg TV*, Musk said "a few hundred" customers canceled orders for the Model S after Broder's review. But there is more to this story...

Five days after the *New York Times* article was published, Musk wrote an article on his company blog titled, "A Most Peculiar Test Drive" and basically dismantled Broder's review on many different levels, saying at one point that "Model S never had a chance with John Broder." He also called out the *New York Times* directly saying:

> When the facts didn't suit his opinion, he simply changed the facts. Our request of the *New York Times* is simple and fair: please investigate this article and determine the truth. You are a news organization where that principle is of paramount importance and what is at stake for sustainable transport is simply too important to the world to ignore.

Apparently Broder didn't know that the entire driving experience was being monitored and documented via Tesla's GPS and computer system. Figure 3.1 illustrates two inaccuracies in the graphic attached to Broder's article according to Musk.

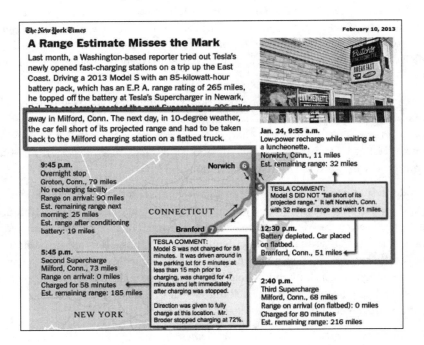

Figure 3.1   *Elon Musk's rebuttal of* New York Times *review*

Fast-forward three days, and the *New York Times* public editor Margaret Sullivan said that she did find problems with reporter John M. Broder's note-taking and judgment after his negative review of the Model S. So without specifically apologizing to Tesla Motors, she apologized.

What makes this story even more interesting is that Musk wasn't the only one who challenged the *New York Times*. A group of six Tesla owners live-tweeted a road trip from Tesla's super-charging station in Maryland to the other in Connecticut to prove that Broder's review was completely wrong as illustrated in Figure 3.2.

Figure 3.2 *Tesla Model S owners challenging the way the* New York Times *reported the story*

The moral of this story is simple. Five or ten years ago, this would never have happened. Traditionally media companies like the *New York Times* or the *Wall Street Journal* have had complete control over the hearts and minds of consumers. They monopolized our attention spans. They dominated the news cycle and could publish anything about any product or service without the worry of a rebuttal on any level. But the evolution, or I should say revolution, in today's media landscape has changed that, and companies like Tesla Motors are now standing on equal ground with the mainstream media.

Tesla Motors is a media company whether they know it or not—they are agile storytellers that produce relevant content that show up across the entire ecosystem. Today, your brand needs to start thinking, acting, and operating like a media company, too, and it's so much more than just refuting negative media coverage.

Unfortunately, it's not like you can turn on the "media company" button and change operations and behavior overnight. It requires a change in attitude, behavior, and thinking, coupled with processes and governance models. You also must have technology in place that can facilitate the transformation. This change starts with building a centralized, editorial team—otherwise known as a Social Business Center of Excellence.

Building Your Social Business Center of Excellence (CoE)

The trend over the last several years in many large companies has been the development of centralized teams, often referred to as a Centers of Excellence (CoE). Many times, these teams are responsible for creating standards and governance around the use of social media both internally and externally. I talk a lot about this in my first book, *Smart Business, Social Business*.

In the context of transforming your brand to a media company, the CoE can be considered more of a content and editorial team. I'm certainly not saying you need to create two separate teams because they are essentially one and the same. It's just a different way of looking at it.

The goal of the CoE should be more than just driving social media adoption, governance, technology (community applications, social CRM), deployment, and training. To achieve true business results, it has to succeed at changing organizational behavior—the way it thinks, communicates, and markets to customers. In doing so, the members must adapt and change their own behavior at the same time. They must become change agents if they truly want to see the transformation come to fruition.

Jeremiah Owyang, Principal Analyst at the Altimeter Group, defines the CoE more from a social business adoption standpoint, highlighting how companies in general are becoming more social. He states that the CoE is a centralized program that provides resources, training, and strategy to a variety of business units that are deploying social media in order to reduce costs, increase efficiency, and provide standardization (webstrategist.com). He writes that this team is often managed by the Corporate Social Strategist, who's the business stakeholder and program champion. Figure 3.3 illustrates a framework needed to deploy a CoE.

**Common Requirements for Social
Media "Center of Excellence"**

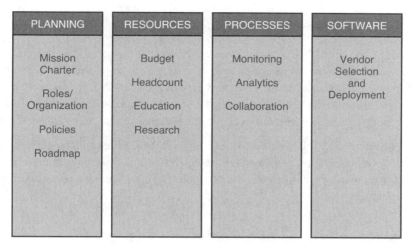

Figure 3.3   *Common requirements to deploy a Social Business Center of Excellence*

In the 2011 research report by the Altimeter Group, titled "How Corporations
Should Prioritize Social Business Budgets," Owyang shares four different business
cases for deploying a CoE:

- **Provide Customers with a Consistent Social Experience:** Business
  units can either be coordinated in their efforts or fragmented and
  decentralized. Without a common program in place, each business unit
  develops its own programs, resulting in wasted resources and a fragmented experience for customers.

- **Obtain Efficiency Throughout the Organization:** The cost of social
  business will only increase as more business units develop social efforts
  on their own without proper "guardrails." Second, this increases time-
  to-market by enabling various business units to communicate with
  each other.

- **Foster Accountability Across Business Units:** Corporations are sad-
  dled with hundreds of social assets, which they have difficulty tracking,
  let alone the risk of a single vendor selling multiple instances to various
  business units. This central group helps to sunset abandoned efforts
  and increase success of all moving parts in the organization.

- **Coordination Among Business Units:** Companies need processes and policies to handle negative situations and mitigate potential PR crises in social channels. This centralized group can quickly work with various arms of the company in a coordinated way to reduce risk and increase responses to PR dilemmas.

Although many of these business cases are important for social business adoption and showcasing organization maturity—and may even be relevant to you and your journey—there is an additional business case that should be front and center as you read through the rest of this book. The first step of transforming your brand to a media company requires you to create and/or champion a center of excellence.

There are certainly other cases that exist beyond these for establishing a centralized team. It will depend on your business objectives and/or challenges that are preventing your company from reaching that next level or solving a particular business problem.

The Responsibilities of a Center of Excellence

If you are a part of a CoE, thinking about building one, or just curious, you need to understand that it's not easy. There are uphill battles and political issues you must navigate through to make progress. Change is difficult in business and generally in life. And, most people reject it unless it's delivered in doses or communicated in a non-threatening way, especially when it can potentially affect others' job responsibilities.

A CoE cannot just be a committee that meets once per month or be someone's part-time job. In most cases, it starts out that way, but eventually it must evolve into something bigger. Otherwise, the team will never get anything done and scaling will be difficult. The CoE must belong to a reporting organization with the autonomy to make specific and calculated business decisions as it relates to marketing communications and brand strategy. Making the successful transformation from a brand to a media company requires the brain power and hard work from a highly specialized team with skill sets ranging from content strategy to technology integration and deployment.

Defining your brand's content strategy will undoubtedly be the most difficult task yet one of your most important responsibilities. Later in this book, I go into great detail on exactly what you need to do succeed. But on a high level, developing a content strategy requires you to analyze several key conversations and analytical inputs and to formulate a content plan that adds value to your customers and also aligns to your brand's objectives. This isn't easy.

Building a content governance plan, which is covered in Chapter 10, "How Content Governance Will Facilitate Media Company Transformation," is a task that needs to be high on your priority list. It's about optimizing your content supply chain, which will ensure control and consistency in the content you create and distribute. Real-time analytics, content performance, and general measurement will also be a part of the CoE's responsibility.

Internal training of employees is also a huge part of the CoE's responsibility. Employees (and customers) can help you feed the content engine by acting as content contributors and brand journalists. But employees must be trained before they're unleashed on the public. The training curriculum should include how to use the latest social media tools and platforms, the best practices for engaging with customers, and how they can contribute content and help tell the brand story within their own social media channels.

One of your last major responsibilities is to assess, deploy, and implement various technology solutions in your organization—from content publishing platforms like Kapost or Contently to real-time content optimization platforms like Social Flow or the Dachis Group Real-time Marketing Dashboard.

The Organizational DNA and Team Dynamics

Every company is different, but most have similar functions that are responsible for specific tasks such as marketing, IT, and customer support. A successful CoE will ensure that there is participation and engagement from multiple business units and from different teams in the company. Figure 3.4 is an example of how a CoE can work in your organization.

Figure 3.4 *One example of organizational structure of a Social Business Center of Excellence*

As you can see in this figure, there are two circles that surround the CoE. The inner circle makes up the core team and involves employees from the social media team (or potentially corporate communications), digital marketing, customer support, analytics, brand/creative, and regional leads. This core team is responsible for

- the content strategy
- how the content strategy is executed across paid, owned, and earned media
- technology deployment and adoption
- best practice sharing
- training of employees and partners

The outer circle represents the supporting roles of the CoE. The core team will tap into their collective knowledge and support for specific initiatives or projects. For example, during the research phase of the content strategy, the segment marketing team may be responsible for sharing any reports or data about current customer segmentation. This is a vital input of the content strategy. Another example is planning for an upcoming event. The events team is crucial to ensure that the CoE is involved in planning and content creation and customer engagement specifically at the event.

The most important element in the outer circle of the CoE are the employees of your company. If you think about how media companies like the Huffington Post generate so much content, it's because they have several hundred contributors fueling the content engine day in and day out. You can leverage the support of employees in a similar fashion and help them become brand journalists. Of course, you wouldn't just open the floodgates without getting their buy-in for participation, training them, and having already established workflows that ensure consistent storytelling.

Considerations for Building a Social Business Center of Excellence

As you prepare to build your team and assign roles and responsibilities, you should consider several things before beginning.

What Is the Vision and What Message Will Be Communicated to Others?

Having a clear and articulate vision for your CoE determines its success. And the message to the rest of your organization must articulate the value of "what's in it for me" and answer questions such as:

- Can I do my job better and more efficiently if I buy into this vision?
- Will it make my job easier, and will I be happier?
- Is this the right vision for the company to achieve its business goals, and does my role play into that vision?

One crucial factor that plays a key role in determining whether others will buy into your vision is what Malcolm Gladwell, author of the *Tipping Point*, describes as "the stickiness factor." This refers to a unique quality that compels a message to "stick" in the minds of others and influence behavior change. After all, that should be the goal of the CoE—to influence and change behaviors of others, ultimately transforming your brand into a media company. The message must dig much deeper than just collaboration and innovation too. It must correlate back to the needs, wants, and desires of employees and at the same time align with your business and marketing objectives.

Find the Willing Participants (Change Agents)

It's one thing to have smart strategists and business leaders as a part of your CoE, but it speaks volumes if the team members have the ability to influence others. Call it the *Law of the Few.*

Borrowing again from Malcolm Gladwell, your CoE should consist of "connectors, mavens, and salespeople." Connectors are the employees who know everyone in every department and have the ability to serve as conduits between each group, helping to find connections, relationships, and "cross-fertilization" that otherwise might not be possible.

Mavens are "information specialists" and are the people within your company many rely on to learn about new information. A maven is someone who wants to solve other people's problems, generally by solving his or her own. According to Gladwell, mavens have the ability to start "word-of-mouth epidemics" due to their knowledge, social skills, and ability to communicate. Even with internal change management initiatives, the ability for a message to spread word-of mouth (from employee to employee) like an epidemic could mean the difference between success and failure. Mavens are information brokers—sharing and trading what they know with whom they know. The goal of transforming your brand to a media company requires an epidemic of change for it to truly spread.

Salesmen are those within your organization who have a natural gift of charisma to be extremely persuasive in inducing others' behaviors. They usually have powerful negotiation skills and tend to have a unique quality that makes others want to agree with them.

You will need people like this on your team if you truly want change implemented within your company.

Defined Roles and Responsibilities

It should be clear from the beginning what your CoE's roles and responsibilities will be—whether it's strategy, change management, technology deployment, or something else.

Unclear roles can quickly give birth to organizational conflict and unnecessary silo creation between internal teams that may have social media as a part of their job responsibility. This is where the "soft" skills of your CoE team can make a difference because much of their jobs will be to evangelize and educate the rest of the organization about your vision. One way to avoid push back and general conflict is to co-create the roles and responsibilities with your team as well other internal stakeholders.

Celebrate Short Term Wins

Social business transformation can take years, and a renewal effort risks losing momentum if your team is not given short-term goals to meet and celebrate. While keeping laser focus on your long-term strategy, it's imperative to try and establish smaller-scale tactical objectives that your CoE can meet within a reasonably short period of time. Examples can include:

- Defining the brand content strategy
- Training employees
- Determining a social media measurement framework
- More effective/collaborative team meetings

These are certainly tactical in nature, but having tangible outcomes of your team's change efforts are important. Consider the following:

- What do you want your team to accomplish this week/month/year?
- What do you want your team to accomplish in two to five years?

To track the progress, it's important to pay attention to small, identifiable changes in your day-to-day business operations such as:

- New ideas/innovations proposed from internal meetings
- Technology vendors (content publishing, communities, social CRM, online monitoring) selected, contracts signed, and deployment schedules finalized
- Social media training started and completed or certain milestones reached

When these positive changes have been observed, it's also important to keep the momentum going and celebrate by:

- Publicly recognizing your team's work
- Giving monetary rewards (bonus, promotion)
- Just saying "thank you" (it goes a long way)
- Gamification (rewarding and incentivizing certain behaviors)

> The goal of transforming your brand to a media company requires an epidemic of change.

A few small wins does not mean that the change has been successfully completed. There will surely be roadblocks in the future if they haven't already surfaced. Using these victories as a stepping-stone to the next achievement will keep your team's momentum going strong. It's important to remember that organizational change doesn't happen overnight, and neither does the transformation from brand to media company.

How the Center of Excellence Integrates into Your Organization

Figure 3.5 illustrates how your CoE can integrate into the organization, from strategy and planning, execution, measurement, and best practice sharing.

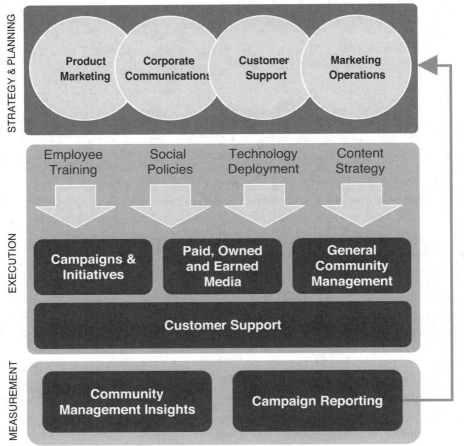

Figure 3.5 *How the Social Business Center of Excellence integrates into the organization*

The top of the figure represents traditional siloed organizations: Product Marketing, Corporate Communications, Customer Support, and Marketing Operations. But this might look completely different for your company and may even include other cross-functional teams such as specific sub-brands, products, or regional teams. Nonetheless, the role of your CoE is to ensure that every team is communicating with each other for a variety of different reasons. Not only is collaboration healthy for your company, it's imperative when deploying enterprise-wide employee training, social media policies, technology deployment, and defining your brand's content strategy.

The ability to tell a consistent brand story across the social ecosystem is fundamental to reach customers, as discussed in Chapter 1, "Understanding the Social Customer and the Chaotic World We Live In." Your CoE is responsible for doing this in several communication channels that include:

- Campaigns and Initiatives
- Paid, Earned, and Owned Media
- General Community Management
- Customer Support

Additionally, the CoE will be responsible for consolidating the collective data points and measurement initiatives from each of these channels and feeding the best practices and learning back into the respective teams so that they can iterate and/or pivot their content strategies if needed. You can almost consider them as facilitators of knowledge sharing.

As you can see, much of the CoE's responsibility will require them to tear down organizational silos and attempt to communicate and collaborate with others. This is a difficult task given that silos have plagued business progress for years. And unfortunately (or fortunately depending on how you look at it), email just won't work in today's business environment. Jive CEO Tony Zingale reiterated this point in a 2012 interview with the *Computer Business Review*. He said that the willingness for employees to collaborate and communicate together is something that companies aren't used to today. The traditional email models are used in a random way, and cultural and behavioral change is necessary to embrace and adopt a new way to communicate and to get work done. The good news is that there are technological solutions that can help facilitate collaboration.

The Jive Social Business Platform is one technology platform that can enable you and your teams to guide collaboration in a more efficient way when deploying your content strategy and driving organizational change across your business.

Vendor Spotlight—Jive

Jive is a social business platform focused on enterprise collaboration. In November 2012, a global business consulting firm analyzed Jive customers and learned that their platform is making a difference in areas like corporate productivity, sales, marketing, and customer service. Jive offers a wide array of product features and capabilities, but here I focus on only the ones that will help you start the transition into a media company.

No one can argue that planning and executing a content strategy is complex, especially if you work in a global company. As I mentioned in Chapter 1, the media landscape is dynamic, and there is a proliferation of delivery channels and devices, multiple partners and players, and an explosion of data—and constantly shifting technologies are coming to the market everyday. The Jive platform gives you the ability to create a virtual war room to monitor all the aspects of your strategy, from planning to execution. It's essentially a dashboard where all of your internal stakeholders can share content, discuss deployment tactics, and manage the entire content supply chain from beginning to end. Regardless of physical location, your teams can stay aligned with the campaign strategy, launch, content plan, and ongoing community engagement. Figure 3.6 is an example of a team collaborating and planning the launch of a new product.

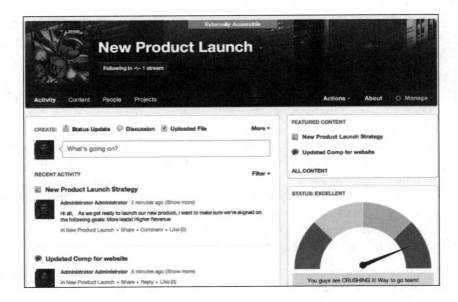

Figure 3.6 *Virtual team members collaborating and planning in real time for a product launch*

Jive also gives you the capability to support disparate teams (sales, marketing, countries) by providing the right content at the right time—when they need it. Instead of using email to solicit feedback on content and to consolidate edits, Jive takes the guesswork out of knowing which version is the latest and provides one channel for your team to communicate important updates to your internal stakeholders. By using Jive's rich text editor, your team can collaborate and edit drafts, solicit feedback, and mark documents as final in one place.

The value of Jive is that it can provide your team with several tools that facilitate internal communication, collaboration, content creation, and sharing. They have built-in activity streams that allow you to see updates from your team members, the projects they are working on, and the content they are uploading and downloading from the platform. You can also create your own custom "Attention Streams" to track particular people, groups, and projects. Their built-in program for Microsoft Office (Word, PowerPoint, and Excel) allows you to turn these documents into a real-time collaborative platform so you can co-author, comment, and revise content with your team without disjointed email attachments and version control madness. This is extremely helpful as your team is documenting best practices from others in the organization and sharing them across the company.

The built-in game mechanics and rewards capabilities encourage your team to participate and provide incentives to actively engage within the platform. As teams participate, they earn more points and get more rewards. So if you have employees who are responsible for writing, editing, or approving content, this is an excellent way to encourage them to do more of it.

Although Jive is excellent for internal collaboration, it's worth mentioning that they also power external communities as well. Figure 3.7 is a screenshot of SAP's Community Network where customers, partners, and SAP employees are engaging in real-time technology and industry discussions.

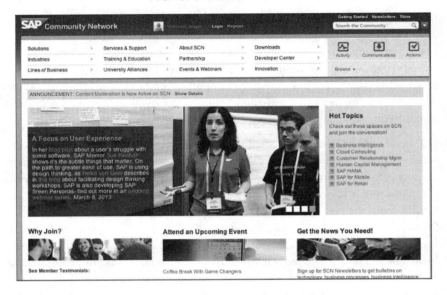

Figure 3.7   *Jive enables SAP to engage directly with customers and partners.*

4

Empowering Employees, Customers, and Partners to Feed the Content Engine

Tweetable Moment: *Smart marketers will enable employees, customers, and partners to feed the content engine and help tell the brand story. —#nextmediaco*

If I were a PR guy and shared a press release on Facebook or broadcasted a Tweet announcing a new product or service, chances are you wouldn't notice. And if you did notice, you probably wouldn't care. I am a marketer by trade and I have an agenda. I want you to buy my product, click my link, download a whitepaper, Like my status update, and then tell all your friends about it. This is one reason I'm not trusted or credible in the eyes of the consumer.

But what if a random employee does the same? Will he or she get the same reaction? It will certainly depend on the context and tone of the message. But if the employee is just excited about the company they work for or demonstrating a level of thought leadership, that message has the ability to influence others. This is called brand advocacy. An advocate can be an employee that loves the company, a customer that loves the products, or a channel partner that values the relationship.

An Overview of Employee Advocacy

Several variables are involved when discussing employees tweeting or promoting content about their company and/or it products. The obvious one is whether or not employees are simply spamming their online communities with deliberate marketing messages or retweeting brand messages offering zero value. If it is spam, readers will undoubtedly ignore those messages and brands may find themselves the focal point of case study on "what not to do" when activating their employees.

But what if the employees were adding value to the conversation? What if they were transparent with the information they were sharing and it was actually helpful? Would people still feel the same? Jay Baer, author of *New York Times* bestseller *Youtility: Why Smart Marketing Is About Help, Not Hype,* makes the case that marketing, whether directly from a brand and/or its employees, must add value (or be helpful) when communicating directly with customers. It could be as easy as providing how-to videos that offer customer value. In 2013, Lowe's released a series of amazingly simple Vine videos of home improvement tips and tricks—unscrewing a stripped screw, taking off a stubborn sticker, and cleaning a dirty cookie sheet. Or, it can be as simple as employees offering low-level support to customers who are seeking additional information about the brand's products (such as customers looking for the latest software download).

In this case, the power lies with both the tone and context of the actual message and the person delivering it. Why? Because humans relate to humans more than they do to a brand message, assuming that the person sharing content isn't copying and pasting scripted marketing material. It's in our DNA to relate to others. When is the last time you had a conversation with a sign on a brick wall with a logo on it? Hopefully, never. But I am sure you remember receiving stellar service at a restaurant or from an airline flight attendant. You might even remember his or her first name. This happens all the time.

Do a search in Twitter for Zappos, and you will find customers and employees tweeting about how much they love the brand. And guess what? If you ever tweet about having an issue with an order being late or never arriving, those same customers and employees will respond in no time asking you how they can help.

It's called *brand advocacy* and you can fuel your brand's content engine by enabling employees and customers to help you tell your brand story. Media companies today are doing this but in a slightly different way.

Let's take *Forbes* as an example. *Forbes* has always been known as a magazine that features original articles about finance, investing, and marketing topics. As of a few years ago, Forbes.com barely had an online presence worth talking about. Even though the site itself has been online since 1996, it wasn't until 2008 that something shifted. It's unclear when they started allowing for contributing authors, but since then the content has really started to make an impact. Today, several hundred contributing authors write topics daily about marketing, business, and social media. And all that content not only lives on Forbes.com, but it's also indexed in Google and drives mass amounts of web traffic back to the site, which is definitely a good thing for Forbes.com's advertisers.

You might ask, "What's in it for the contributing authors if they aren't staff?" Well, contributing authors do get paid based on the amount traffic they drive back to Forbes.com. It's also advantageous to add "*Forbes* Columnist" on their LinkedIn profiles. *Forbes* blogs and articles reach quite far across the social web, giving contributing authors a wider range of visibility for their content. In fact, I see content daily from *Forbes* shared on Twitter, Facebook, and LinkedIn coupled with hundreds of comments, Likes, +1s, and retweets. You need to think of your employees as contributors (or brand journalists) that can help tell your brand story in a human and authentic way.

In a 2012, HootSuite CEO Ryan Holmes wrote a blog post in LinkedIn citing three reasons why you should hire employees specifically to use social media. According to the post, he said

- **#1:** It helps hire better people.
- **#2:** It breaks down hierarchies in the workplace.
- **#3:** It empowers employees to be brand advocates.

Although #1 and #2 are certainly important and can have a positive impact on your business culture, #3 illustrates this point of employee advocacy. In his post, Ryan says that there's absolutely no requirement that his employees talk about HootSuite on social media channels, but he is fully supportive of them building their individual brands and social media following while cultivating the company brand at the same time.

Of course, any CEO can write a blog post and preach about employee empowerment, culture, or management issues. But in HootSuite's case, it's much more than just lip service. I have experienced his philosophy firsthand on several different levels over the last few years. Let me give you a few examples.

I first started using Twitter in 2007. Back then, there weren't any apps to tweet from, so all functionality and usage had to be managed directly from Twitter.com. In 2008, TweetDeck was launched, and the application not only allowed you to manage Twitter accounts more effectively, but it also made content publishing and community management so much easier. It was the first app of its kind in the market and it was easy to use.

In 2012, one of my clients asked me to facilitate a training session for his global marketing team's offsite. The topic was "How to use Twitter to Engage with

Customers and Influencers." It seemed easy and straightforward at first. After all, I do this type of training all the time. It got complicated after he told me that they had just signed an enterprise agreement with HootSuite and that he wanted a hands-on demo to be included in the training session—screenshots, how-tos, and step-by-step instructions on how to set up accounts and workflows. I had never used the platform before, so I had to learn it quickly. At first, I didn't understand the platform at all. I was confused about how HootSuite managed various accounts, and the entire user interface seemed foreign to me. I was frustrated and anxious at the same time because I was on a strict timeline.

So I sent out a few public tweets asking for help. The responses were overwhelming, and they came flooding in not just from HootSuite employees, but from their customers as well. Several tweets directed me to an online library filled with white papers, videos, how-to guides, and blog posts. One employee even offered up a phone call and gave me a personal walk through of the platform. After a few short hours reading the material, watching the videos, and using the platform, I felt confident enough to create the training session.

Later in 2012, HootSuite's University Director Kirsten Bailey demoed their platform via Skype for my social business strategy class that I teach at San Jose State University. She spent an hour and a half in the evening with my class answering questions about a variety of topics related to their software and also walked them step-by-step through the platform.

And for months thereafter, she spent valuable time with students answering additional questions, which isn't even a part of her job.

Many other HootSuite employees have become my personal friends. I have written several guest posts on their blog, participated in speaking engagements with various team members, and been involved in a webinar series as a part of HootSuite University. Although they have become a recent client of Edelman, I have always been an advocate of their brand, even before I started working with them. I often tell others about my experiences and it's not just because they have an excellent product. They have great employees, too. They are a textbook example of a company that has truly humanized its brand by empowering its employees to engage externally with customers and prospects. Oh, and I still use HootSuite today.

Though these personal stories are certainly inspiring, let's examine some data to see if there is more to this story.

Advocacy, Trust, and Credibility Are Synonymous

Every year, Edelman conducts an annual report and surveys more than 31,000 people in 26 different markets around the world (see Figure 4.1 for 2012 and 2013 results). The report measures the level of trust people have in institutions, industries, business leaders and within various markets. When asked about trusted sources and credible spokespeople, respondents speak loud and clear about who they find credible when seeking information about a brand or company:

- 67% of those surveyed find a technical expert in the company as credible.
- 61% of those surveyed find a "a person like yourself" as credible.
- 51% of those surveyed find a regular employee in the company as credible.

TRUSTED SOURCES ARE EXPERTS AND PEERS
CREDIBLE SPOKESPEOPLE

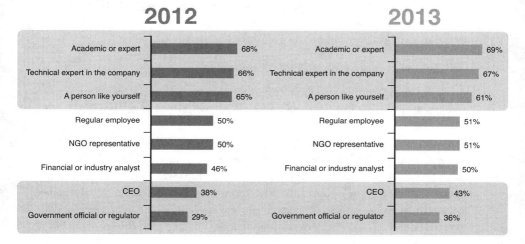

Figure 4.1   *2013 Edelman Trust Barometer—trusted sources are experts and peers.*

Additionally, 2012 research by the Society for New Communications Research (SNCR) titled the "Social Mind" surveyed 300 business professionals and found that by far the most frequent use of social media among business professionals was interacting with their peers within online communities like LinkedIn, Facebook, Twitter, vertical-specific communities like Spiceworks, and even branded communities. Key findings of the study include:

- Professionals spend 40% of their time online interacting in peer-based communities, closely followed by online interactions with friends (31%) and family (13%).
- Sixty-five percent of users participate to engage with a professional community of colleagues and peers via social media networks.

- Eighty percent participate in groups online to help others by sharing information, ideas, and experiences.
- Eighty-two percent exchange information with professional networks, and 78% exchange information online with friends; 37% exchange information with "experts."
- Nearly 80% of respondents participate in online groups to help others by sharing information and experiences; 66% participate in a professional community of colleagues and peers; 41% participate in groups to be seen as someone knowledgeable.
- Educational information was by far the most frequently shared at 61%.
- For seeking information about companies, nearly 50% of respondents said that visiting company websites was most meaningful, 45% read blogs; followed by micro blogging (41%), direct email (40%), and information exchange in online groups or forums (41%).

So what exactly does this research mean for you?

Well, we know from the Edelman Trust Barometer that employees (technical experts and "people like yourself") are trusted and viewed as credible. We also know that business professionals spend a lot of time in social networks interacting with others, seeking advice, and looking for information. So by combining these two pieces of research, it makes sense to empower your employees to engage online with customers, especially if you work in a B2B (Business to Business) environment. It gives you the opportunity to demonstrate thought leadership, influence others through the buying cycle, and feed the content engine with relevant and trusted content. It also provides an opportunity to have employees become brand journalists.

Employees as Brand Journalists

As humans, we love to hear good stories. You probably know "that guy" who can capture the attention of everyone around him during a dinner party when he's telling a story. He's always with an entourage of people laughing and agreeing with just about everything he says. This might explain why when someone is telling you a good story, you may not even realize it. You are too fascinated with the actual story itself. That's the power of a well-told story. From a brand standpoint, storytelling allows a company to be "human" and being human is about having a real, honest connection with people, being transparent, responsive, and, above all, accessible. We can all thank social media for all that.

This is why your brand must empower employees to become storytellers, or rather, brand journalists.

One of the earliest references of brand journalism came from Larry Light, McDonald's CMO, at the 2004 AdWatch conference where he proclaimed that mass marketing no longer worked and no single approach told the whole story. Here is what he said:

> Brand Journalism is a chronicle of the varied things that happen in our brand world, throughout our day, throughout the years. Our brand means different things to different people. It does not have one brand position. It is positioned differently in the minds of kids, teens, young adults, parents, and seniors. It is positioned differently at breakfast, lunch, dinner, snack, weekday, weekend, with kids, or on a business trip.
>
> Brand Journalism allows us to be a witness to the multi-faceted aspects of a brand story. No one communication alone tells the whole brand story. Each communication provides a different insight into our brand. It all adds up to a McDonald's journalistic brand chronicle.

Light's speech didn't go well with everyone. Seth Godin, marketing genius and author of over 12 best-selling marketing books, responded in a blog post just a few days later:

> The marketer doesn't get to run the conversation. It's not really brand journalism that's happening, you see. It's brand cocktail party! You get to set the table and invite the first batch of guests, but after that the conversation is going to happen with or without you. (sethgodin.type-pad.com)

And Godin was absolutely right. Back in 2004, brands were still confused on how to use social media to actually have a conversation. Today, things are different.

The philosophy of brand journalism is simple. It's about combining the core tenets of journalism with brand storytelling, thereby creating conversational value to all stakeholders, both customers and the media. Brand journalism is much more than employees tweeting or sharing company news on Facebook. It's about finding good stories about the brand, its products, or employees and using long-form content to tell a story. There is no real difference between an employee brand advocate and a brand journalist. One just has superior writing skills and can tell better stories.

The idea of brand journalism is easy. The execution isn't. But the good news is that this book will show you how to do it. But as you prepare to empower, train and mobilize your employees, you can't forget the power of your customers either.

An Overview of Customer Advocacy

I talked a lot about customer advocacy in my first book, but it's probably even more important today. Customers are influencing their peers through the purchase funnel through organic conversations they are having online and offline. Their voices and opinions are trusted. Consider these three powerful data points:

- Ninety-two percent of consumers around the world say they trust earned media, such as recommendations from friends and family. (Nielsen)
- Eighty-two percent of U.S. consumers are influenced by friend's social media posts, compared to 78% for brands' posts. (WOMMA)
- There are a total of 500 billion word-of-mouth impressions every year. (Forrester)

But do we even need data to support these findings? Most of us intuitively know that we as customers trust each other. How many times have you been influenced to purchase a specific product or fly on a particular airline because someone told you about his or her personal experience? On the other hand, how many times have you changed your mind about purchasing a specific product because one of your friends shared their negative experience? It happens all the time. As I mentioned in Chapter 1, "Understanding the Social Customer and the Chaotic World We Live In," we are all influential, regardless of our Klout scores or how many friends, fans, and followers we have.

The good news today is that customer advocacy is becoming an increasingly important topic for marketers. But the opportunity is more than just building intimate relationships with those customers who have a strong affinity for your brand. The opportunity is enablement; that is, enabling those customers to help tell your brand story. According to a 2013 study facilitated by Brand Advocacy Platform Zuberance and UBM Tech, producers of the Online Marketing Summit found

- Eighty-nine percent of marketers said advocacy is important or very important in 2013.
- Seventy-nine percent of marketers said advocacy is more important in 2013 than it was in 2012.
- Seventy percent of marketers planned to increase spending on advocate marketing programs in 2013.

So we have established that empowering brand advocates (employees and customers) is important to help feed your brand's content engine; and it's great news that companies are now realizing the opportunity and making financial investments in this area. But the challenge with empowerment is that it's not actionable. Any CEO or business leader can send out a corporate-wide email empowering the workforce to engage in social media. And at the same time, any community manager can ask friends, fans, and followers to upload photos to their Facebook timeline. But just because you ask doesn't mean they will listen. For you to scale your content operations, you need to *enable* brand advocacy, and this means you have to have a plan.

There are three types of advocacy programs that you can leverage as a part of your media company transformation: employees, customers, and partners. Each of these groups can play a significant role in your content strategy with each one taking on the role of a contributor, writer, or brand journalist. However, there are certain fundamentals you must carefully think through before you launch your programs that will enable you to scale and plan accordingly.

How to Scale and Plan an Enterprise Advocacy Program

A successful enterprise advocacy program is comprised of four pieces: the program infrastructure, the content strategy, the measurement framework, and the technology platform. But you should always remember what it is you are trying to accomplish when thinking about your advocates. Most brand advocacy programs are designed solely to build more intimate relationships with customers, gain customer insights, or share future product roadmaps with them. While these factors are surely important, there is much more to it. If you are serious about transforming your brand into a media company, you need to ensure that your advocates (employees, customers, or partners) are given the opportunity to contribute content and help tell your brand story.

Program Infrastructure

You can think of the infrastructure as the terms and conditions or plan of record for your advocacy program. The infrastructure documents a variety of information and can even serve as your "pitch" internally for financial support from other business units:

- **Selection Criteria:** It's important to document a process for selecting your advocates. This can be anything you choose, and it's quite possible that your criteria will change as you learn and expand the program. You can randomly select advocates based on their individual levels of influence or how large their personal communities are. You can decide whom to include based on how often they engage with the brand. You can have advocates apply to be a part of the program. Or you can you use platforms such as Kred, SocMetrics, Appinions, or Flow140, which are tools that can help you identify your most influential advocates within specific areas of interest. For employees, you can pick and choose who you want to participate based on their interest and social proficiency. You can even open it up to your entire company. However, it's a best practice to start small and hand select a few employees, establish a few small wins, learn some best practices, and then begin to open up the program to other employees gradually.

- **Longevity of Program:** In many cases, advocate programs have an infinite life span. Some companies rotate advocates in and out every 6 to 12 months or simply leave it open for anyone to join. This depends on your resources and/or budget constraints. The one thing to remember is that when you build a thriving community of advocates, you cannot abandon or forget about them—ever. The Microsoft MVP (Most Value Professional) program has been around well over a decade and still going strong today. Out of 100 million technical community members globally; roughly 4,000 of them are MVPs. MVPs are nominated into the program by their peers, Microsoft employees, and other MVPs who participate in the program. Each year a panel of Microsoft employees reviews the contributions of each nominee for quality, quantity, and level of impact of content created within the technical community. The MVP program has been cited in hundreds of blog posts, white papers, and several articles in the *Harvard Business Review* as "best in class" advocate programs.

- **Customer/Employee Expectations:** You must be completely clear when you communicate your expectations to your advocates and also outline what they can expect from you in return. For example, an advocate program might consist of you soliciting feedback from your advocates about new products or services. This should only be done if you are actually willing to implement their feedback (if it makes business sense of course). Bobbi Brown Cosmetics did this back in 2012. They ran a Facebook promotion to crowd source which new shade of lip color the company would put back into production. CEO Bobbi Brown posted a video on the company's Facebook page, inviting its near 250,000 fans to vote for their favorite from a list of the 10 most-frequently requested colors. Bobbi Brown then made those products available to buy exclusively through Facebook—a good way to measure ROI as well. Other companies, such as Nissan, Volkswagen Canada, Levis, and Expedia, have done similar programs.

Or if you are enabling employees to write, tweet, or contribute to your brand's Facebook page, Twitter account, or blog, you should ensure that their content is actually getting published and not sitting in your email inbox.

- **Organizational Support:** Regardless of which team is responsible for managing this program, there must be internal support from executives, product organizations, customer support, compliance, privacy/security, and legal *before* your program is launched. This requires collaboration across job functions and maybe geographies, which is always a good thing to do anyway.

- **Contract or NDA:** Not all advocate programs require a contract or NDA. If you are sharing product road maps or giving them confidential information, then yes, there should be controls in place that protect you and your company's intellectual property. There should always, however, be documented terms and conditions that contain language explaining that advocates can leave the program at any time and for any reason or can be asked to leave the program at any time and for any reason.

- **Social Media Policy:** Specifically for employee advocacy programs, you must ensure that there is not only a social media policy in place, but that employees are familiar with it and trained accordingly.

Content Strategy

As much as your content strategy must include curating and distributing content from your advocates to help tell your brand story, you must also have a content plan for engaging directly with them. Unfortunately, many teams that manage these programs often overlook a content plan and then struggle to keep the conversations alive and fresh with advocates—more so with customers than employees. Your content should be planned weekly, monthly, and even quarterly and take into consideration several factors such as the following:

- Upcoming events or industry tradeshows
- Upcoming product launches or new releases of an existing product
- Fun things like contests, polls, and research questions
- Asking for user generated content (such as uploading and sharing photos on Facebook orTwitter)

Smart and innovative companies take it one step further and co-create new products and services with the community. GiffGaff, a mobile virtual network operator based in the U.K., is a textbook example of a brand that has built their entire business with their community members. Using the software application, Lithium, they reward active community members for running various portions of the business including answering questions in the community, attracting new members, or using content to help promote the company.

As a thank you, community members are rewarded with virtual praise and an elevated personal reputation. These points are accumulated for referring people to the service, helping people by answering specific questions or solving technical issues in the community, or even creating promotional content for the company. The points can be applied against their monthly mobile services, taken as a cash reward, or donated to a charitable cause.

Measurement

Measurement cannot be ignored when managing and scaling your enterprise advocacy programs. Some companies measure reach and impressions of content that are shared externally from advocates. Others simply measure the amount of activity and participation from advocates. And even others measure actual sales generated through an advocate program. Zuberance, the brand advocate platform mentioned earlier in the chapter provides this level of measurement and engagement to its clients.

Whatever your measurement criteria, it should be used as a benchmark internally for all other (and future) advocate programs. More importantly, the KPIs need to be in alignment with business goals and should be shared internally with each of your stakeholders before you launch your program.

Technology

A decision should be made early on about which technology platform you want to use to manage, communicate, and mobilize your advocates. Using email will not be an option because it can't really scale, track, or measure anything. You can always take the "limited budget" approach and use private LinkedIn and/or Facebook groups. Although using these platforms is affordable, this approach doesn't give you the ability to customize the look, feel, and functionality of the program. It's also more difficult to enable your advocates to create, share, and amplify content using these free platforms. You might also want to look into using private communities built with popular applications, such as Lithium as mentioned earlier. This option gives you more flexibility to match the look and feel of a corporate website as well as integration with other social CRM, customer service, and online monitoring technology solutions.

There are also several new players in this space that can help you communicate with advocates, manage and promote their content, reward them, and run various measurement reports and analytics:

- **Dynamic Signal:** A platform that manages and scales both employee and customer advocate programs with the ability to create private and/ or public facing communities.

- **Zuberance:** A platform that finds advocates based on their Net Promoter Scores and then gives you the ability customize various flows depending on their scores.

- **Fancorps:** A platform that allows you to ask advocates to perform certain tasks and then get rewarded for completion; usually lives within a Facebook page.

- **Influitive:** A platform similar to Fancorps but more focused on the B2B audience and lives on a separate microsite. They also have built-in rewards and badging.

- **Crowdtap:** A platform that's focused on collaborative marketing with customers with built-in rewards.

- **Social Chorus:** An influencer marketing platform that allows you to upload various forms of content that advocates can then use for their own blogs and social communities.

- **Extole:** A platform that allows you to tap into the power of your customer advocates to drive brand awareness, new sales, and acquisitions through word of mouth marketing.

- **Addvocate:** A platform mainly for employees that makes it easy for them to share content about the brand or any other topic.

Though many of these platforms offer similar capabilities, functionality, and pricing, you have to ensure that they can meet your internal requirements and business goals instead of the other way around. And as you begin transforming your brand into a media company, one requirement is how you can leverage these advocates to help create and distribute content. Remember, this is what media companies do.

Three vendors in this space do this really well: GaggleAMP focuses on enabling employees; Napkin Labs position themselves for customers; and Pure Channel Apps prides itself as being the only vendor in the market place that caters to channel partners in the supply chain.

GaggleAMP Helps Scale Employee Advocacy

This entire chapter is about advocacy, and there is no better place to start than with your employees. As mentioned earlier, your employees can serve as brand journalists if they have the right training and know how to tell stories. Or, more generally, they can at least be content contributors and amplify branded content, very similar to the *Forbes* example mentioned in the earlier section "An Overview of Employee Advocacy."

GaggleAMP is best described as a social media amplification platform that enables employees to share branded content and also fuel the content engine with their own thoughts and ideas. They have two core products: Amplify and Distribute. Both products are cloud-based platforms that allow you to invite employees into what the platform calls Gaggles. Each employee of these Gaggles is notified via email whenever there is a new piece of content to be shared. The employee can then choose to share the content with the click of a button or click "No Thanks." In some cases, you can use built-in controls to ensure that some content remains compliant and can't be edited, which is good if you work in a regulated industry. Figure 4.2 shows you how employees can edit content and then share it to their personal social media accounts.

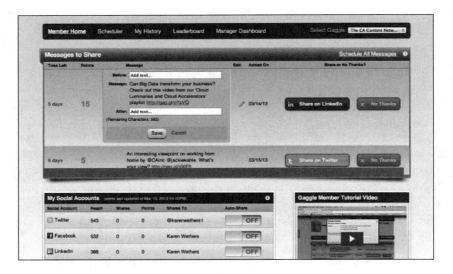

Figure 4.2   *2013 GaggleAMP enables employees to edit content before they share it.*

The difference between the two products Amplify and Distribute depends on who you are distributing content to, an individual or an entity. The Amplify product is solely for employees. The Distribute product is more for franchisees like Cold Stone, Subway, or insurance companies that may have several local retail outlets. Both products provide an amplification effect by having content, which previously would have been shared on one social media account to be shared on a large number of accounts over a period of time. The result extends both the reach and the shelf life of your content marketing initiatives.

Finally, GaggleAMPs products can be integrated into marketing automation platforms and web tracking tools such as Marketo, Google Analytics, and HubSpot.

Napkin Labs Helps Scale Customer Advocacy

While GaggleAMP is good for scaling employee advocacy programs, Napkin Lab's core focus is on customer advocacy. Their platform turns Facebook pages into social hubs that gather feedback and ideas that can help you collaborate with your most valuable customers. With their "Fan Center" platform, you can crowd source content, ask questions, and capture insights about your customers globally and in real time.

As a primary step, their platform captures two years worth of social data about how each fan has interacted with your brand page in the past. Based on millions of comments, Likes, shares, photos, posts and polls, they give each fan a ranked score, helping you identify your top advocates. They offer a series of leaderboards and analytics that give you insight into which of your fans are most active and influential, as well as what they are talking about. They also provide tools to sort and segment top users geographically and provide rewards and badges for those who are most active in your Facebook community.

In the context of this book and as you think about content, Napkin Labs' tools push beyond just the first phase of measuring consumer-to-brand interaction. Insights into top fans become the stepping stone to mobilizing advocates to create and share powerful content that influencers others. You can choose from over 15 activities to crowd source content from your top advocates. For example, they have a brainstorm tool to gather ideas around a topic you pose or a storytelling tool to capture relevant stories from customers. The tool then gives you the ability to reward a fan or easily repurpose content to be posted on your Facebook timeline. Figure 4.3 shows how easy it is for you to use the Fan Center almost as a content library to highlight customer stories.

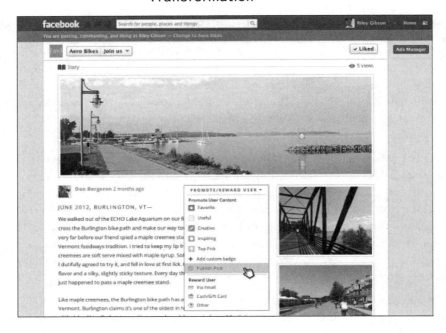

Figure 4.3 *Napkin Labs makes it convenient to share fans' content on your brand's Facebook timeline.*

Using this platform, advocacy, content creation, and even consumer insight gathering becomes intertwined and mutually reinforcing. You can form a richer community within a Facebook experience by giving your fans a greater voice and enabling them to help you tell your brand story. Meanwhile, you are capturing invaluable content and forming a deeper understanding of your most valuable customers.

Although tools like Napkin Labs work well for B2C brands, which sell products or services directly to consumers, you can't forget the content opportunities of working with your channel partners in the supply chain, especially if you work in business-to-business (B2B).

Pure Channel Apps and the Channel Partner Content Opportunity

Pure Channel Apps and their SocialOnDemand platform enable channel partners to share and distribute relevant content up and down the supply chain. Using this platform is a win-win for everyone involved because it gets your message in front of the right audience and also helps feed your channel partner's content engine.

Here is how it works.

The first step in the process is content creation—whether you work for a vendor, manufacturer, distributor, or retailer. The content can be in any form, such as a blog post, tweet, Facebook update, infographic, whitepaper, or video.

Then you enter that content into the SocialOnDemand platform and select a series of filters or tags that correlate to a specific territory, country, post category, and/or customer segment. This is done to ensure that your channel partners only receive the content that's relevant to their customers. Figure 4.4 illustrates how to enter in a new piece of content.

Figure 4.4 *SocialOnDemand enables B2B companies to share content with their channel partners.*

After the content is in the system, your channel partners will receive an email informing them that there is content waiting to be approved. From there, they can decide if they want to publish it or not. If they decide to publish the content, they can log into the portal where they'll be able to edit the post, assign it to one or more of their social media accounts, or publish directly from the SocialOnDemand platform. Figure 4.5 is a sample email that channel partners receive notifying them that there is content for them to approve or not.

At any time, you can log into the system and see how many of your partners are registered; how many social media accounts they have added; what social media accounts these are; and how many friends, fans, and followers each partner has within his or her community. You also have the ability to see which channel partners have generated the most engagement with your content, the potential reach and impressions, as well as the number of clicks.

Figure 4.5   *Channel partners are notified via email that there is content waiting for them to approve.*

Vendor Spotlight—Expion

Expion is an enterprise-grade social media management platform that allows for large brands and multi-location companies to engage in social media channels. At a very basic level, the platform allows you to post content to multiple social media channels like Facebook, Twitter, Google+, and LinkedIn; monitor brand-related conversations; and engage in two-way dialog with customers and partners. Their platform also helps brands analyze and engage with various audiences; build, manage, and deploy social media apps; and provide reporting and analytics dashboards. Though their platform is certainly robust and supports various enterprise capabilities their Social Advocator feature is what is being spotlighted here.

As discussed throughout this entire chapter, empowering customers and employees to engage online on your behalf is a challenge to scale. These two groups of advocates need to be enabled to feed your content engine, and it has to be convenient for them to do so. Social Advocator solves this problem. This value-added feature can give you the opportunity to build on your employee and customer advocacy programs and enable them to share branded content online and within their own social networks very easily. As depicted in Figure 4.6, Social Advocator is a browser plugin compatible with Chrome, Safari, Firefox, and Internet Explorer. Advocates are notified when there is new content that they can share, and they can simply click a browser icon to view the content.

Figure 4.6 *Social Advocator allows advocates to share branded content easily from a
browser plugin.*

As you can see from the figure, the plugin is visual, almost Pinterest-like, so that
advocates can easily scroll through the content and share what they are most interested in sharing. Currently, Social Advocator can publish to Facebook, Twitter,
Google+ and LinkedIn.

On the back end, marketing, communication teams, brand teams, or just about
anyone else who you give access to within your company can add content for each
of the social networks and store it into this content library. Content can be scheduled or updated in real-time with push notifications, and each time you add new
content, a notification appears in the browser plugin icon. Advocates can share this
content if they wish.

What makes this platform even more robust is the integration with the Expion
engagement dashboard. As you are executing your content strategy and engaging
day to day with your customers, the content generated from your advocates can
be integrated into the platform and be shared or amplified directly by the brand.
The platform can also give you robust metrics to showcase the reach/impressions
of your advocate's communities, detail their level of engagement, and help you
identify which advocates participate the most, as well as identify which ones are the
most influential.

5

Building Your Social Business Command Center

Tweetable Moment: *Listening to customers and not taking action is worse than not listening to them at all.—#nextmediaco*

There is a scene from the 2002 Matt Damon movie, The Bourne Identity, *in which several high-ranking CIA officials at the Pentagon are tracking Jason Bourne's every move through satellite and GPS and displaying it on several large screens. They basically want him captured or dead before he reaches the media and exposes Operation Treadstone. The room is filled with data scientists and analysts who are updating Bourne's movements in real-time and passing that information to hired mercenaries who are on the ground hot on his trail.*

Of course this is just Hollywood, but scenarios similar to this actually exist.

The North American Aerospace Defense Command (NORAD) is a bi-national United States and Canadian organization responsible for ensuring air sovereignty and air defense of North American airspace and for monitoring against potential threats to both countries.

Some of these warnings include the monitoring of man-made objects in space and the detection and warning of attacks against North America whether by aircraft, missiles, or space vehicles.

I spent eight years in the U.S. Marines, so I can talk about NORAD all day long. And though I am certainly glad that we have them protecting us citizens from UFOs and such, this chapter is more focused on how brands, large and small, are using similar command centers to monitor "brand" conversations and how you can use them to engage with customers.

A *Social Business Command Center* is a dedicated area (either virtual or in a physical space) where a brand's social media or customer service team can monitor real-time conversations about the brand and its products as well as engage in conversations with influencers, customers, prospects, and the media. Whether it's a Pentagon-like setup, a few LCDs in a conference room, or virtual dashboards manned by community managers and support agents in various offices, the Social Business Command Center can acquire real-time intelligence and help you make informed business and marketing decisions.

To give you additional context and a slightly different point of view, Jeremiah Owyang, Analyst at the Altimeter Group, defines command centers as the following:

> A command center is a physical space where companies coordinate to listen and engage their market in social channels to achieve business use cases in marketing engagement, customer care, risk management, or operational efficiency of coordination and contact center deflection.

Command centers can be used to solve a variety of business challenges, such as managing crises, solving customer problems, or listening for trending topics so that your brand can capitalize on real-time content marketing. However, you must first have a well-documented plan of action so that you can stay laser-focused on what it is you are trying to achieve as you build and launch one. This includes ensuring you have alignment from all your internal stakeholders, documented keywords and phrases that you will be monitoring, technology selection, processes/workflows, and reporting frequency.

The Strategic Importance of a Social Business Command Center

Before you launch your command center, it's important to ensure that you have the right goals and objectives, buy-in and support from internal stakeholders, as well as the budget needed to make this financial investment because it's not cheap. The following are eight use-cases why your business should have a command center. You can use this information to create your proposals and answer questions from upper management—especially the executives who have financial authority.

1. **Listen**: This one is the no-brainer. Several of the technology platforms that power command centers pride themselves on their listening capabilities. They have software that scrubs the Internet and captures all mentions of your brand in forums, blogs, Twitter, Facebook, YouTube comments, Instagram—you name it. It then provides reports that measure share of voice, volume of mentions, sentiment, community growth, engagement metrics, and so on. Just like any relationship, whether online or in real life, most of what you should do is *listen*.

2. **Action**: What's the point of listening if you aren't prepared to take action? Ask any married couple how important this is. Most will tell you that it's imperative in relationship building and nurturing. At least my wife thinks so. Deploying a command center gives you the opportunity to find relevant conversations about your brand and then allows you to add value to the conversation by participating. If you aren't prepared to add value to the discourse, you might want to rethink your strategy or postpone it until you are ready to do so. This is especially important for customer service teams and them having the autonomy to solve customer issues quickly and efficiently.

3. **Community**: When you listen to the conversation and add value to it, you and your brand become trusted members of the community. And as Seth Godin wrote in his book, *Permission Marketing*, over 11 years ago, you can then "ask permission" to market your products and services to them. The same holds true today. Both Facebook and Twitter spent years building their communities before they decided to monetize them, and today they are both doing extremely well.

4. **Brand Advocacy**: Friends, fans, and followers are great, and it sure looks good in a PowerPoint presentation when you have a lot of them. But what's next? Your goal should be to turn those friends, fans, and followers into brand advocates. Chapter 4, "Empowering Employees, Customers, and Partners to Feed the Content Engine," not only pleads the case that you need to create brand advocacy that can help you feed the content engine, but it also shows you how to do it, step-by-step.

5. **Content**: Command centers can also give you the opportunity to capture trends that are happening in real-time and allow you to insert your brand into the news-cycle if it makes sense to do so. In this case, you wouldn't necessarily be monitoring "brand mentions" but rather topics that are trending from the people who follow your brand in social media. Though "content is king," the ability to create the right

content, at the right time, in the right channel, and to the right customer is where the true value is. Command centers can give you this ability.

6. **Innovation**: Companies such as Dell, GiffGaff, Lego, and Starbucks rely heavily on the community for innovation. They are not only "listening to the conversation," but they are taking the collective feedback from their communities and taking action by innovating their products and services based on customer insight. Not only does this strategy help you build products that people will actually buy, but it also creates a sense of advocacy because your community feels emotionally invested in your brand and its products.

7. **Research**: Command centers can also work as real-time focus groups or be used as research initiatives. Many of these technology platforms pull in customer data like basic demographics and psychographics; as well as give you insights into customer pain points about your products or services. In 2011, Clemson University launched their Social Media Listening Command Center specifically to support their Creative Inquiry program. Undergraduate students involved in this program can use the command center to research topics of their choice under the guidance of faculty mentors and get credit for it.

8. **Customer Support**: Many command centers today are managed by customer support agents who have the responsibility of listening specifically for "brand mentions" and then solving customer issues quickly and efficiently. Many times these command centers also have built in processes, escalation workflows, and ticketing systems, much like a traditional call center operation.

Once you decide on your goals and objectives for your command center operation, you will have to think internally about all the moving parts that will bring it to life. This includes the actual strategy—what problem are you trying to solve for? You will also have to determine the various dashboard views, which is really the "eye candy" of the entire operation. You will have to coordinate with the right stakeholders to determine who needs to be involved to make the command center work to everyone's benefit. This may include various marketing and PR teams, product or brand teams, IT, customer support, and country/regional marketing teams as well. Lastly, you will have to document all your internal and external requirements, which is really the engine of the command center technology.

Figure 5.1 is an example matrix of what your strategy can look like as you plan to launch your command center.

STRATEGY	DASHBOARD VIEW(S)	STAKEHOLDERS	REQUIREMENTS
Brand, Competitive Monitoring	Share of Voice, Sentiment	CMO / C-Suite	Integration With Other Brand Monitoring Software
Competitive Analysis	Brand/Community Engagement, Community Growth	Marketing, Analytics	Integration With Facebook Insights, Competitive Integration, Historical Data
Solving Customer Issues	Brand & Product Mentions	Customer Support	Workflows, Ticketing System,
Crisis Communications	Negative Brand Mentions, Issues Monitoring	Corporate Communications & Crisis Teams	Email Alerts, Escalation Workflows
Community Management	Community Engagement (Likes, Comments, Shares, RTs), Web Traffic	Marketing, PR, Social Media, Customer Support	Integration With Facebook Insights, Web Analytics, Escalation Workflows

Figure 5.1   *An example strategy matrix for command center deployment*

The Social Business Command Center Framework

So far in this chapter, I have provided several use-cases that you can adopt if you are thinking about building your command center. And the truth is, you should build a command center whether one use case makes sense for your business or all of them make sense. Figure 5.2 gives you a high-level and general visual framework of how a command center can work within your company:

- **Monitoring:** The command center staff monitors online conversations and determines which conversations to respond to and what kind of content to create.
- **Content Creation:** Reactive content is usually managed by community managers or customer support staff. Proactive content creation is managed and executed by the content marketing team (community managers, designers, copy writers, and producers) or even a team of brand journalists.
- **Publish:** After the content is created and shared in your brand's owned media channels, it can be published to paid media channels if applicable.
- **Amplify:** After it's published, the content is spread across your brand's social media ecosystem for the community to amplify, resulting in earned media for your brand.
- **Measure:** In some cases, the content is measured and iterated in real-time to take advantage of what's trending within the news cycle.

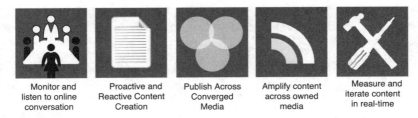

| Monitor and listen to online conversation | Proactive and Reactive Content Creation | Publish Across Converged Media | Amplify content across owned media | Measure and iterate content in real-time |

Figure 5.2   *The social business command center framework*

How to Build a Social Business Command Center

Building a command center isn't like building Legos. There aren't sets of instructions that are going to walk you step-by-step to show you which pieces go where. It's more like a puzzle and often requires you to force-fit certain pieces to make it work. Every company is different. Culture, marketing philosophies, go-to-market strategies, and technology deployments are unique to each organization and are often times dynamic. Whenever new leadership revolves in and out of a company, you can find yourself taking two steps back with each step forward. The good news is that I have developed a five-step framework that will not only make your life a little easier, but will also help you stay on track as you plan to launch a command center for your brand.

Discovery

If you have ever worked in consulting, you already know that the first step in any project plan is the discovery phase. In this phase, you have to do an internal audit and document your findings related to your internal stakeholders—marketing, public relations, customer support, IT, operations, and others. This alone can take some time, particularly if you work for a large and matrix-structured company.

After your stakeholders are identified, you have to get a firm understanding of their current responsibilities and set expectations with them very early on about what their roles will be in the command center deployment. These discussions should also involve asking for any financial support you need from each of these teams. Partnering with the IT team will be critical in this process for a variety of reasons. First, you need to know which current technology platforms are being used for CRM, online monitoring, content publishing, and any other applications that might be used alongside your command center operation. You also have to find out if there are any existing firewall restrictions as it relates to application development and/or current contractual obligations that exist with any vendors. It's always wise to make IT your friend and involve them in the decision-making process early on. If you do this, there will be fewer roadblocks as you go. It's important not to work in a silo when planning for your command center.

You should also interview several leaders in your company to get a better understanding of what they perceive to be the most pressing business challenges facing the company. Which competitors are keeping your CMO up at night? What are the biggest challenges your CIO is having when deciding on technology? Ask your CEO how he or she feels social media will help elevate the brand or business. All of these conversations are going to help you frame your strategy.

Externally, you should plan to do an audit of all of your social media activities. This should include documenting how many Facebook, Twitter, YouTube, and other accounts that your brand is responsible for, which ones are active, and/or which ones can be consolidated and shut down. A content audit is just as important. This involves looking at each of these communities and measuring the past and present content performance of each. Part of your internal stakeholder audits consist of determining who is responsible for managing each of these communities.

Planning

After you have all of your interviews and information documented, you need to begin planning your launch. The first thing you need to do is determine which technology vendor(s) to partner with. The next section gives you an overview of several vendors you can consider using that have productized command center offerings successfully.

Deciding on the taxonomy of key terms you want to monitor is a part of the planning process. Obviously, you want to monitor for brand-related terms, but there are several other things to consider as well. If your brand name or products are difficult to spell, you should also monitor for common misspellings. Competitive terms should also be on your list as it allows you to get a better understanding of the conversation volume and share of voice that your competitors have over your brand or vice versa. Industry terms are just as important. If you work for Nike and basketball shoes are a strategic initiative for your brand, you could consider monitoring "basketball shoes" as an industry term. You are able to extract the data and see of those "basketball shoes" conversations, how many also mentioned Nike, or better yet, your competitors. If your percentage numbers are lower than your competitors', then you know you need to work on your brand positioning and content strategy.

Simultaneously, you need to start talking with your internal stakeholders and come to an agreement on a measurement plan. As discussed in Chapter 2, "Defining Social Business Strategy and Planning," one of the biggest challenges that most companies face is that they aren't measuring their social media efforts or that everyone internally is measuring it differently. Either way, this is not the way to go. You must establish what you want to measure and deliver a reporting schedule that everyone is brought into, ensuring that it's a collective decision between you and all of your stakeholders before the command center launches.

Training is critical to the launch plan. Whenever you deploy a new set of technologies, the learning curve is usually massive, so having a solid training plan should help alleviate many of your challenges. Part of your training should include "how" to use the command center (set up accounts, running reports) but also contain process and workflows so that community managers know how and when to escalate social conversations to customer support and/or crisis teams.

After you have sorted out the technology situation and the terms for monitoring and created the training and workflows, you have to define your team's new roles and responsibilities. This includes creating monitoring schedules for your teams and then determining who is responsible for running reports, creating content, and engaging directly with your customers.

Implementation

Implementation happens the day you turn on your command center. You might already be engaging with your customers in two-way conversations, but now you will have additional data about what they are saying as well as what the larger community is saying simultaneously. This gives you better context on how you want to respond.

One of the key things to remember when you launch is that you should document any and all best practices, key learning points, or insights that you gain and share that knowledge with your internal stakeholders. It is particularly important to share these best practices with the teams that support your initiative financially. It helps validate their financial investment in case you need to ask for additional funds in the future.

Companies like Dell and Gatorade made a big splash about launching their command centers mainly because they were among the first to do it. This resulted in some great media attention, and they are often cited in white papers, blog posts, and various industry reports. But as command centers are slowly becoming the norm, you might not want to spend your time trying to get external coverage and instead focus on listening and engaging with your customers.

Reporting

One of the first things you will find out after the command center launches is that you get a line of new stakeholders that want you to run reports for various product launches and initiatives. It happens all the time, and it requires you to iterate your reporting schedule. You should already have a report lined up that you will send to the CMO and marketing leadership. This report should include data points around share of voice (brand and competitive) and brand sentiment. Your marketing teams might find this data useful, but they want more granular metrics such as content performance, community growth, community attrition, and general engagement. Digital campaign marketing teams might want all of the above and "campaign-specific" data points such as captured leads, conversions, and click-through rates.

Kaizen

Kaizen, meaning constant improvement, is a Chinese term that has been adopted by Japanese carmakers such as Toyota. Toyota uses this concept to help eliminate waste on their assembly lines so that workers are more efficient and productive when performing specific tasks. In this case, it's important to remember you should constantly be trying to improve—not just the technology, workflows, and the terms you are monitoring, but also the way you generate content and engage with the community. The great thing about launching a command center is that you can acquire data at your fingertips that will help you create content that's more meaningful and relevant and that will help you build stronger relationships with your customers.

Social Business Command Centers in Action

Several brands, including NGOs and universities, are finding value in deploying command centers. Following are a few organizations that are using them within a physical location for a variety of reasons.

University of Oregon

Oregon has one of the highest nationally ranked college sports programs. With 18 varsity teams, the Oregon Ducks are best known for their football team and track and field program, which has helped to make Eugene become known as "Track Town, USA." Their top-ranked football team regularly plays in high-profile, nationally televised games and draws the attention of social media users everywhere—resulting in one of the largest social communities with well over 500,000 fans on Facebook and Twitter combined.

In 2012, Oregon was the first university to launch a command center. They call it the QuackCave, and it's used to share news and content from social media channels including the @GoDucks and @QuackCave Twitter accounts. Additionally, the QuackCave serves as a hub for all of the athletic program's social media communications where staffers distribute promotional content through Twitter, Facebook, YouTube, Instagram, and other social networks. They also monitor fan conversation to answer questions and interact with passionate students, alumni, and random followers, especially when the Ducks are playing in prime time. It's currently manned during workday hours by a rotating cast of students and athletic department staff.

Cisco Systems

Cisco Systems launched their command center in October 2012, which they call their Social Media Listening Center. They have six touch-enabled LCD screens showcasing real-time information about Cisco conversations happening in social media. The command center's visualizations are powered by one of Cisco's core products, the Cisco Interactive Experience Solution, which uses the network as the platform to transform customer experiences with interactive digital media. The solution allows you to deliver interactive content and information in real time, improving loyalty and revenue, while increasing efficiencies in business processes. The platform is managed in the cloud and is a Linux-based solution that has a proprietary Enterprise-grade browser that allows for data-rich visualizations to be loaded onto the screens.

Today, Cisco currently views and monitors all Cisco brand-related conversations, their suite of products, competitive conversations, and share of voice. They also find and monitor which influencers are talking about which products, and they have also deployed specific event-based command centers for past events like the London Olympics and the Cisco Collaboration Summit 2012, where conversations were monitored and viewed in real time.

Clemson University

In 2012, Clemson University also built their Social Media Listening Center (SMLC) with support from Dell and Salesforce Radian6. Its command center enables students and faculty to monitor thousands of online conversations about organizations, brands, products, and services on a global scale and in real time.

The SMLC has six large LCD screens featuring different content and data visualizations. Salesforce Radian6 provides the platform to listen, discover, measure, and engage in conversations across the Internet and captures more than 150 million sources of online conversations from Facebook, Twitter, YouTube, LinkedIn, blogs, and other online communities. The Radian6 summary dashboard provides a graphic display of social media content to convey sentiment, share of voice, trend information, geo-location, and other demographic data.

American Red Cross

In 2012, the American Red Cross launched their Digital Operations Center. They currently use it to monitor and respond to real-life disasters that threaten human life. Most recently they used their command center to monitor and respond to victims of Hurricane Sandy. A team of 23 Red Cross staffers and volunteers monitored more than 2.5 million #Sandy mentions in Twitter, tagging 4,500 for on-the-ground follow-up.

The Digital Operations Center aggregates social media conversations from numerous sources to include Twitter, Facebook, and blogs and delivers all the data into visualizations that are easy to track and view. In a 2012 *Information Week* article, Red Cross President and CEO Gail McGovern said that the Digital Operations Center gives the Red Cross a better idea of what's happening on the ground during a disaster, helps the organization detect and track trends, and helps connect affected individuals to resources they need. The command center is modeled after Dell's Social Media Listening Command Center, which Dell opened in December 2010. They were one of the first companies to build a command center.

Gatorade

In 2010 Gatorade launched its Mission Control Center in partnership with Radian6 and IBM to track conversations customers were having about their sports drink. The command center features six large-scale LCD screens where they monitor a visualization of tweets that are relevant to Gatorade; tracking terms relating to the brand, including competitors, as well as its athletes and sports nutrition-related topics. They also measure blog conversations across a variety of topics that display how viral those conversations are across the social media ecosystem. They display detailed sentiment analysis around key topics, product launches, and campaign initiatives.

Their Mission Control is physically located in a conference room right in the middle of Gatorade's marketing team, and the monitoring dashboards are available for employees to view directly from their computers.

The New Form of Command Center Operations: Real-Time Marketing

Although many of these command centers discussed above are used to react to conversations, there is a new form of command center that gives you the ability to be proactive, monitor "what's trending" within your communities, and then create content that capitalizes on the real-time news cycle. Some call it the *creative* or *brand newsroom*.

Take for example Super Bowl XLVII after the lights went out during the halftime show. No one could have anticipated that this was going to happen, so planning for it would have been impossible. But there were a few brands that were able to capitalize on the power outage. Oreo was one brand that seized on the opportunity and they have now popularized this concept of real-time marketing.

"Power out?" Oreo posted to Twitter and then linked to a photo with this caption, "No problem. You can still dunk in the dark."

The tweet was retweeted 10,000 times within one hour of the power outage at the Mercedes-Benz Superdome and has since been cited in *Ad Age*, *Adweek*, *New York Times*, *Mashable*, *Digiday*, and *Fast Company* to name a few (see Figure 5.3).

Figure 5.3   *Oreo tweet during the Super Bowl halftime show.*

The Oreo photo was "designed, captioned, and approved within minutes," according to Sarah Hofstetter, president of the cookie brand's digital agency of record, 360i, in an interview with *Ad Age*. All the decisions were made in real time quickly because marketers and agency members were sitting together at a "mission control" monitoring what was happening during the Super Bowl.

A few other brands jumped in as well. Audi, whose TV commercial aired just before the blackout, used the power outage as an opportunity to take a soft jab at rival luxury car manufacturer Mercedes-Benz (the prime sponsor of the *Mercedes Benz* Superdome in New Orleans) tweeting

> Sending some LEDs to the @MBUSA Superdome right now.

Another example happened in the summer of 2012. It was an exchange between Oreo Cookies and AMC Theatres Twitter accounts. Here is how it played out:

> **Oreo:** Ever bring your own Oreo Cookies to the movie theater? #slicksnacker

> **AMC Theatres:** NOT COOL, COOKIE. RT @Oreo Ever bring your own Oreo Cookies to the movie theater? #slicksnacker

> **Oreo:** Fair enough @AMCTheatres, but don't hate the player, hate the game:)

> **AMC Theatres:** GAME ON. RT @Oreo Fair enough @AMCTheatres, but don't hate the player, hate the game:)

In the last exchange by AMC Theaters, the community manager snapped a picture of himself with two Oreos covering each of his eyes and pointing his fingers directly at the camera insinuating that he was watching Oreo's every move.

What's interesting about these two brands bantering back and forth is that Oreo never tweeted directly to AMC Theaters. They did mention the word "theater" in the original tweet, but there was no @mention, which is a basic practice when purposely trying to mention someone on Twitter. The community manager at AMC Theaters was undoubtedly monitoring the term "theaters" to see if there was an opportunity for him to insert the brand into a creative conversation, and he found one. Another takeaway is that he was given the power and autonomy to create a piece of visual content on the fly and respond quickly—two important characteristics of real-time marketing.

Not Everyone's Onboard with Real-Time

Although this new trend is gaining traction with many brands building their own newsrooms, some don't necessarily believe the hype.

Shiv Singh, head of Digital at Pepsi, believes that creative newsrooms are just a buzzword. In a 2013 *Digiday* article titled, "Should Brands Have Newsrooms," he said, "For all brands to wake up one day and have a newsroom, I wouldn't recommend that by any means. It scares the living daylights out of me to think of if all brands had a newsroom and were culture-jacking every event." The article goes on to say that operating a newsroom is expensive and difficult to do. This is definitely true if you consider agency resources, head count, and the technology investment needed.

Joe Lazauskas, Managing Editor at Contently, disagrees with Shiv. In a response blog post, he said that "those who push back on the creative newsroom concept are stuck imagining a newsroom from 1993." In either case, real-time marketing is alive and well today. Virgin Mobile has its own creative newsroom, staffed by internal and agency team members, including Ron Faris, head of global marketing. According to the same *Digiday* article, the Virgin Mobile newsroom publishes content 12 times a week on average.

My view on brand newsrooms is straightforward. Brands cannot sit idle and wait for the news cycle before they create game changing content. They should be doing this day in and day out, no questions asked. The reality is that real-time content should only be a small percentage of your brand's content strategy anyway; unless, of course, you are actually reporting news or your products are relevant to pop culture. That said, your brand should be prepared at all times in case the opportunity does arise to "culture-jack" the news, but understand that there must be some correlation between what's going in the news and your content narrative, even if it's just a small one.

Real-Time Marketing Technology

Although most command centers today are reactive and used to monitor for brand mentions, a few platforms are positioned to lead the way for real-time marketing deployment, SocialFlow being one. SocialFlow is a content publishing and ad platform that uses real-time analytics and a predictive algorithm to publish content at the right time when customers are actually paying attention (see Figure 5.4). They have two core products, Cadence and Crescendo, which I discussed at length at the end of Chapter 1, "Understanding the Social Customer and the Chaotic World We Live In." If you use their software, you also have the option to use their real-time command center dashboard that surfaces trending topics (as well as topics that will start to trend) from your brand's set of followers as well the entire social web. Their features include

- Real-time conversations among an audience or a segment you determine
- Content ranked or scored against an audience based on real-time interest and relevance
- Specific views of all of a company's brand's followers (Likes, retweets, community growth) in aggregate and the ability to compare these data points with other accounts (including competitors)
- Trending topics, accounts, and hashtags
- Total interactions with the accounts of a company's top engagers and where they are located geographically

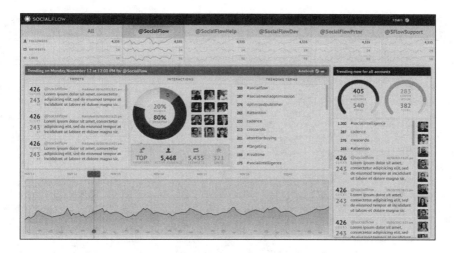

Figure 5.4   *SocialFlow's real-time command center dashboard*

In August 2013, the Dachis Group announced their Real-time Marketing Platform, a scalable real-time marketing solution that makes it easy for brands to find and join the trending conversations of their customers, prospects, and advocates.

The platform engine solves several challenges that you may be facing when attempting to execute real-time content marketing:

- **Targeting:** The hyper-fragmentation of media has made it extremely difficult to find your target audiences using most forms of traditional media monitoring and measurement. This platform finds the live conversations of your most coveted audiences so that you can create content in an environment where you know you have your audience's attention.

- **Attachment:** Most brands struggle to adjust their marketing processes and workflows from a world of a few major initiatives a year (product launches, events) to a world with thousands of opportunities to engage every single day. This platform can help you identify the trends that you should pursue today so that you can join the conversations with an added value piece of content.

- **Measurement:** Real-time conversations move too quickly for traditional marketing analytics. This platform is built on top of Dachis's social analytics engines and provides the detailed insights and reporting marketers need to be effective.

According to Jeffrey Dachis, founder and CEO of Dachis Group, real-time marketing is the discipline that finally allows brands to get in on brand relevant conversations happening in the highly fragmented media universe we now live in, and with big data analytics, we can deliver targeted scale and efficiency for brands in ways that were unthinkable before (dachisgroup.com). Figure 5.5 is an example of their real-time dashboard.

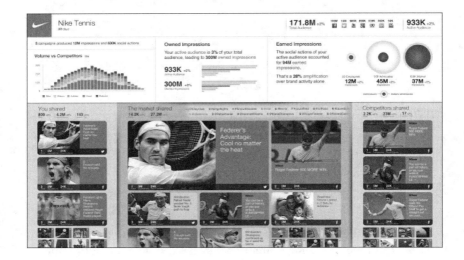

Figure 5.5   *The Dachis Real-time Marketing Platform surfaces trending topics about or related to the brand.*

Although it's not necessarily a dashboard or command center, Trendspottr is another platform that can help you surface real-time, trending content. TrendSpottr is a web service that identifies real-time trends happening in social media for any search term or topic of interest. The algorithms used by their platform are tuned to identify real-time trends at their acceleration point to provide early and predictive insights. TrendSpottr identifies trends and trending information hours or even days before they become "popular" and reach a level of general awareness. These early insights can keep you "ahead of the curve" to prepare for and predict market and social behaviors, consumer preferences, impending crises, and real-time marketing.

In 2013, Bit.ly, a popular URL shortening service, launched a set of social application programming interfaces (APIs) that includes real-time search, attention spikes, and metadata about URLs being shared across the social web. Their real-time search platform (Rt.ly) allows you to run a query and get back the top URLs and stories that are trending. Queries can be specific phrases such as "Sons of Anarchy" or filtering by criteria with stories about news that people are reading about in Austin, for example.

The platform works similarly to Twitter's Trending Topics feature. If you go Rt.ly, you find a number of filters that let you search all Bit.ly links by city, social network, keywords, languages, and even topics. You can also "create a story" for a particular search, for example "Apple iPhone," that displays a report with a map showing click-through rate, geographical distribution of readers, link referrals, related stories, top domains, and more.

There are only few vendors in the space that offer real-time monitoring of trends, content performance analytics, and audience analysis. This will certainly change as real-time marketing become prominent and as more brands will demand diversity of services from the technology vendors they work with.

Vendor Spotlight: HootSuite, MutualMind, PeopleBrowsr, Tickr, and Tracx

The following vendors have productized their command centers and focus more on "brand and industry monitoring" for reactive purposes, which is just as important if not more important than real-time, opportunistic marketing purposes.

HootSuite

In 2012, Social Media Management Software Company HootSuite launched their 2012 Election Tracker. The tracker monitored both the Barack Obama and Mitt Romney campaigns up through and after the election. The dashboard as seen in Figure 5.6 monitored all the conversations on Facebook and Twitter about each candidate in real time. It not only displayed the latest tweets from both parties, but also pulled in any mentions of either candidate as well as the conversation sentiment.

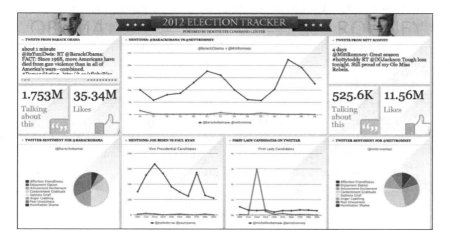

Figure 5.6   *The HootSuite Social Media Command Center*

The dashboard also displayed Facebook data including the number of Likes as well as how many people were talking about both candidates. Last, the dashboard displayed trending graphs of spikes and valleys of online conversation.

HootSuite's main component of their command center offering is the multi-platform KPI (Key Performance Indicators) visualization for social analytics. This extends the current HootSuite dashboard by providing optimized, live data feeds and visualization that can be configured for large screens (TVs), PCs, and mobile devices. You can also add data feeds from other providers, such as web analytics or social CRM applications. Their platform also works with HootSuite's existing enterprise engagement solution and mobile applications so that their customers can monitor real-time conversations from the browser and/or mobile phone.

MutualMind

The MutualMind Command Center (MCC) integrates social listening, multilingual sentiment analysis, pre and post-collection filtering with real-time response, advanced visualization, and workflow management. Their platform delivers 360-degree visibility by combining listening analytics from all major social media channels (Facebook, Twitter, LinkedIn) with visual and location data analytics from social sites such as Instagram, Foursquare, and Tumblr.

In addition, real-time event tracking is supported via MutualMind's Authentrix series of metrics, measuring influencer impact and giving you the ability to quickly gauge marketing promotion success and ROI. Their features include:

- **Modules:** Customizable, widget-based views with advanced visualizations for social data (see Figure 5.7).
- **View builder:** The ability to create custom command center views using drag-and-drop widgets from a library of templates.
- **Business data integration:** The ability to create new widgets in user interface, which import and overlay business data with social and marketing data.
- **ROI Calculator:** A built-in, customizable, data-driven ROI calculator.
- **Analytics:** Text, location, and visual media analytics; brand and competition comparisons, share of voice, activity and multi-lingual sentiment heat maps, topic discovery, authentic reach and authentic influence of brand advocates and influencers, social channel analytics, and target audience listening.

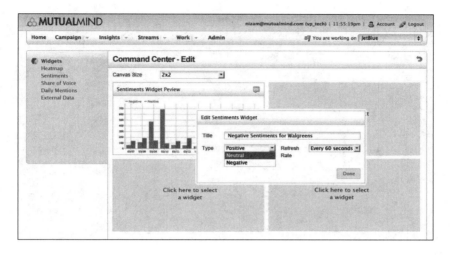

Figure 5.7 *The MutualMind Command Center (MCC)*

PeopleBrowsr

PeopleBrowsr's Command Center product displays many of the same data points as those command centers mentioned previously. One of the main differences is that their dashboard screens are interactive. Figure 5.8 shows that if you click any of the data points on the dashboard, a popup displays with all of the conversations tied to that specific data point.

Additionally, they have an interactive, global heat map that displays the same conversations globally. Their platform is fully integrated with Kred—an influencer platform that enables you to identify influential people within interest-based communities. Kred scores are generated by observing a social network user's content, who it reaches, who acts upon it, and whether the user relays the content of others.

Similar to HootSuite, PeopleBrowsr has an engagement platform with Twitter conversations broken down in streams: @mentions, @replies, and searches. It also gives you the ability to interact with your community and influencers in real time.

Figure 5.8   *PeopleBrowsr Command Center*

Tickr

Tickr describes their product as "a 360° view of your brand and business within social media and beyond." As such, you shouldn't think of Tickr as limited to social media monitoring, but more as a way to help understand the impact of social media on other parts of the business—web traffic, news mentions, even online sales data. The key value proposition of Tickr is the way the platform brings together all this data in one place with a clear and simple interface. Tickr is currently used by project managers to track projects in real-time, C-level executives to get a holistic view of how various parts of their organizations relate to each other, agency account managers to track brands and campaigns, and operations centers to monitor IT systems status. Figure 5.9 is one dashboard illustrating the conversations that are happening about your brand globally, with an interactive heat map indicating the volume and frequency of these conversations.

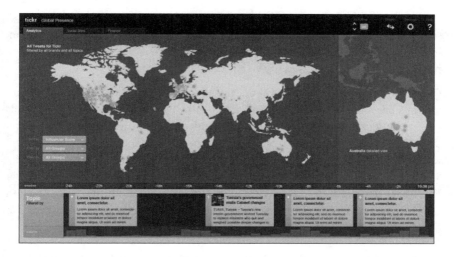

Figure 5.9   *Tickr Command Center*

One key feature that sets Tickr apart from other platforms is that the initial set up takes literally minutes. Basically, all you do is either enter a simple keyword string or an advanced Boolean search query that you want to begin monitoring. And as much as I stressed that you need to collaborate with the IT organization, the Tickr platform is a SaaS-based solution (Software as a Service), so there is no engineering or IT support required. You can quickly configure reporting screens that combine social media, news, blogs, campaign metrics, and enterprise reporting in one interface. (And for those of you who can't quite let go of paper, there is an export to PDF option as well.) Obviously this saves time and money compared to hand-created reports, but a key strength of Tickr is that it allows managers to see correlations between data across all kinds of sources—correlations that might otherwise go unnoticed (such as an influencer who retweets the brand which sends hundreds of people to the website who then make product purchases).

Tracx

Tracx is a social intelligence software platform that supports various job functions including marketing, customer support, sales, customer insights, product management, and even HR. Tracx integrates social monitoring and listening with full engagement, as well as social analytics and reporting. Tracx also mines social conversations to find people in the active buying phase and automatically categorizes them based on where they are in the buying process (awareness, research, opinion, purchase, or loyalty).

This tool also allows for monitoring social conversations across a broad range of social sites including Twitter, Facebook, LinkedIn, Google+, YouTube, Instagram, Flickr, Tumblr, Reddit, Foursquare, community forums, news sites, blogs, and even popular retail forums such as eBay and Amazon.

One the most powerful features about the Tracx platform is the capability it provides its users to pivot on social data in real-time by topic, network, demographics (age, male/female), geography, sentiment, and so on. This will help you shift your content strategy in real-time by monitoring the performance of your marketing activities and how it's affecting the broader conversation about your brand. Tracx also monitors across both owned social media (corporate Twitter accounts, Facebook pages, and so on) and earned (social mentions by third parties on all the sites mentioned here) and lets users easily toggle between them or view them combined. Figure 5.10 illustrates their command center technology.

Figure 5.10   *Tracx Command Center*

6

Understanding the Challenges of Content Marketing

REC

Tweetable Moment: *It's time to move past the content marketing buzzword. It will not help transition your brand to a media company. —#nextmediaco*

Content marketing is the real deal. The term itself has been gaining currency over the last several years, slowly becoming the new buzzword for marketers and gurus everywhere and eye candy for brands. But what is it? Well, there are several definitions floating around the Web so I will take the one directly from Wikipedia:

Content marketing is "any marketing format that involves the creation and sharing of media and publishing content in order to acquire customers. This information can be presented in a variety of media, including news, video, white papers, ebooks, infographics, case studies, how-to guides, Q&A's, photos, etc."

Using Google Trends, I searched for "content marketing" and the results speak for themselves. Figure 6.1 shows graphically how popular "content marketing" has become over the years based on total number of Google searches. The horizontal axis of the main graph represents time (starting from 2004), and the vertical is how often a term is searched for relative to the total number of searches, globally.

 Tip

In case you are new to using and understanding Google Trends, the online (and free) tool shows you how often a particular search term is entered relative to the total search volume across various regions of the world, and in various languages.

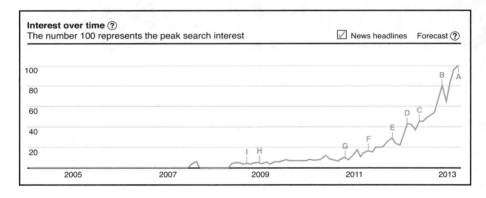

Figure 6.1   *Google Trends shows that content marketing is gaining in popularity.*

The hockey stick growth of content marketing started a few years ago in 2011 and continues to rise year after year. In addition, doing a quick search in Twitter reveals hundreds if not thousands of conversations, blog posts, and tweets of people sharing content about content marketing. A quick scan of recent headlines includes titles such as

- 12 Challenges that Stop Marketers from Creating Epic Content Marketing
- A Basic Game Plan for Content Marketing Done Right

- 5 Proven Tips for Crafting Relevant Content that Attracts, Convinces & Converts
- 5 Tips for Mobile-Friendly Content Marketing
- Tips for Creating an Editorial Calendar for Content Marketing
- 3 Offbeat Content Marketing Programs that Inspire

Take some time to read these articles (some were even written by a few personal friends of mine). Each article is well written, educational, and informative. They can teach you how to create stellar content, ensure that it's searchable and optimized for Google, video, and mobile; they also include advice and tips about what *not* to do in content marketing.

There is no shortage of good "content marketing" content available to you online. And there are several examples of brands that are doing an exceptional job executing content marketing programs. Before we examine the challenges of content marketing, let's take a look at a few successes first.

Examples of Brands Taking Content Marketing to the Next Level

Brandon Gutman, *Forbes* columnist and founder of Brand Innovators, published a blog post in 2012 that tells a story about how some large brands use content marketing in different ways. In his *Forbes* article titled "5 Big Brands Confirm That Content Marketing Is The Key To Your Consumer," Gutman writes how these brands such as Virgin Mobile, American Express, Marriott Hotels, L'Oréal, and Vanguard are adopting and using various forms of content to achieve their marketing goals.

Virgin Mobile

Virgin Mobile, a prepaid wireless mobile service provider recently launched Virgin Mobile Live. Figure 6.2 shows a Pinterest-like social newsroom that publishes and aggregates a compilation of tweets, photos, and videos several times daily. Featuring new music, apps, web memes, and streaming music player, Virgin Mobile Live shares content across a host of social communities including Facebook, Buzzfeed, Twitter, and Instagram. To date, the site is averaging over one million unique views per month, spreading virally by over 50,000 "super-sharers" on Facebook and Twitter.

Figure 6.2   *Virgin Mobile's Social Newsroom that aggregates content about music*

According to Ron Faris, Head of Brand Marketing at Virgin Mobile,

> ...scaling our content efforts isn't just about expanding the size of our
> social reach across new platforms. It's also about deepening the level
> of engagement we have with our fans in the social communities they
> hang out in. We've been successful so far in rewarding our fans with
> Virgin experiences on Facebook and Twitter. The next step is to evolve
> our social platform to allow fans to reward one another with special
> moments.

American Express

American Express, one of the world's largest financial services companies, has
participated in many content marketing programs. One of their most successful
and long-standing is American Express Unstaged—a program that live streams
concerts by some of the biggest names in music through the lens of a well-known
director, Werner Herzog, to fans across the globe. Fans are viewing not only the
event during its live performance, but also exclusive videos before and after the
event. When American Express Unstaged presented Coldplay in 2011 it became
(and continues to be) the largest single-artist event on YouTube.

"Content is an important piece in all of our marketing efforts...extending our messaging through content is a great way for us to continue to convert our customers
from simply seeing a message to considering our brand," explains Walter Frye,
Director of Entertainment Marketing and Sponsorships at American Express. Frye
also shares that American Express will continue to invest in content through its
partnerships with music but also sports and other entertainment properties:

These partnerships allow us to create memorable experiences for our Cardmembers; through our content use, we are able to scale out that experience to prospective and current customers and ultimately exposing more people to our brand and driving consideration.

Marriott

Renaissance Hotels is Marriott's experiential "lifestyle" brand, designed for business travelers who see travel as a way to explore the world. Hence, the brand designed two platforms to help guests "Live Life to Discover." The Navigators platform helps guests to discover the local city outside their hotel, and the RLife LIVE program helps guests to discover new music, films, arts, food and drinks inside the hotels. Both programs provide rich content for engaging guests online. In May of 2012, Marriott relaunched RenHotels.com as not just a hotel website but as a discovery site. All the curated local discoveries (over 6,000 and growing) from their 155 hotels around the world now live online. And the brand promotes them to start conversations in their social channels. The brand's site is seeing record traffic and exponential growth in engagement, and its Facebook community has grown to 270,000 Likes.

Dan Vinh, Vice-President of Global Marketing at Renaissance Hotels at Marriott International, said

As a global brand with limited awareness and limited marketing budget, we have to find ways to be relevant and drive consideration. Content is critical for us because it's the currency that drives our relevance and therefore consumer consideration for our brand. And content for us lives first and foremost in the offline world through our hotel guest experience. This is how we ensure that what we do and say is authentic. Then we extend it to online to continue the dialogue with existing guests and their network (our prospects).

L'Oréal

L'Oréal, the largest cosmetics and beauty company globally, recently partnered with *Rolling Stone* to create content around the discovery of new, emerging musicians and their styles. In 2011 they made history by searching new artists in the country and asking consumers to vote and decide who would become the first unsigned artist ever to be featured on the cover of *Rolling Stone*. They developed specific content around this program, which culminated with the winner artist signing a contract with a record label and looking to engage and connect with consumers throughout the process with the ultimate goal of building stronger affinity and emotional connection.

In 2012, L'Oréal evolved the program to leverage *Rolling Stone*'s "Women Who Rock" annual issue, inviting consumers to get involved again, voting and deciding which female emerging musician would be in the flip cover of this celebratory issue that featured Adele in the cover. "We are very satisfied with the program having much stronger results this year achieving or surpassing our targets and benchmarks from number of page and video views, earned impressions to brand health tracking metrics," shared Debora Koyama, AVP Marketing, L'Oréal USA.

Koyama is excited about what the brand is planning for 2013:

> My vision has been to take this strategic platform for the brand to the next level by comprehensively integrating all initiatives and touch points and by expanding our footprint on content creation appealing to Millennials in a much stronger and relevant way.

Vanguard

Vanguard, a financial investment and management company, launched a campaign called "Vanguard at the Movies" in 2012, which spoofed classic movie genres of horror, drama, and suspense to convey what using Vanguard doesn't feel like. The initiative was launched during the summer blockbuster movie season with in-theater trailers and a heavy digital presence on sites like Hulu and Rotten Tomatoes. Vanguard used the movies not only to extend the brand, but also to cross-merchandise its existing video content on YouTube. The movies became a focal design point in relaunching the brand's YouTube page via a movie theme.

Michael Ma, Head of Retail Advertising and Prospect Marketing at The Vanguard Group, explained that in days after its release, the movies became the most watched video on the brand's YouTube channel and more than doubled its traffic. "Within weeks the Vanguard's YouTube channel went from tens of thousands to hundreds of thousands of views—half of them being our spots, but roughly the other half staying to learn more about our brand through other video content."

There are certainly more examples of large and small brands leveraging content marketing practices to build brand awareness, reach customers, and drive sales. And many of them are successful. But along with some of these successes comes several challenges as well.

Content Marketing Challenges: What the Experts Say

Creating content is the number one challenge today, but don't worry. You're not alone. All brands struggle with creating and distributing relevant content to their customers. Giselle Abramovich, writer for Digiday, wrote an article in 2012, "Why Brands Struggle With Content Creation" that highlighted several leaders from top brands about why they struggle with content. Perhaps you can relate to some of these issues.

Nestle Purina

Julie Brown, Manager of Digital Insights at Nestle Purina, said that speed is a huge challenge for her brand today and that creating quality content at a pace that "feeds the beast" of socially relevant content is challenging. She says there is a need to work increasingly with scrappy production houses to produce great, high-quality content that is timely and will resonate with what consumers are already talking about.

As discussed in Chapter 5, "Building Your Social Business Command Center," the ability to create real-time content is not easy to do and requires a social business strategy in order to execute it flawlessly. A strategy helps you define what the brand is comfortable talking about as well as what the brand isn't comfortable talking about; identify roles and responsibilities of the team; and identify the internal resources needed to execute properly.

Greg Samarge, Digital Marketing Manager also at Nestle, said that the single largest issue is being able to create break-through content and still have the budget to fund distributing that content. It's hard enough to justify the budget to create that content, he said, but it's even more challenging to then push for sufficient budget above and beyond the content creation to distribute this great content.

In this case, the challenge isn't only creating relevant content, but also finding the right distribution channels for Nestle content. A good content strategy not only helps determine "what" you want to say from a brand strand point, but also "where you want to say it," which will help solve the distribution channel dilemma. I call this the content supply chain. A social business strategy alone does not guarantee you more budget, unfortunately. But it can help you make the case for it by demonstrating the business value of having a content strategy. It will also help you deliver a specific action plan as you prepare to transition your brand to a media company. Usually a content strategy starts with a content audit that identifies current gaps with existing content, content performance metrics, competitive audit, and recommendations on how to take content to the next level and begin to change your customer's behaviors in a positive way.

AARP (American Association of Retired Persons)

Tammy Gordan, Director of Social Communications at AARP (American Association of Retired Persons), said that one of the biggest challenges is the blurring of the line between content creation and journalism. She says AARP creates content involving advertising, public relations, and marketing and also produces television, radio, web, mobile, and print content. Figuring out workflow, marketing, and job descriptions has been one of the most interesting struggles of 2012 for them.

A content governance plan (part of a social business strategy) solves the challenge of content approvals and workflows. If done correctly, workflows can be created that manage the entire content supply chain—the creation, approval, distribution and integration of content. This helps ensure brand storytelling across multiple channels is consistent and also prevents disjointed content and community management practices. Platforms like Kapost, which is discussed at the end of this chapter, can help you manage content through these processes.

Kellog

Bob Arnold, Associate Director of Global Digital Strategy at Kellogg, said the biggest challenge for them is balancing adding value to the customer experience and communicating the brand message at the same time.

As discussed in Chapter 1, "Understanding the Social Customer and the Chaotic World We Live In," creating content that adds value to your customers yet stays consistent with the brand is a huge challenge. The good news is that creating a robust content strategy can solve it. With a good content strategy you can determine the brand's tone of voice, categorize your content into various themes, and then determine which content should be shared within specific online channels. It consists of a culmination of various inputs:

- Brand narrative (core values, brand positioning, product news)
- Non-business issues that are important to the brand (sustainability)
- How the media contextualizes the brand when they write stories
- How the community contextualizes the brand when they tweet, leave comments, or write blog posts
- What other topics your community cares about
- Historical content performance
- How consumers search for your brand, product
- The top 10 or 15 customer support issues

Chapter 7, "Defining Your Brand Story and Content Narrative," goes into great detail about each of these inputs.

Cisco

Karen Snell, Content Lead at Cisco Systems, said that the biggest challenge they face is getting buy-in for their approach to content creation from their peers. As storytellers first, she said, our team is dedicated to finding and telling stories that make a connection with our audience and producing them in such a way that they will make an impact, an impression and hopefully result in a social action—sharing, tweeting, republishing, and so on. She went on to say that they are continually explaining their strategy and "selling" their approach to internal stakeholders.

At Cisco, enterprise collaboration presents a challenge, as it does at most companies. Organizational silos have always plagued business progress and continue to stunt the growth of collaboration. But the transition from brand to media company requires internal teams to work together to build a content organization that adds value to all stakeholders—internal teams, partners, and customers. This is why it's so important to invest in a social business strategy that helps you tear down organizational silos and build collaborative and innovative teams and business models, allowing the company as a whole to become a content machine.

Capri Sun

Orion Brown, Brand Manager of Capri Sun, said that the biggest challenge is creating both consumer-relevant and brand-building content. Some brands (namely, passion brands) lend well to this as they are already ubiquitous and are intimately integrated into the daily lives of consumers. A passion brand is one that delivers emotional equity to its customers and has the following characteristics, according to media agency MediaCom:

- Adventurous/Rebellious
- Desirable/Sexy
- Playful/Fun
- Creative

So their hurdle to find touch points that feel natural and relevant to the consumer might be lower. But for many brands, he said, it's a delicate balance between creating a branded message that doesn't sound like a sales pitch but still drives consumers ultimately to purchase. In his experience, he continued, identifying the consumer need that a brand meets, then laddering that back up to a higher emotional need helps drive relevant content creation. But even then, brands need to be mindful of not getting too arrogant in their brand promise to keep the content grounded and believable to the consumer.

Capri Sun, a brand I grew up with and now buy for my family, has the same challenge as Kellogg. But providing meaningful content that builds on the passions and motivations of consumers yet stays true to the brand promise is not easy to do. Finding the right balance is difficult, but it can be done with a sound content strategy.

To dig down a little deeper into some of these content challenges, I thought it would be good to spend some time with several leaders in the space, do my own qualitative research, and get their opinions. I asked them about the challenges with content in organizations today. Although some mirrored many of the same issues as those mentioned above, some were completely new.

Mindjet

Jascha Kaykas-Wolff, Chief Marketing Officer of Mindjet, a Collaborative Tools and Work Management Software company, explained to me that it's about lack of resources and priorities. He said that the content strategy needs to match to the business objectives and map to current and relevant cultural and social issues that are important to the brand. Additionally, he stressed that poor organizational design is a huge factor that's causing brands to miss the mark on creating and distributing content to the right customer at the right time. Most community and content strategies, he said, are splintered among multiple members of a marketing team and have a lack of ownership other than tactical execution.

Sears

Sean McGinnis, Marketing GM at Sears Holdings Corporation, has a slightly different take to the issue. He believes it's more of a leadership issue and said that a strong leader pushes the need to disassemble silos and have a unified content strategy that delivers value to each of the brands stakeholders and that benefits the business at the same time. Instead, there is too often infighting among departments that results in politics and arguments over budget, personnel, and roles/responsibilities that result in fractured content and communities. He also believes that brands suffer from a lack of a cohesive strategy, a complete investment in the right resources, and a plan to achieve the goals of the organization through content. Workflow and processes are a huge part of the problem, he said, but without the strategy, commitment, and resources, all the workflows and processes in the world will not create a winning content program.

Kinvey

Joe Chernov, Vice-President of Marketing at Kinvey, a Mobile Cloud Backend as a Service Provider, looks at it more from a psychological perspective. He suggests that brands struggle to create relevant content because they can't empathize. They have a hard time seeing the world through the lens of the buyer. Instead, they insist on trying to persuade the buyer to see the world through their own perspective. Relevant content is the byproduct of empathy. Everything else is just selling.

Ricoh

Sandra Zoratti, Vice-President of Marketing at Ricoh, an electronics company, believes that to create cohesive communities and content, brands need to look at content as a strategic infrastructure instead of a tactical execution. Identifying a brand persona that represents the authentic culture of the company—and its people, products, and practices—is important. Then, she said, a content approach can be crafted that create value for your audience, engage prospects and customers, and cut through the clutter. She emphasized that creating and curating content takes time. Marketers and brands who choose to proactively outline an approach prior to content generation and curation benefit from the harmony of communities and content, thus maximizing engagement and ROI.

ArCompany

And finally, Danny Brown, Chief Technology Officer of ArCompany, a social business intelligence agency, believes it's a workflow issue. He said that there are still too many processes and hoops to jump through and that company politics are plaguing business progress. When an organization requires multiple sign offs just to approve a tweet, status update, or blog comment, then you know you have an issue with time and context. He stressed that company leadership must deliver trust to their teams so that they can execute content programs that provide value.

So here we have several different points of view from a variety of different perspectives about the challenges of content marketing. On one hand, it's a matter of not having the right resources or enough time and then balancing the content mix with brand messages and content that adds real value to consumers. On the other hand, it might be more about organizational management—leadership, psychology, company politics, and the amount of processes needed to get things done.

Now let's take a look at some quantitative data to see if there are any parallels.

Content Marketing Challenges: What Does the Data Show?

In the 2011 Annual Content Curation Adoption Survey by HiveFire, and as depicted in Figure 6.3, 73% of respondents said that their biggest challenge with content marketing was "creating original content" with the same percentage of respondents also citing that they don't have enough time to do it. What is not surprising is that 39% of the respondents were unsure of how to staff their teams correctly to execute content marketing programs successfully.

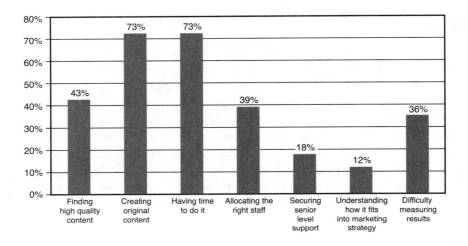

Figure 6.3   *HiveFire study reveals that creating original content is the number one challenge for brands.*

In this case, it's not just the challenge of creating original content, but it's the lack of internal resources needed to execute these content programs. This could be a result of your organization not being structured properly, not having a unified vision of how you view content and its importance, lack of prioritization, or just being blind to the opportunity. So perhaps it's more of a business challenge than it is a marketing one. And although this study is a few years old, I see the same challenge plaguing businesses today, mainly due to the "bright and shiny" object of social media as discussed in Chapter 2, "Defining Social Business Strategy and Planning."

Also in 2011, the State of B2B Content Marketing Survey by Marketing Automation Firm, TechValidate, reported that 43% of B2B marketers said that the amount of time needed to produce content was their biggest challenge with content marketing (see Figure 6.4). According to the report, the respondents said that it took between four and eight weeks on average to produce relevant marketing content, and nearly 13% of those surveyed reported that they often spend over three months creating content.

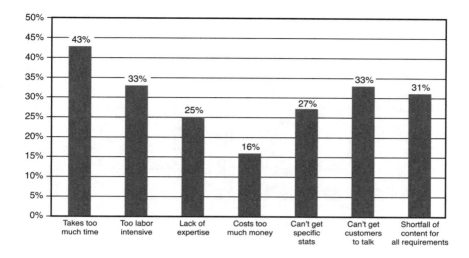

Figure 6.4 *TechValidate study reveals the amount of time needed to produce content is the biggest challenge with content marketing for B2B marketers.*

As mentioned in Chapter 3, "Establishing a Centralized 'Editorial' Social Business Center of Excellence," media companies have several distinct qualities that allow them to capitalize on consumer attention, especially in a world where there is a content surplus and attention deficit. The ability to tell good stories, mass amounts of relevant and ubiquitous content, and agile teams are necessary to build an "always on" content organization.

More importantly, to make even the smallest impression on consumers, you need to ensure that it doesn't take your company four to eight weeks to create original content. One week is even too long. The ability to move quickly and create good content fast (and in real-time) is a business imperative in today's environment. Trust is even more important. Without trust from company leadership, you'll never get things done in a timely manner because they want to see and approve everything before it gets published. Streamlined operations and having the right team structure are also needed to cut down on the lead-time to create high quality and relevant content.

A more recent study validates some of these same concerns. The B2C Content Marketing: 2013 Benchmarks, Budgets, and Trends–North America Report by the Content Marketing Institute and MarketingProfs shows that a lack of budget is the top challenge faced by B2C content marketers today (see Figure 6.5). In fact, 52% of B2C content marketers are challenged with lack of budget, compared with 39% of B2B content marketers.

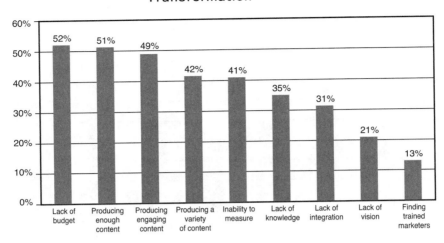

Figure 6.5   *Fifty-two percent of B2C content marketers are challenged with lack of budget.*

With the exception of budget issues, the top three challenges plaguing content marketers today have to do with the inability to produce enough content, engaging content, and a variety of content. What is surprising is that 31% of respondents are not integrating with other communications channels. This is a major concern. Lack of integration equals disjointed content, failed community management, and irrelevant storytelling. How can you tell a consistent brand story across a variety of channels if you aren't communicating internally with other teams? Although these are more tactical challenges, they certainly stem from the same root cause mentioned previously—lack of trust and collaboration.

Though many of these top challenges are consistent with the other reports as well as the statements made by those I interviewed, the following study paints a somewhat different story.

The 2012 Content Marketing Survey Report by eConsultancy and Outbrain illustrates a few differences of opinion from both in-house marketers and agencies and what each believes to be the main barriers to effective content marketing. As illustrated in Figure 6.6, the two most commonly cited barriers for in-house respondents were a lack of human resources (42%), followed by a lack of budget (35%); whereas, agency respondents were more likely to cite a lack of understanding or training (46%) and a lack of content creation skills (39%) as areas that prevent effective content marketing. What's interesting about this study is that the top three content marketing challenges have nothing to do with content marketing at all—lack of human resources, lack of budget, and company politics.

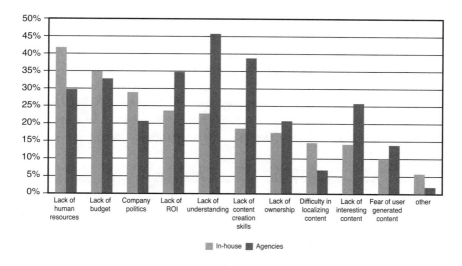

Figure 6.6   *The 2012 Content Marketing Survey Report illustrates what marketers (in-house/agency) believe to be the biggest challenges to content marketing.*

In looking at the first two studies from HiveFire and TechValidate, it's clear that the challenges many marketers face is tactical. The ability to "find" good content, creating original content, and finding time to do it are consistent in both reports, and it actually makes sense. If you work in a silo and fail to collaborate with other teams and even customers, you can see why these are such huge pain points.

The more recent reports from eConsultancy and the Content Marketing Institute/MarketingProfs paint a slightly different picture. The commonalities in both dig much deeper than just marketing challenges. Lack of budget, human resources, collaboration/integration, and company politics seem to be barriers to effective content marketing. These challenges were also validated by many of the leaders who gave their points of view earlier in the chapter.

And here lies the issue at hand with content marketing.

Content marketing is by nature, tactical. It can easily be done in a silo. If you are a marketer, there is absolutely nothing stopping you from creating, aggregating, and curating content and then posting it up in social media channels without having a strategy. You can hire consultants, agencies, and even third-party journalists and bloggers to create content and campaigns on your behalf. It's fairly easy and afford-able to use services like Poptent or Genius Rocket to crowdsource highly produced video content. And guess what? You can do all of this without actually talking to anyone in your company. Now, the content itself might not be epic or change any specific consumer behavior but it's not hard to do, and it's not that expensive.

The reason why many of the companies surveyed struggle with content, storytelling, and scalability is because they are looking at content from an elementary point of view. Content is not a box you check, a bubble you fill in, or a bullet point in a PowerPoint presentation. It's more than SEO (Search Engine Optimization); it's more than videos, Infographics, Instagram photos, and real-time marketing. You can't learn about content from clever blog titles like "10 Proven Tips to Learn This" or "5 Smart Tricks to Learn That." Content must be considered a strategic imperative for your business. You must become a content organization if you want to take your business to the next level.

Just as there is an art to storytelling; there also needs to be a strategic and operational plan that can help you create and distribute content; integrate it across paid, earned, and owned media; and measure it effectively. As a marketer, brand manager, or small business owner you must move beyond the content marketing buzzword and commit to building a content strategy that will allow you to execute your tactical content marketing initiatives flawlessly and at scale.

Moving Past the Content Marketing Buzzword

So let's recap.

As previously mentioned, content marketing is any marketing format that involves the creation and sharing of media and publishing content in order to acquire customers. This information can be presented in a variety of media, including news, video, white papers, ebooks, infographics, case studies, how-to guides, Q&A's, photos, and so on. This is a self-explanatory definition, and there are thousands of resources that can help you create compelling content.

But this book isn't about content marketing. This book is about change. It's about helping your brand evolve into a media company. This change starts with understanding how to implement a social business strategy (Chapter 2). It then continues on to help you build your centralized editorial team—the Social Business Center of Excellence (Chapter 3). The next step to facilitate this change involves building your army of content contributors and brand journalists—employees, customers, and partners (Chapter 4). And then it's about building a real-time listening center, also known as the Social Business Command Center, which allows you to react to conversations about your brand and also be proactive in capitalizing on real-time content creation based on what's trending in the news cycle (Chapter 5). This change must also help you think beyond the content marketing craze and focus on building a content strategy instead.

Kristina Halvorson, CEO and Founder of Brain Traffic and coauthor of *Content Strategy for the Web* has a robust definition of content strategy:

Content strategy plans for the creation, publication, and governance of useful, usable content. The content strategist must work to define not only which content will be published, but why they are publishing it in the first place. Otherwise, content strategy isn't strategy at all: it's just a glorified production line for content nobody really needs or wants. Content strategy is also—surprise—a key deliverable for which the content strategist is responsible. Its development is necessarily preceded by a detailed audit and analysis of existing content.

A content strategy also requires support, collaboration, and integration from a variety of internal teams—marketing, public relations, customer support, brand and/or product teams, analytics, IT and even internal communications. Each of these teams play a pivotal role in helping you deliver a content strategy with a strong operational plan that can help you scale. That is, if you want stellar content that actually changes consumer behavior.

The deliverables of a content strategy include the following:

- Storytelling principles and tone of voice
- Content themes and storytelling pillars
- Distribution and frequency of content
- Platform-specific content and engagement considerations
- Creative newsroom and converged media modeling
- Content supply chain (that is, content creation to distribution workflows)
- Key insights and observations from a content audit

Each of these content strategy deliverables is discussed in depth throughout the rest of this book. And as a result, you will be able to deliver a robust plan that will help turn your brand into a media company.

Vendor Spotlight—Kapost

Imagine you work for Intel as their blog editor or community manager. Now, Intel has well over 100,000 employees globally, many of whom engage online on Twitter, Facebook, and LinkedIn. Now imagine if some of those employees want to become brand journalists and write stories on the company blog. This is certainly a good thing. Those employees understand—and can write knowledgeably about—a variety of topics related to Intel's expertise and that potential customers would find interesting. But how would you manage the workflow from content ideation to content distribution and all the processes and approvals in between?

You can certainly test the waters with your collaboration and community software, but it probably won't work for you. Collaboration software is meant to collaborate and share documents and knowledge but not manage a process as robust as this. And email is certainly out of the question. These workflow challenges alone will not only contribute to your lack of sleep at night, but might also discourage employees from wanting to contribute in the first place. And while you are trying to make the transition from brand to media company, the last thing you want to do is give publishing authority to every employee who wants to contribute. Doing so leads to a whole new set of marketing and business challenges. In a situation like this, you need a platform that can automate editorial workflow, and this is exactly what Kapost delivers.

Kapost is a content marketing software platform that organizes complicated content marketing operations into a structured business process. Their platform manages the entire content marketing process to include

- planning (persona/buying stages)
- ideation (crowdsourcing form shared with internal or external ideas)
- production (marketing calendar, workflows, and approvals)
- distribution (including social media channels, marketing automation software, and CMS platforms)
- analytics (such as lead conversions, shares, earned links, and pageviews)

Kapost centrally organizes all your content, including emails, landing pages, blog posts, white papers, eBooks, infographics, videos, and social media content into a single platform. The platform also integrates with all major content platforms like Marketo, most CMS platforms, social networks, YouTube, Brightcove, and Slideshare to name a few.

The Kapost platform is built to manage four key areas in the content marketing process: planning, production, distribution, and analysis.

As depicted in Figure 6.7, Kapost has a robust content dashboard that displays a set of columns that can be easily customized based on the details that are important to you or any user that has access to the platform. As illustrated, the columns have several pieces of important information. Because these column headers are customizable, you can set them up as you and your team see fit:

- **The type of content:** Blog post, article, tweet, YouTube video
- **When the content was last updated:** Important to quickly see when that content was touched last
- **The author:** In case there is any follow-up needed
- **Next task:** Where the content currently stands in the workflow

- **Publish deadline:** The date that the piece of content is scheduled to be published
- **Submission deadline:** The date that the piece of content must be submitted for approvals

The dashboard gives you a high-level overview of all of your content, the status of each piece of content, and where it currently stands in your customized workflows. This is extremely important regardless of whether you have a small team or several hundred contributors helping you execute your content strategy. You can quickly get a status check without having to sift through Excel data, and the worry about whether or not you have the latest version is non-existent.

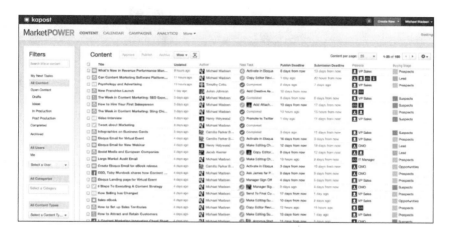

Figure 6.7 *Kapost dashboard gives specific details on each piece of content in the platform.*

One of the most challenging aspects of managing content is streamlining all of the great ideas that keep you up at night, hit you while you are driving in traffic, or come to mind during a conference call. Even if you are taking notes in an old-school paper notebook or if you use the note-taking application Evernote, the content ideas still must go from concept to fruition. And as mentioned many times in this chapter, the ability to manage this process from beginning to end is a major challenge for many.

Still today, much of editorial planning still happens in multiple Excel or Google Docs. The good news is that Kapost has a calendar feature that helps you get rid of Band-aid solutions (see Figure 6.8). At a glance, you can see all of the content and campaigns planned by the day, week, or month. The calendar has unlimited views, and customizable filters allow you to slice and dice your content by specific dimensions. For example, you could filter your calendar by various employees' content submissions, business unit, region, brand, and more. The calendar items drag and drop, open with a click to provide more information, export to a PDF for reporting purposes, and sync to your inbox calendar (Outlook, Gmail, for example). This makes the editorial process much easier to manage and scale.

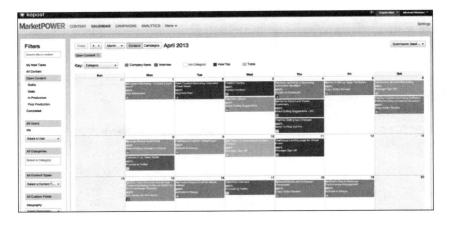

Figure 6.8 *Kapost editorial calendar has multiple customizable views.*

Also as you publish content across multiple channels, Kapost aggregates performance metrics from all those channels and displays them in one central reporting dashboard. The system aesthetically displays metrics from every step of the process in any specified date range including

- Ideas submitted
- Content published
- Links (to content) earned
- Content views
- Content conversions (that is, the number of leads or sales that the specific content has generated)
- Social analytics (Likes, comments, shares, tweets)

Kapost can further slice and dice this data by any dimension (that is, by author, category, business unit, brand, buying stage, or persona).

A favorite feature of Kapost is that the platform can be easily customized to automate various types of content and approval workflows based on your company's structure and needs. So if you work for a large company with several brands and need multiple approvers before a piece of content goes live, the platform can support it. Or if you work for a smaller company and need legal approval before any and all content goes live, the platform can support this simple workflow as well.

Also for global organizations with different needs based on business units and regions or agencies managing multiple clients, the Organization feature allows each division, business unit, or client to have its own platform. These platforms operate independently of one another, and users can only see the content within their specific instance. However, each platform falls under the supervision of a "parent" instance, which means the managing body or agency can see all content, analytics, and workflows in their "child" instances. For example, if Intel wanted to have separate instances for their teams in China, North America, and Argentina, this feature makes it possible. Or an agency can see how each of their clients are doing without different clients having access to one another's content.

SECTION III

Developing Your Content Strategy

Too many pundits put content marketing into a box. Content is so much more than SEO, link bait, videos, infographics, and social media status updates. Although these are certainly important, delivering a content strategy is about thinking holistically about the organization and all of its moving parts. It takes into consideration the content narrative, platform strategy, content governance, converged media, as well as culture, organizational behavior, and structuring your teams to maximize the content supply chain.

All media companies are content machines. They have the correct structures in place, aligned teams, and a robust editorial process, and they execute the distribution of their content flawlessly. Your brand must follow this model. Realizing that you still have rigorous business goals, you must challenge the status quo and think about content the way media companies do. Red Bull has done it. Coca Cola and Intel are doing it. What are you waiting for?

Chapter 7: Defining Your Brand Story and Content Narrative

Before you think about where and how you want to tell your brand story, you must first understand the story you actually want to tell. This chapter will help you craft a content narrative that's relevant to your brand and at the same time changes customer behavior:

- The Inputs Needed to Build Your Content Narrative
- The Output Should Equal Your "Hero" Content Narrative
- Simplifying Your Content Narrative
- Vendor Spotlight—Compendium

Chapter 8: Building Your Content Channel Strategy

Once you have crafted your content narrative, you can then decide where and how you want to tell your brand story. This chapter will give you examples on how you can build your channel strategy, taking into consideration content relevance and native "social" platform behavior:

- Finding and Preventing Gaps with Your Social Media Channel Strategy
- Mapping Your Content Narrative to Social Channels
- Building Your Content Tiers by Channel
- Laser Focused Storytelling by Channel
- Diversifying Your Content Types per Channel
- The Importance of Visual Storytelling
- The Importance of Long-Form Content When Telling Stories
- Striking a Balance Between Long-Form Content and Short-Form Storytelling
- Best Practices for Writing Long-Form Content—It All Starts with the Title
- Vendor Spotlight—Contently

Chapter 9: The Role of Converged Media in Your Content Strategy

Consumers must interact with your brand message three to five times before they start to believe. Delivering converged media models will help you spread your brand story consistently across paid, earned, and owned media channels to reach them:

- Defining Converged Media
- Why Converged Media Is Important to Your Content Strategy
- Converged Media Models
- The Promise of Real-Time Marketing
- Real-Time Marketing Is More than Just Being in Real Time
- 'The Creative Newsroom
- Creative Newsroom 5-Step Activation Process
- Creative Newsroom Models
- Vendor Spotlight—Newscred

Chapter 10: How Content Governance Will Facilitate Media Company Transformation

Building your content supply chain is imperative to ensure consistency and control in brand storytelling. This chapter will show you how to build processes and workflows starting from content ideation, creation, approval, distribution all the way to content optimization:

- Defining Content Governance
- Building an Effective Collaboration Model
- Proactive Content Workflows for Planned and Unplanned Content
- Reactive Escalation Workflows and Risk Assessment
- Governing New "Brand" Account Creation
- Managing the Security of Social Media Passwords
- Vendor Spotlight—Spredfast

Chapter 11: Structuring Your Teams to Become a Content-Driven Organization

Having the right team in place is important in becoming a media company. This chapter will help you decide how you can structure and align your teams so that you can become a content-driven organization:

- A Quick Lesson in Change Management
- Tearing Down the Organizational Silos
- Identifying Roles and Responsibilities
- Structuring Your Content Organization by Channel
- Structuring Your Content Organization by Brand or Product
- Structuring Your Content Organization by Region
- Structuring for Converged Media and Real-Time Marketing
- Choosing the Right Technology Platforms
- Vendor Spotlight—Skyword

Defining Your Brand Story and Content Narrative

> **Tweetable Moment:** *Brands can't wait around for news to happen before creating content. They should have a story and tell it consistently.*
> *—#nextmediaco*

Red Bull has done what few other brands have been able to do successfully—become a media company. If you go to RedBull.com, put your thumb over the logo and scan the page, you'll see that their site looks just like CNN.com. It's filled with flashy headlines, visual imagery with both videos and photos of epic sporting events. That's what Red Bull is known for. That's their story.

But there is certainly more to their story than a flashy website.

Red Bull's holistic approach to storytelling ensures that every brand expression, conversation, tweet, status update, and video—from product announcements to corporate culture—is a part of its content narrative. With the continuous stream of extreme sports and epic content aimed at youth culture, the "giver of wings" story has instantly become what every brand should strive to be. And they go "all in" when delivering that message.

For example, when Red Bull sponsors the X games, they don't just post large banners throughout the event with their logo plastered all over it. Instead, they capitalize on their story and build a snow ramp for Olympic Gold Medalist and professional snowboarder Shaun White. And when that wasn't enough, they helped Felix Baumgartner skydive from outer space as a part of the Red Bull Stratos project. In October 2012, Baumgartner flew approximately 24 miles into the stratosphere over New Mexico in a helium balloon before free falling in a pressure suit and then parachuting to back to Earth. The total jump, from leaving the capsule to landing on the ground, lasted about 10 minutes.

Sounds epic to me.

Red Bull Stratos was a huge win with over eight million people watching the event online and seven million people engaging with the content in various social media channels. For the month following the space jump, anytime someone talked about space or space travel, the conversation inherently included a mention of Red Bull. They owned the conversation. And months later, when a dad launched his son's Skylanders Tree Rex action figure into space, Red Bull jumped in with words of encouragement. @RedBullStratos spotted the conversation on Twitter and joined in on the celebration, tweeting, "Tree Rex needs his wings too."

In a 2012 *Fast Company* interview, Red Bull founder and CEO Dietrich Mateschitz talked about the transition from his brand becoming a media company. In the beginning, he said, when the company first launched Red Bull, a product that stimulated body and mind, the message was more about the roots of where the product came from. Today and after 20 years, it's now called adventure sports, extreme sports, and outdoor sports.

When asked what the Red Bull brand stands for, his response sheds clarity on how brand storytelling and the content narrative has evolved from just company history, product announcements, and traditional marketing messages:

> What Red Bull stands for is that it "gives you wings..." which means that it provides skills, abilities, and power to achieve whatever you want to. It is an invitation as well as a request to be active, performance-oriented, alert, and to take challenges. When you work or study, do your very best. When you do sports, go for your limits. When you have fun or just relax, be aware of it and appreciate it.

Notice that Mateschitz's response has nothing to do with the actual product. This story works for Red Bull. They are using the "gives you wings..." messaging to enable athletes, students, and just about anyone else to experience life to the fullest, be adventurous and enjoy every minute of it. And Red Bull is executing this message flawlessly across every form of media.

Red Bull's narrative has evolved over the last 20 years. It didn't start out talking about extreme sports. The company has adapted over the years to deliver a message that resonates with its target customers, which is one reason why Red Bull leads in the energy drink category. They have a good story and it's that simple.

Red Bull might be the exception to the rule, but as you think about your story and how you want to tell it, you must consider several internal and external inputs before you can establish a narrative that resonates with consumers.

The Inputs Needed to Build Your Content Narrative

Your *content narrative* is not synonymous with your brand positioning, brand personality, or brand attributes. These are certainly inputs into the content narrative, but they are not the same thing and are certainly not meant to be replaced. In most cases, your brand narrative will not impact consumer behavior when shared in its purest form, as today's consumers ignore marketing messages with no relevance. Instead, your content narrative should translate the core tenets of your brand into a story that demonstrates how your business relates to its consumers.

Figure 7.1 is an example of the various inputs needed to craft your content narrative.

Each of these inputs must be carefully analyzed and thought through before your content narrative is established to ensure you are telling the right story.

Figure 7.1   *Inputs needed to build your content narrative*

Brand Messaging & Product Benefits

This isn't a branding book, but it's important for you to understand what a brand narrative is because it's a vital input into your overall content. The following is a common and very basic definition of a brand that's taught in most business schools and universities.

> A brand is a product, service, or concept that is publicly distinguished from other products, services, or concepts so that it can be easily communicated and usually marketed. A brand name is the name of the distinctive product, service, or concept. Branding is the process of creating and disseminating the brand name. Branding can be applied to the entire corporate identity as well as to individual product and service names.

For the most part, and there are certainly exceptions, brands are often expressed and communicated in the form of logos, campaigns, and other creative executions. Red Bull has obviously turned this definition completely upside down. In the technology industry, a more recent example of this is Intel's extension of "Intel Inside," a creative brand initiative that differentiated Intel from its competitors and helped them engage in a direct conversation with consumers, essentially bypassing their channel partners. What started out as a clever campaign has become a core part of Intel's brand position.

There are five key elements that make up holistic brand strategy:

- **Brand Position:** Describes what your company does and for whom it does it, what your unique value proposition is, and how a customer will benefit from using your product or service. For example, when you think of Wal-Mart, you might imagine low cost products. That is their brand position. And if you are in the market for a new car and safety is your number one concern, you might consider purchasing a Volvo. They own that positioning.

- **Brand Promise:** The single most important thing that your company promises to deliver to its customers—at *every* single touch point. To decide what that is, consider what customers, employees, and partners should expect from every possible interaction with you. Every business and marketing decision should be weighed against this promise to be sure that it fully reflects that promise or at the very least it does not contradict it (for example, Nordstrom's promise to deliver exceptional customer service or Southwest Airline's promise of convenience when booking/changing flight plans).

- **Brand Personality:** Illustrates what your company wants its brand to be known for. Think about specific personality traits you want prospects, clients, employees, and partners to use to describe your company and brand. Consider well-known weight loss program, Weight Watchers. Of course their business model is selling weight loss solutions, programs, consulting, and diets. But their brand personality is selling empowerment and empathy. Many of their corporate spokespeople like Jennifer Hudson express this sentiment in television commercials and online video advertisements.

- **Brand Story:** Illustrates your company's history, along with how the history adds value and credibility to your brand. It should include a summary of your products or services. A great example of this is what Google did for Chrome. They released a video of a dad keeping a journal about his daughter, Sophie Lee, from before she was born and then highlighting her life milestones—first birthday, crying, laughing, becoming a big sister, and much more. The video concludes with

Google's suite of products circulating and showcasing how their products can help you "the customer" tell this same story.

- **Brand Associations:** The specific physical artifacts that make up your brand. This is your name, logo, colors, taglines, fonts, imagery, and so on. Your brand associations must reflect all that you promise to your stakeholders.

There is an old saying that is still relevant today: "Features tell, benefits sell." Well, despite its age and the fact that I am probably dating myself, it's still true today and is an integral part of your storytelling initiatives. I am sure you remember buying your first laptop. The sales rep over at Best Buy was most likely explaining something along the lines of "This ultrabook is equipped with Windows 8; it has an Intel Core I7 64-bit processor; it has full HD with a 15.6" screen; it comes equipped with 8GB of memory and a 500GB 1600 MHz DDR3 hard drive with Intel Smart Response Technology."

Unless you know about laptops or consider yourself a technology enthusiast, none of this technical jargon matters to you. What you want to know is how it will benefit your life. Questions like "How fast is it?" "Can I watch high definition movies and browse Facebook at the same time?" or "How many photos and videos can I store on it?" are more important. So as you think about your content narrative, consider the brand, the products, and what they promise to deliver to you customers. These are all extremely important.

The Non-Business Issues Important to Your Brand

If you don't own a pair of TOMS shoes, you should. TOMS designs and sells shoes based on the Argentine alpargata design. Alpargata shoes have a canvas or cotton fabric upper and a flexible sole made of rope or rubber material and molded to look like rope. The shoes have been worn by Argentine farmers for hundreds of years and were the inspiration for TOMS.

What's unique about TOMS, if you remember from Chapter 1, "Understanding the Social Customer and the Chaotic World We Live In," is that when they sell a pair of shoes, another pair of shoes is given to an impoverished child; and when TOMS sells a pair of eyewear, part of the profit is used to save or restore the eyesight for people in developing countries such as Argentina, Cambodia, Haiti, and the United States. In a recent interview on Treehugger.com, the founder of TOMS Shoes, Blake Mycoskie, goes on record to explain his inspiration for starting the company.

> I'm a serial entrepreneur. I've started five companies in the last 12 years, mainly in media and technology. I was just kind of burned out. I went down to Argentina looking for some time to relax, experience the culture, take it all in. I spent a couple of weeks doing that. In the

process, I met some expats that were down there doing some really great social work in some of the villages on the outskirts of Buenos Aires. I asked them if I could tag along.

I'm always looking for new experiences. When I went with them to one village in particular, I noticed that most of the children did not have shoes and that if they did have shoes, they had a shoe that was way too big, or duct-taped, or a flip-flop with a hole in it. It just shocked me to some degree. Shoes aren't that expensive, so why don't they have shoes? And even more so, after I stopped a few of the kids and looked at their feet, they had cuts. They had hookworm. They had infections.

He goes on to talk about the implications of not having shoes in some of these countries.

I would say that there are really three things that you find. Number one is just that having shoes helps someone with their personal security and understanding. It gives them self-worth. It shows that they're valued. It's almost a sense of wealth in these communities. It almost becomes a passport into other things that are very important. School, for instance, is probably the easiest example. A lot of kids cannot go to school unless they have a proper uniform, and a proper uniform includes shoes.

So, literally, I've met thousands of families that the first thing they say to us when we give them shoes is, "Oh my God, my kid will now get to go to school." That's a big deal. To think that there are schools with open seats in the developing world that don't allow kids to come in because they don't have a pair of shoes. To me, it's just ridiculous. But that's just the custom that they have. So giving them a pair of shoes allows education.

In Blake's case, he built his entire business model on helping others, and everything you see online—TOMS.com, Twitter, Facebook, paid advertising, and various customer conversations deliver on this powerful message. This is what TOMS stands for.

Your company's business model might not be rooted in philanthropy, but most likely, your brand is involved in some type of corporate responsibility or citizenship. Issues around sustainability, energy efficiency, poverty, or human trafficking should be considered to be a part of your content narrative in some way.

If your company does not have a corporate social responsibility program, perhaps that should be considered—and not just for the sake of storytelling. It's just the right thing to do.

Media Perceptions of the Brand

Tesla Motors is a car company that designs, manufactures, and sells electric cars and electric vehicle powertrain components. The company first gained widespread attention by producing the Tesla Roadster in 2008, the first fully electric sports car. Its second car is the Model S that was released in 2012.

If you scan the media headlines about Tesla, you will see a wide array of different headlines. As discussed in Chapter 3, "Establishing a Centralized 'Editorial' Social Business Center of Excellence," there was a negative review of the Model S written by *New York Times* reporter John Broder in February 2013 titled, "Stalled Out on Tesla's Electric Highway." More recent headlines include

> **"Sarah Palin echoes Romney: Tesla Motors 'losers' who build 'bricks'":** In this article, Sarah Palin commented on a Facebook post saying that Tesla Motors was launched after receiving a loan from the Department of Energy but has since been plagued with problems and laid off 75% of its workforce.
>
> **"Facing opposition from auto groups, Tesla looks to change Texas law so it can sell cars in the state":** In this article, it appears as if Tesla Motors is in a legal squabble with the state of Texas. They are facing opposition from the state's auto dealers association who want to stop Tesla from selling, delivering, and servicing its vehicles in the state of Texas.
>
> **"Tesla expects its first-ever profit":** In this CNN article, Tesla Motors is expecting to report its first-ever quarterly profit after sales of its all-electric Model S exceeded expectations and that the announcement about the just-ended first quarter pushed Tesla Motors (TSLA) shares nearly 16% higher.

There are hundreds of articles written every day about companies, brands, CEOs, products, and services. Gaining insight into how the media talks about and perceives your brand is important. I am not referring to the sentiment of the conversation or volume of conversation. These are certainly important but aren't the focus of your narrative. I am talking about the context in which they talk about your brand. It will either help you craft a message that resonates with the media or validate that your current narrative is actually working.

In the Tesla example, the above CNN article states, "The company is sticking with the larger 60-kilowatt hour battery pack option, with a range closer to 230 miles. That model sells for $62,400 after a $7,500 federal tax credit." The interesting thing about this is that "tax credit" saving message is very much a part of the way that Tesla persuades buyers to purchase the car, both on the company website as well as when you visit the sales center. In fact, they calculate the purchase price based on that savings even though it's more of a rebate than a discount taken at the time of purchase.

Community Perceptions of the Brand

Just as it is important to understand how the media talks about your brand, it's even more important to understand what your customers are saying. Are they validating your narrative? Do they refer to your brand the way you want them to refer to it? Extracting these insights helps you craft a content strategy that is more relevant to your customers.

Let's build on the Tesla example. I went to their Facebook page to see how their fans were "reacting" to the content on the page. Again, not necessarily looking at the sentiment or engagement, but more to understand the way they talk to and about the brand. The Tesla Motors community manager recently shared an article about the opening of 20 service centers in Raleigh Durham, North Carolina. A quick scan of the Facebook comments show that their customers are excited naturally, saying "No wonder it was the unanimous car of the year...beauty, power, sophistication, and non-polluting...all in one machine" and "I'd add +1 to that group if I had the means to buy a Tesla. I'm a Leaf owner in Raleigh though, so I'm still helping to push EV adoption here."

I then clicked over to the article on WalterMagazine.com to get more context and get a better idea of how the writer perceived and talked about Tesla. Seeing the commentary in the actual article gave additional insight:

> That cherry on top is no joke. Model S owner Otto Kumbar insisted on nudging Walter into the driver's seat of his new car, and while there's no mistaking the Tesla's style, it's the instantaneous, rocket-like zoom that erupts with a tap on the pedal—zero-to-60 in four seconds—that could make an eco-warrior out of anyone. ("It's So Easy Being Green When Your Ride Looks Like This").

I then did quick search of "Tesla Motors" in Twitter, which gives even more insight into the way the community is talking about the brand.

- @azizonomics Electric cars economically unviable? Nope. Tesla Motors just made a first quarterly profit.
- @drgrist Can we please have electric cars NOT rely on sexist advertising? RT @TeslaMotors Chick Magnet.
- @hunterwalk Imagine @TeslaMotors-operated drive-in movie theaters in LA, SF for Tesla owner meetups. C'mon @elonmusk, make it happen!

- @amandatapping Voila le Tesla!! Totally electric. Totally fun, gorgeous and fast. Loving it! @TeslaMotors!! Xo

And last, in response to the article where Sarah Palin was quoted, there is a tweet directly from Mr. Elon Musk himself:

- @elonmusk Sarah Palin calls Tesla a loser. Am deeply wounded. Btw, Model S warranty does cover "bricking."
- @IshanShah Keep up the good work @TeslaMotors! Palin=trolling. @elonmusk: "Sarah Palin calls Tesla a loser...Btw, Model S warranty does cover bricking."

Again, the purpose of this analysis is not to track sentiment, conversation volume, or community engagement. It's to get a better understanding of the community and "how" they talk or refer to the brand. Does that context match Tesla's content narrative or brand positioning? Or does it provide insight that would influence how Tesla creates content? In some cases, it might make an impact, and other times it might not prove to be as valuable.

Fan Interests

It's no secret that Facebook limits the number of fans that see your content unless you pay to promote your posts. It makes sense. That's their business model. So unless you have a huge budget to promote all of your posts, you need to figure out a story that resonates with your Facebook fans. And even then, you cannot ignore a paid media strategy in Facebook. You need to understand what interests your fans when they aren't talking with you or about you. Unfortunately, much of this data is private, so it makes it difficult. You can certainly go to random fans' personal pages and do it manually, but this isn't a scalable solution if you have a large Facebook community.

MicroStrategy is one of the largest vendors of business intelligence software, competing with products such as SAP Business Objects and IBM Cognos for reporting and analysis of data. In 2012, they launched their Wisdom Application that takes Facebook data to the next level. Their application makes it simple to drill down into information shared by millions of Facebook fans. Currently the application has data from about five million people, and MicroStrategy says that it's growing by about 100,000 people a day. The app has two main functions. The first allows you to analyze and compare the information from almost half a billion Facebook Page Likes. The second provides you detailed statistics about your personal Facebook network.

Their enterprise product lets you access and analyze big data from a variety of sources and provides them in several analytical views based on demographics, psychographics, check-in locations, and interest. Figure 7.2 shows all the data points that Wisdom can provide to you.

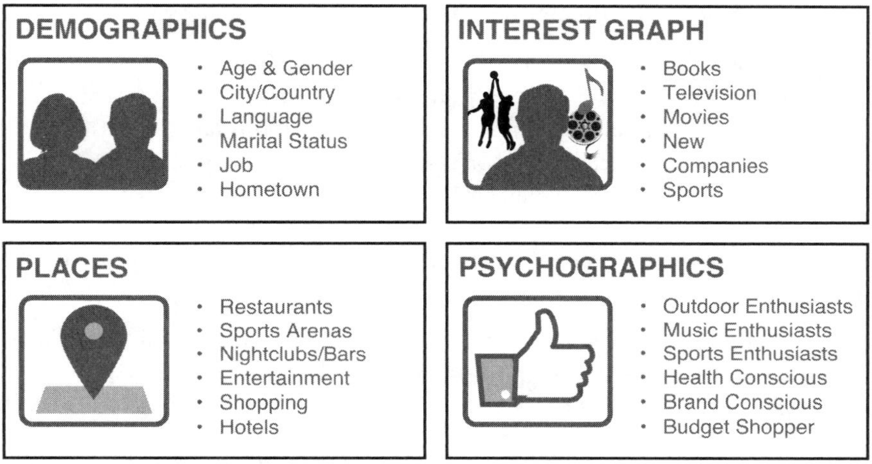

Figure 7.2   *Wisdom's Enterprise product can give you information about your fans.*

Also if you work directly with Facebook, you can request the Connection Analysis Report that provides a deeper look into the demographics and psychographics of your fan base. These insights can help you to determine how well your brand is connecting with your customers on Facebook and understand deeper insights into what they are interested in. The report details specific demographic data, how your fans access the page (mobile, which device, and so on), as well as what other brand pages your fans also like.

Similar to the Wisdom application for Facebook, Demographics Pro can help you get a better understanding of your Twitter followers. CEO Paul Hallett describes his product as the "Nielsen for Twitter," which can give you a detailed demographic and psychographic breakdown of your Twitter followers. I ran my Twitter account through the product and received the following summary at the beginning of a 27-page detailed report:

> @Britopian's followers are in their early thirties, typically married with high income. The account has a noteworthy audience concentration in San Francisco.

> **Professionally,** @Britopian's followers are employed as senior managers, customer service professionals, entrepreneurs, HR professionals, and consultants. The account ranks within the top 10% of all Twitter accounts in terms of density of sales/marketing managers.

In their spare time they enjoy beer, political news, nightlife/partying, wine, and yoga. People following @Britopian are charitably generous, environmentally aware, and health conscious. Sports that rise most notably above Twitter norm include hockey, cycling, and skiing.

As consumers they are relatively affluent and fashion conscious, with spending focused most strongly on nightlife/entertainment, technology, and wining/dining. Main street brand affiliations far stronger than Twitter average include Morton's Steakhouse, Trader Joe's, Caribou Coffee, Pei Wei, and Capital Grille.

I never knew that I attracted beer-drinking politicos who also enjoy yoga and partying.

Although this data is certainly helpful, it's important to remember that it should also be considered one of several inputs that will help deliver your content narrative.

Seattle-based Simply Measured provides deep analytics when researching your brand's Twitter followers as well. The following example is a report analyzing Starwood Preferred Guest's (SPG) Twitter account. As illustrated in Figure 7.3, the platform analyzes the top keywords within your followers' profile descriptions. In this example, 9% of SPG's followers have "travel" listed in their profiles. This shouldn't be all too surprising because SPG owns several hotels—The W, Westin, Sheraton, and ALoft. What is interesting, though, is that 3% have "music" and "business" listed in their profiles. Though these percentages are fairly low, it might prove to be an opportunity to create more business and/or music-focused content.

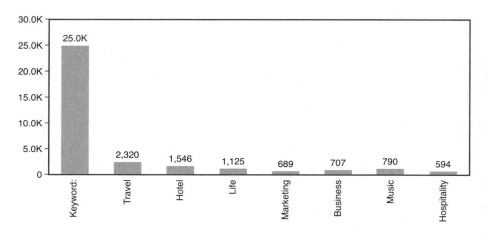

Figure 7.3 *Top keywords within followers' profile descriptions*

Simply Measured also surfaces the top keywords within tweets. In the following example and analyzing Jet Blue's Twitter account, 18% of Jet Blue's followers are also mentioning "flight" followed by "#JetBlueApp" at 11%, "Ipad" at 7%, and "giving" at 6%. In this case, it would be smart to get a better understanding of some of the tweets that mention "flight" specifically, as this could be a customer service issue or current customers complaining about the brand for some reason. And it's quite possible that the "giving" keyword could be associated with a campaign of some sort, perhaps a partnership with a cause-related organization. Figure 7.4 illustrates the breakdown of the top keywords associated with the tweets that also mention Jet Blue.

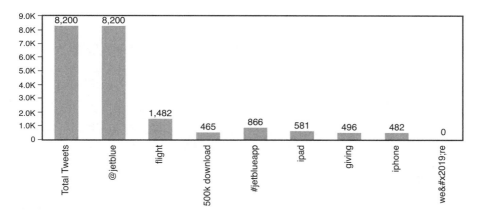

Figure 7.4 *Top keywords within followers' tweets*

And finally, Simply Measured also integrates with Influencer Platform, Klout. This integration enables you to see influence scores for all of your followers. More importantly, it breaks down the topics within which your followers are influential. Figure 7.5 shows all of Time Warner Cable's followers based on their topics of influence. For example, 12% of their followers are influential about photography.

Most Popular Klout Topics

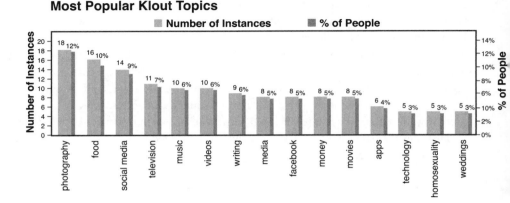

Figure 7.5   *Most popular Klout topics of Time Warner's Twitter followers*

Historical and Current Content Performance

It's also a smart idea to analyze historical content performance to help determine what's currently working and what isn't. Simply Measured also provides this level of data for both your Facebook pages and Twitter accounts as well as several other social media channels.

Simply Measured can give you basic engagement data such as average "Likes, comments, and shares," top performing posts, reach and impressions, and community growth metrics in Facebook, but they also provide you with the engagement numbers by time, day, and content type. There are several takeaways about data like this. One is that it will help you get smarter about day parting your content and answer questions like, "Is it more effective to post on Monday mornings at 9:00 AM PST or Friday afternoons at 4:00 PM PST?"

Second, the data sheds some light about which types of content are the most effective—video, photos, general status updates, or posts with/without links. This is important because as you build your content narrative and decide how you want to tell your brand story, this data gives you insight as to how you want to execute it and in which media type.

Consumer Search Behavior

Many social media marketers often forget about the power of Google. It is true that Google is the home page for just about everyone with an Internet connection. It is the gateway into the content that we are looking for. When I need to make a financial transaction online, I Google "US Bank," click the link, and login. When I want to access my personal email, I Google "Gmail," click the link, and log in. And whenever I speak at a conference or lecture at a university, I usually ask if anyone else does the same thing, and the answer is always an overwhelmingly "Yes!"

So the question is, how can you capitalize on understanding how people search for information in Google? Well, it just so happens that Google gives you this information for free. If you go to https://adwords.google.com and search for any keyword, it provides a report and tells you how many people, globally and locally, search for that specific keyword in a given month. It also gives you other, similar keywords and their corresponding search volume numbers.

Using the tool, I did a search for "makeup and acne." I explain why in the next section. Figure 7.6 shows that there are several thousand searches per month for that and similar keywords. Specifically, 33,000 people search for this every month, globally. This is valuable to you as you think about your content narrative. You never want to create content just for the search engines, but it's good to understand how people are searching for information, especially if you work for a makeup manufacturer in this case.

Keyword	Competition	Global Monthly Searches	Local Monthly Searches
makeup acne	High	33,100	22,200

Keyword ideas (100)

Keyword	Competition	Global Monthly Searches	Local Monthly Searches
best makeup for acne	High	9,900	6,600
best makeup for acne prone skin	High	3,600	2,900
makeup for acne	High	33,100	22,200
makeup and acne	High	33,100	22,200
makeup for acne skin	High	8,100	5,400
makeup for acne prone skin	High	6,600	4,400
good makeup for acne	High	1,300	880
makeup to cover acne	High	5,400	3,600
makeup for acne scars	High	2,900	1,600
mineral makeup for acne prone skin	High	390	260
makeup causes acne	Low	1,000	720
best mineral makeup for acne	High	720	480
best makeup to cover acne	High	1,000	880
acne makeup	High	33,100	22,200
cassandra makeup acne	Low	46	16
mineral makeup acne	Medium	1,600	880

Figure 7.6 *Google Adwords tool gives you specific data on how people search for information.*

It's also helpful to see how people search for your brand, specifically. Do they spell it correctly? What other terms are they associating with your brand? This data can give you a frame of reference into consumer behavior when they type your brand name into the search bar.

Understanding how and what consumers are searching for in Google will give you direction on the how you execute your content marketing initiatives, specifically when writing long-form content.

Customer Service Pain Points

You can't argue that customers are more empowered, connected, and vocal than ever before. It's one reason why your brand should act more like a media company. Social, mobile, and cloud platforms can give you the opportunity to invite your customers to play a completely different role in the company. There are several technology solutions in the market today that enable you to do this effectively. One platform is Lithium's Social Web product, a social media management platform that equips customer service agents to respond to posts across social channels such as Facebook, Twitter, Lithium Communities, industry forums, and other social destinations.

What's great about this tool is that it bridges that gap between a branded Lithium community (generally hosted on a brand's website) and brand pages on Facebook. Lithium uses Q&A boards, discussion forums, and search capabilities within their Facebook apps so that posts appear in both places, creating seamless conversations across both ecosystems. This is important because when a user asks/responds to a question in Facebook, it's dynamically updated on the branded site (and vice versa). This means that all the Q&A that happens within Facebook is not only game for Graph Search, but will also be indexed in Google. Win-win, if you ask me.

If you take a look at the Sephora Facebook page (https://www.facebook.com/Sephora) and click Beauty Advice, you'll see a form that allows you to ask a question or search the community for specific answers. This experience is powered by Lithium. I typed in "makeup and acne," and a drop-down menu of several conversations appeared. I clicked one thread "Do makeup primers aggravate acne?" and saw that there were about seven answers from others in the community giving their specific points of view. I then went to Google and searched for "does makeup aggravate acne," and the same conversation appeared in Google, specifically in the fourth position in the search results. Clicking the link took me to Sephora's Lithium branded community and specifically the same thread I came across in Facebook.

Using a tool such as Lithium's Social Web can help solve customer problems quickly and efficiently. It can also provide insight into what is bothering your customers so that you can create content around these issues and dominate Google at the same time. This tactic can also decrease calls into your call center if done right since many people search Google for answers before dialing customer service.

It's also good practice to use video when creating customer support content. The number one search term in YouTube is "how to," and it's the perfect opportunity for you to create proactive videos that answer questions your customers are asking about (such as how to unscrew a stripped screw). Home improvement retailer,

Lowe's, used Vine (six-second video social network owned by Twitter) to create six-second tutorials for their customers on this very topic.

What's important to realize is that most social content—specifically tweets and Facebook status updates—do not appear in Google's search results. So when you think about creating and using video content, think YouTube and other types of long-form content.

The Output Should Equal Your "Hero" Content Narrative

Building your content narrative isn't easy. You will have to spend a significant amount of time understanding the different data points (qualitative and quantitative) to get a 360-degree of view of your customer and your content. Each input plays a critical role in your content and your channel strategy, which is discussed in Chapter 8, "Building Your Content Channel Strategy."

Obviously, you have to take into consideration your brand and what it stands for. Skipping this step would be a huge miss, and you could find yourself creating and sharing content that doesn't align to your business goals. The nonbusiness issues might or might not play a role, depending on the size and culture of your company. But it would be a good idea to go through the exercise and understand if your brand is involved in corporate responsibility initiatives. Getting a firm understanding of how others talk about you is extremely important, whether it be the media, bloggers, or your customers.

Understanding their interests and passion points allows you to relate to them on a more personal level. Historical content performance is important as it will inform your channel strategy and give you insight into the types of content that delivers the most engagement and value. Search behavior helps you shape how you talk about your products, brand, and the value proposition that you deliver to your customers. Last, customer service can be much more than just responding to and answering customer questions online. By understanding your customer pain points, you can create content that aligns to those pain points, capitalizes on search, and potentially decreases calls coming into your call center.

After you gather all of this data, you need to collaborate with your internal stakeholders and prepare for a content innovation exercise. Depending on the size of your company, this could take one week or several weeks. But the goal of this exercise is to come to a collaborative decision on how you want to tell your story. You need to prioritize the importance of each of the content inputs and plot each one by the goals of your brand, the strategic importance of each, and your operational capabilities to execute.

Assuring that you get all of your internal stakeholders involved is imperative to the success of your content strategy. If you work for a small company or have a limited budget, you might not be able to execute a fully robust content strategy. You might only have the time, budget, and capabilities to focus on the top three content initiatives and build from there. However, going through the exercise just described will prove to be valuable to you in the long run.

Part of this exercise is also determining what your brand's tone of voice will be, specifically within social channels. For example, the following is one way this can be crafted if your brand is a clothing manufacturer or retailer:

- **Approachable:** Your brand is fun, easy to talk to, and answers questions even when they may not make complete sense. Your brand is a friend to all and gives good advice to those customers who seek fashion advice. You brand is not the fashion police and believes that everyone is beautiful even if their clothes may not match.
- **Fun/Humorous:** Your brand will never sound like a robot or share corporate gibberish. Going shopping is fun and you should have fun when talking about it. Your brand is clever, witty, and makes people smile.
- **Smart:** Your brand is a subject matter expert in all things fashion. No room for error when it comes to talking about important things in life, like making your customers look and feel good in some new threads.
- **Enthusiastic:** Your brand must strive to get customers excited and pumped for life events and milestones such as bachelor parties, anniversaries, back to school, or girls' night out.

Keep in mind that your brand's tone of voice should be unique to your brand's core values, culture, and content narrative.

The output resulting from these considerations will help you craft a content strategy that can scale and produce content that can have a strong, positive impact on customer behavior—whether it's selling more products, repositioning your company in its industry, or raising your company's profile and its public perception.

Simplifying Your Content Narrative

As complex as all of these inputs into your content narrative might be, you have to simplify it as best you can. If you recall from Chapter 1, there is a content surplus in the market place, and customers have an attention deficit. So telling a complex story in several different channels is going to be challenging. You should have a simple story to tell in the limited amount of time you have your customers' attention. This is certainly more difficult if your company sells extremely complex products or services.

I used to read the popular children's book *Love You Forever* to both of my girls when they were little. Even thinking about it today, I still get choked up and emotional. Go ahead and call me a softy. What I remember most about the book is that it uses imagery to tell a significant part of the plot (as with most children's books). The story is about a mother's unconditional love for her son. It chronicles her son's life growing from an infant to an adult and starting his own family. The sad conclusion shows how he reciprocates his love to his mother who has grown to be an elderly woman. There are just a few sentences on each page, but the story and illustration is powerful, and you can even follow along without actually reading the text.

This is how you should think about your content narrative. Visual storytelling is certainly top of mind for marketers today and something that consumers are demanding. With the rise of Instagram, Pinterest, Vine, and Facebook's recent Timeline redesign, it's even more important to keep your content narrative as simple and visual as possible.

Vendor Spotlight—Compendium

Compendium is a content marketing platform that can help you capture and create original content in a branded hub for distribution to any marketing channel. What differentiates Compendium from other platforms is that they host and manage all the content, hosting, and web services for their clients. They break down their platform down into the 5 Ps of Content Marketing:

1. **Plan Your Story**: Compendium can help you stay laser focused about the story you want to tell. From topics, timelines, tasks, and tracking to managing and growing your sources and library of original content, their platform can help you conceive, curate, and refine the story that makes you most appealing to your target audience.

2. **Produce Your Story**: Compendium helps you create a more effective story and provides workflows that help manage the content life cycle from beginning to end. With their StoryCapture feature, you can turn community conversations and customer stories directly into fresh content for your story, naturally.

3. **Publish Your Story**: Compendium offers a wide variety of templates, matching, or fully custom designs to ensure that your storytelling hub matches your brand and/or other online assets. Compendium hosts every site and handles all tech support.

4. **Promote Your Story**: With Compendium's "from anywhere, to anywhere" approach, your content can be distributed in a multitude of social media channels, and they help you build a repository of content you can repurpose for the future.

5. **Prove Your Story:** Compendium keeps you up to speed on what your audience is responding to and how your content is performing with their measurement and reporting dashboard.

Following is a case study that illustrates how Compendium can help you solve your content challenges.

Cvent is the world's largest provider of online event management, meeting site selection, and web survey software solutions. With four distinct product offerings, Cvent communicates differently with each of its target audiences through various marketing channels. They have an army of writers, content contributors, and editors who are responsible for feeding the content engine. To accomplish this task efficiently, Cvent needed tools with enterprise reliability to help guide writers to stay on message and to help administrators manage content with customizable workflows.

In the fall of 2008, Cvent launched a content hub (http://blog.cvent.com/) with Compendium, using two blogs to target their event planning and surveys offerings. Leveraging Compendium's tools to help with content creation, moderation, and broadcasting, Cvent has since been able to launch two more blogs within their content hub—each targeted at a specific audience with specific goals (for example, thought leadership, brand awareness, lead generation). Features like Compendium's Message Meter help Cvent's 54 writers stay on message regardless of which of topics they are writing on. Meanwhile, Compendium's moderation workflow feature allows Cvent's six editors to create custom approval workflows for each blog, easing the editing process while assuring that every piece of content is proofread before being published. And all of this content is published on pages that are hosted in the cloud—ensuring that up time is reliable and page load speeds are optimal, no matter where their online visitors are located or how much traffic they get to their website.

With this content hub at the core of their content strategy, Cvent has been able to launch several targeted eNewsletters. Each newsletter is populated with the best performing content targeted for its unique audience. In addition, Cvent's content is published on their social media channels using custom tracking. This allows Cvent to get more mileage out of their posts and to understand which content performs the best on each social channel.

Since the launch of their site, Cvent has been able to effectively and efficiently maintain their content hub, 54 authors, and six editors. They have published over

6,300 articles, experienced traffic increases of 175%, and seen an increase in sales-ready leads of 325% between 2010 and 2011. The hub contributed 5% of asset downloads and 1% of demo requests over the last year, with 60% of those coming since launching the new design. Most important, Cvent projects ad sales through its various blogs to reach $1 million in 2013.

Building Your Content Channel Strategy

Tweetable Moment: *Visual Storytelling is critical in how you communicate and tell your brand story but you can't forget long-form content. —#nextmediaco*

I am a huge fan of Whole Foods Market and shop there weekly. It's a supermarket chain based in Austin, Texas, with grocery stores all over the U.S. and currently expanding in Canada and the United Kingdom. All of the products sold are natural and organic, and the company has been ranked among the most socially responsible businesses and placed fourth on the U.S. Environmental Protection Agency's list of Top 25 Green Power Partners.

The shopping experience is amazing, too. Everything you could possibly imagine to fit a healthy lifestyle is sold at Whole Foods. They have an incredible cold bar with fresh salads and vegetables, a hot food bar with freshly cooked chicken and various pastas, and a sushi bar with fresh fish served daily. What makes the experience even better is that every employee I have ever dealt with seems happy and helpful, and they bend over backwards to make your shopping excursion better.

I don't follow Whole Foods in any social network. I am just not that "type of guy," so I decided to look them up on Facebook as I was writing this chapter. I began my search for "Whole Foods Market San …" and before I finished typing my search query, a drop-down menu of several Whole Foods Market Facebook pages appeared. Santa Monica, Santa Fe, Santa Barbara, San Mateo, San Ramon, and San Antonio were the top six results. I didn't actually find the store I was looking for given I live in Santa Clara (San Jose), but I was pleasantly surprised that each of the local pages had fresh, local, and relevant content.. That is certainly a best practice in my book.

From spending some time researching Whole Foods and what they do in social media, it's clear they have a decentralized social channel strategy; meaning that they give autonomy to individual stores to create and manage specific channels. I can only assume that each store has assigned a manager or employee to be responsible for their local Facebook page. It's a good strategy, and they obviously get it.

Like Whole Foods, after you decide on what your content narrative is going to be, you must then map out a strategy on how you want to execute your story across the digital ecosystem.

Finding and Preventing Gaps with Your Social Media Channel Strategy

In Chapter 2, "Defining Social Business Strategy and Planning," I talked about the chaos that social media has caused in companies today and how it's having a negative effect on content and community. I cited the 2012 Altimeter study, "A Strategy for Managing Social Media Proliferation," which found that companies have an average of 178 social media channels. Here is a breakdown of each channel and the volume of accounts:

- 39 Twitter Accounts
- 32 Blogs
- 30 Facebook pages
- 29 LinkedIn Pages
- 23 Forums/Communities
- 6 Foursquare
- 5 Other
- 3.8 Flickr
- .3 Gowalla

There are certainly exceptions to this rule, one obviously being Whole Foods, but with 178 channels, it's almost impossible to keep content fresh, alive, engaging, and locally relevant. Not to mention that 95% of these channels were most likely created from internal silos; and most likely have dying communities because they were created for a campaign or short-term promotion.

So if you are in the process of building out your channel strategy, consolidating your social media channels, or determining if you need additional ones, there are four things you must consider before making a decision. These can help prevent disjointed content, bad community behavior, and customer confusion, which plague so many brands today, unfortunately:

1. **Identify the content narrative:** Do you have a specific content strategy for a specific channel? Chapter 7, "Defining Your Brand Story and Content Narrative," helps you determine your brand story by examining several internal and external factors. Too many marketers today still like to create brand new Facebook pages or Twitter accounts for product launches, events, or campaigns. In some cases, this may make sense but I would at least spend time weighing the pros and cons. I have seen this too many times in the past where several hundred thousand dollars are spent in paid media to drive traffic and build a community on a brand new channel. When the campaign is over, the community is abandoned and forgotten about.

   It's also important to note you should not repurpose the same exact content on one Facebook page to fuel another Facebook page or use tweets to feed content into a Google+ page. Each community is different. They each have different characteristics and functionality. Each channel should have its own content narrative, or at least a different style in how you tell the same story. Otherwise, what's the point of creating something brand new if you already have an existing Facebook page?

2. **Determine the community manager:** With every new community or channel created, there must be a community manager, content marketing manager, or customer support person responsible for that channel. There are two ways to look at this. One is from a proactive perspective. The role of a community manager has certainly changed in the last several years. Today, community managers must posses the skills to create compelling content, analyze data, and even understand the basics of paid media in case certain posts need to be sponsored. Community managers today need to understand content marketing.

   The other way to look at this is from a reactive perspective. Community managers must also monitor conversations that customers are having about the brand (whether a complaint, a potential crisis, or even customers giving the brand praise) and respond accordingly. In many cases, the community manager will be responsible for flagging customer issues and escalating them to a customer support person.

3. **Build a moderation and escalation policy:** There have been several reports published in the last several years that illustrate how customers are seeking customer support within a brand's social media channel, specifically Facebook and Twitter. One study published in 2012 titled, "The State of Social Customer Service" by NM Incite (Joint venture between Nielsen and McKinsey & Company) found that 71% of customers who get a quick and effective response from customer support will recommend that brand to others. This is why it's so important to ensure that your community manager has the power to solve customer problems quickly; or that workflows are in place to escalate customer complaints to someone on the customer support team quickly and efficiently.

Doing so not only keeps your current customers happy, but it also drives advocacy because they will tell others about their experiences with your brand.

4. **Establish a measurement framework:** Chapter 2 went into great detail about the need for your teams to collaborate, and Chapter 3, "Establishing a Centralized 'Editorial' Social Business Center of Excellence," gives you a framework for building a Social Business Center of Excellence (CoE). As previously mentioned, the role of the CoE is to establish a common measurement framework so that the entire organization is measuring social media consistently. Circumstances will certainly arise, for example, when new platforms will need to be used and your measurement framework will need to be adapted. Or if a regional team wants to launch a program into a specific channel that only serves customers in that region, like South Korea's microblogging platform Me2day, you will want to ensure that the team has KPIs that can determine success before launching.

Chuck Hemann, Group Director of Analytics for WCG and co-author of Digital Marketing Analytics describes three ways of looking at measurement. First and foremost is program measurement where you are tracking social channel health (community growth, engagement, reach, and so on). Second is measuring the performance of individual pieces of content, but not just tracking the engagement. It's important to take the second and third steps of tagging content by key message and identifying whether it contained a link, photo, video, and so on. Lastly,

it's important for brands to be constantly analyzing the demographics and psychographics of its community. Ad campaigns, new types
of content and the introduction of new messages all could change the
composition of your community and therefore adversely impact overall
performance.

Mapping Your Content Narrative to Social Channels

One of the outputs of the content innovation exercise discussed in Chapter 7 is cat-
egorizing your content narrative into themes. Consider Figure 8.1 as an example of
how this might look for your brand.

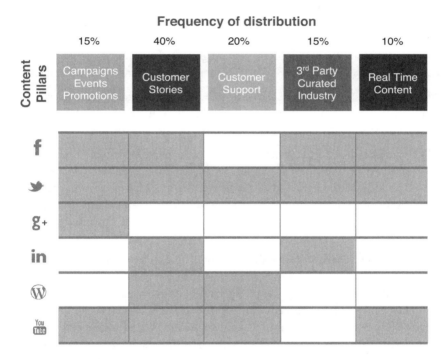

Figure 8.1 *Example of how to organize your content*

In this figure, you see that there are five content themes labeled horizontally:
Campaigns, Events, and Promotions; Customer Stories; Customer Support; Third-
Party Curated Industry; and Real Time Content. Also notice percentages at the
top of each of the content pillars. These are examples and meant to illustrate the
frequency of distribution of each of these content themes. The percentages and
themes will certainly vary, and may even be completely different, based on your
brand's priorities, business goals, the narrative, and the story you want to tell.
Again, this is just an example.

Along the vertical axis are social media channels. This exercise isn't meant to persuade or convince you that you need to use every social media channel to execute your content narrative. Unfortunately, many brands today have this mindset and then struggle because they run out of content ideas to keep the community engaged. You should only launch into these channels if you have the proper resources and capabilities in place, as mentioned in the previous section.

Building from Figure 8.1, let's assume that you have decided to use all of these channels to execute your content narrative and tell your story. In this case, 15% of your content will be campaigns, events, and promotions focused; and this particular content will be spread across Facebook, Twitter, Google+, and YouTube. You might also decide that you want to create customer support related content on Twitter, YouTube, and within a support blog of some sort. What this chart doesn't reflect are the number of channels that you might use if you have more than one Twitter account. Many brands use one main account for general content (brand/ community building) and another to manage support related content and questions. Large brands might have specific regional Twitter and Facebook pages.

Although this is just an example, the distribution percentages do reflect my overall thinking about content. But certainly every brand is different, and these ratios and content themes might or might not work for your brand:

- **Campaigns, Events, Promotions:** If a large percentage of your content is all about "you," "your" brand, "your" campaigns, or "your" event, it will surely annoy your customers, resulting in a high community attrition percentage (number of un-Likes, un-Follows). It's smart to limit this type of content. Remember, content needs to add value to your customers.

- **Customer Stories:** Generally, customers love to hear about other customer stories. This could be success stories, fan photos, or customer testimonials. Take for example a brand like Skype. Their community loves inspirational and emotional content, and it makes sense. The Skype product is all about "making connections" and connecting friends and families to each other, such as the soldier who is stationed overseas who uses the product to see his newly born son or the grandparents who sing happy birthday to their grandchild from across the world. The emotional elements of storytelling are far more effective than "Skype helps me save on my phone bill" type of messaging.

- **Customer Support:** Many believe that customer support is purely reactive. I believe that it's both reactive and proactive. Assuming you have launched your command center, as discussed in Chapter 5, "Building Your Social Business Command Center," and are monitoring conversations about your brand, you should already have an idea of your customers' pain points. Why not take this opportunity to create proactive content to address the issues, specifically blog posts and YouTube videos? YouTube is the world's number two search engine; and guess what the number one search term is in YouTube? The answer—how-to videos. By creating content that addresses customer issues, you are not only solving customer problems quickly and efficiently, but it could also decrease calls coming into the call center.

- **Third-Party Curated, Licensed Content:** Your content narrative must provide value to your customers. So, if that means sharing curated content that doesn't necessarily mention your brand, you should be okay with that. I am certainly not saying you should share competitor content. That wouldn't be smart. But let's assume you work for a financial institution and the U.S. government just passed a law that affects international wire transfers. It would make sense that you share that content with your community and provide context or "expert commentary" about the report. That would be valuable to your fans.

  There are several tools in the marketplace today that can help you curate and distribute third-party content: PublishThis, Curata, and Percolate all provide this service to large and small brands. NewsCred can provide you with a selection of content to license, syndicate, curate, and publish from high-quality, premium publishers, such as the *New York Times*, *Wall Street Journal*, *Forbes*, *Bloomberg*, *The Economist*, *Chicago Tribune*, *Huffington Post*, and many others.

- **Real-Time Content:** The Oreo Super Bowl example mentioned in Chapter 5 certainly made real-time marketing a household topic. I actually missed the tweet because I was depressed, yelling and throwing things during half time. I am a 49ers fan. But the truth is, real-time marketing has been around for quite some time. And though many brands and agencies are jumping on the "real-time marketing" bandwagon, it should not be the focal point of your entire content strategy. You and your brand cannot sit idle and wait for the news cycle before you create compelling pieces of content. You should be doing this day in and day out.

  That said, as you brand becomes a media company, you will naturally have the right infrastructure in place (editorial roles/responsibilities, team structure, and content workflows) to create real-time, valuable content that your customers will find relevant and love.

- **Lifestyle Content:** Although real-time content is making headlines everywhere, some brands, including yours, might not be quite ready or equipped to take it on. If that's the case, perhaps building a content theme that is focused on lifestyle might be appropriate. As mentioned in Chapter 7, there are tools today like the Wisdom application, Demographics Pro, Simply Measured, and Keyhole.co that can help you determine other topics that your fans are passionate about. For example, using one of these platforms, you could get valuable insight that a high percentage of your fans are interested in music, so it would make sense to build that content theme into your narrative. It may even justify your brand creating a new channel (Tumblr or YouTube channel, for example) that would be all about "music." You will just have to ensure that there is a relevant connection to the content theme and what your brand stands for.

After you have determined what your content themes will be and where you are going to share and create that content, you can then build out a specific editorial calendar that illustrates what you will share on a given day within a specific channel. Here is one example of how you can do this on a Facebook page.

- **Mondays** (music Monday): You can execute this numerous ways. You can curate articles from MTV.com or Billboard.com and provide your own context about the story. You can create a weekly Spotify playlist or identify cool mixes on Mixcrate.com and share something clever. Or, if your brand has ever sponsored a band/artist, rapper, or DJ, you can share one of their tracks from YouTube. You should always insert some context into what you are sharing.

- **Tuesdays** (fan of the week): This can certainly be any day of the week, but perhaps one approach to take is to determine which of your fans is the most engaged with your content and thank him for his participation. Another idea would be to share any videos/photos from fans who have uploaded content to your timeline. In some cases, you can ask them directly to do this, or you can use a tool such as Napkin Labs (discussed in Chapter 4, "Empowering Employees, Customers, and Partners to Feed the Content Engine") and do this dynamically.

- **Wednesday** (product tip day): In this case, you can share product-specific updates, video tutorials, or quick tips and tricks. It's always good practice to speak in a tone that your fans will appreciate and not just copy and paste the content from your corporate website or an FAQ document. Again, social media is conversational, and your tone can determine how well (or not) your content is received by your fans.

- **Thursday** (third-party, industry): This could be content about your industry or a mention about your brand from a third-party source. If you work for a start-up, you can easily source third-party content from Techcrunch or AllThingsD about other start-ups and share it on Facebook. Also, there are tools that can easily help you curate content that might not necessarily mention your brand but could be extremely valuable to your community, as just mentioned.

- **Friday** (Friday fun day): This could be just about anything. It can be focused on various community interests or be completely random. It could be memes about cats or dogs, quotes, or polls—whatever matches up nicely with what your brand stands for. It could even be fun games, tongue twisters, or riddles. Intel just recently shared a post asking the community how many words they could make with "Intel"; and then showed a photo from a scrabble game with the brand name spelled out on the tiles. Pretty clever if you ask me.

Building a plan like this helps establish a cadence of content and lets your fans know what to expect on any given day. It also helps you prepare internally so that you can line up your resources well ahead of time and not the night before a piece of content is supposed to be published. And it's certainly acceptable if you change up this cadence every quarter or even monthly. It really depends on what your business and marketing goals are. Plus, your community will let you know what they want and expect and may even tell you directly. Another indicator is simply looking at the content performance metrics.

Not all brands plan out their content this way, and that's okay. You will have to see what works for you, test it, and the change up your content approach if you need to.

Building Your Content Tiers by Channel

Another way to map your content narrative is by adding tiers to your content by specific channel. Figure 8.2 is an example for Facebook specifically. At the top of the pyramid is "marketing-related" content, and the fact that it's at the top of the pyramid and not the bottom illustrates that this type of content should not be the main focus and that it should be limited. Tier 2 content can be anything you choose. In this case, it's combining curated content about the brand, industry-related content, and customer stories. Tier 3 content is the day-to-day community management and encompasses proactive/reactive content and fun/interest-based content. In this model, real-time content spans across all content and illustrates that each tier can capitalize on the news cycle when the opportunity presents itself.

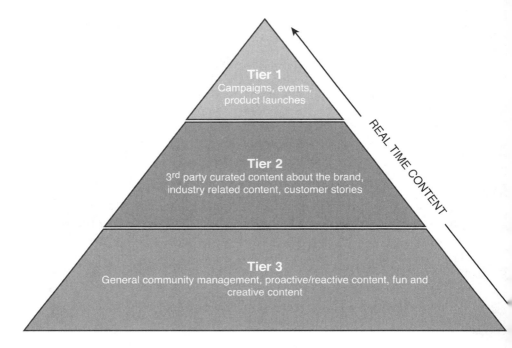

Figure 8.2   *Tier your content by specific channel.*

You will have to repeat this exercise for each channel you manage or for new channels that you launch in the future. In some cases, you might use one specific channel for storytelling, similar to what Burberry has done using Tumblr, which you read about in the next section.

Laser Focused Storytelling by Channel

Burberry, a British luxury fashion house that distributes clothing and fashion accessories globally, has a multitude of social media channels. Their Facebook page alone has 15 million fans, and the content is product and campaign-focused. They have a multitude of Twitter accounts as well; one main account with 1.7 million followers as well as several accounts for a variety of countries and regions. The content there is also very product-focused.

Burberry's Tumblr page is all about one storyline—trench coats. Figure 8.3 is a screen shot of their Tumblr page, "Art of the Trench" (http://burberry.tumblr. com/). The site is described as a "living document of the trench coat and the people who wear it" and that the project is a collaboration among you, Burberry, and some of the world's leading image makers. They even give their Tumblr followers the option to upload their trench coat photos as well.

Figure 8.3 *Burberry's "Art of the Trench" Tumblr page*

Certainly, Burberry could have just shared trench coat related content on their Facebook page as a part of a broader content theme. Instead, they made a strategic decision to create a Tumblr page specifically to tell the "trench coat" story, and they are doing so very effectively.

Sharpie (yes, that Sharpie), manufacturer of writing instruments (mainly marker pens), is dominating Instagram. Their approach hasn't been about sharing marketing messages or tips and tricks. Instead, they use their own product to tell the brand story—yes, their actual product, the Sharpie. Their in-house team of staff and interns create original sharpie artwork, sketches, and doodles that they post daily to engage their audience. The majority of these images are drawn and posted by Whitney Kelly, Associate Manager of Social Media and Public Relations with Sharpie. Who says that you just have to use a Sharpie to label moving boxes?

According to an interview in 2012 with analytics firm, Simply Measured, Kelly said that they wanted to do something different with Instagram to keep their teen audience interested and engaged, so they designed their own sort of Sharpie comic strip ("Sharpie Capitalizing on Instagram"). She went on to say that the fans love the unique, hand-drawn nature of the content (a change from the mostly photo images on Instagram). As a result of this unique approach to storytelling, they have over 100,000 Instagram followers. Figure 8.4 is an Instagram photo from April 2013 titled "April showers! #sharpie" that garnered 5,000 Likes and 55 comments.

Figure 8.4   *Sharpie shares Instagram photos of content sketched using Sharpies.*

Their fans aren't passive about their interest in Sharpie's content either. Sharpie averages over 4,000 Likes per photo and over 31 comments. Although their engagement has grown quickly, it didn't grow without careful consideration and strategic thought. According to Kelly, Nielsen lists Instagram as the top photography site among teens ages 12 to 17.

Other brands such as Comcast (@ComcastCares), Nike (@NikeSupport), and Skype (@SkypeSupport) have decided to tell the "customer support" story or at least respond to customers using specific Twitter accounts. This is becoming a norm for most small and large brands. Creating specific support accounts allows your brand to use its main channels for creating compelling content and engaging the community.

Diversifying Your Content Types per Channel

Just as it is important to diversify your channel strategy, you must do the same with the content you create in each specific channel. The good news is that some channels facilitate content diversity better than others (that is, YouTube, Vine and Instagram for videos, Instagram or Pinterest for photos, and Facebook and Twitter for all of the above).

But the reason content diversity is important to your overall narrative is mainly because consumers learn and consume content differently, just like students in a classroom environment. When I was in college, I excelled in classes like Debate because much of the learning involved me debating others about various topics. I had to learn the content if I wanted to win the debate. On the other hand, I usually fell asleep in History because 90% of the class was just a lecture and the occasional reading assignment.

Chinese philosopher Confucius said, "I hear and I forget. I see and I remember. I do and I understand." And although this quote was said well over 2,000 years ago, it's an important lesson on how you should look at content.

This concept is related to neuroscience, also known as neural science. Neuroscience is the study of how the nervous system develops its structure and how it learns. Neuroscientists focus on the brain, its impact on behavior, and cognitive functions such as learning and understanding. Not only is neuroscience concerned with the normal functioning of the nervous system, but also what happens to the nervous system when people have neurological, psychiatric, and neurodevelopmental disorders.

From a marketing perspective, the study of neuroscience sheds some light on how to assist customers to interact with your content in multiple ways so they can "learn" about you and your brand. Some scholars also refer to this as the concept of *multimodal learning*, which argues that people are more likely to learn and retain information when it is presented in multiple modalities such as written (visual) and aural (auditory) at the same time. At the end of the day, your content will get more attention if you offer people multiple formats by which they can consume it.

Dominic W. Massaro, professor at the University of California, Santa Cruz has defined multimodal learning as an embodied learning situation, which engages multiple sensory systems and action systems of the learner. This type of learning is traditionally emphasized for children with learning challenges and can include a variety of visual inputs in addition to text. Some examples include pictures, art, film, video, and graphic organizers.

Consider Edgar Dale's Cone of Learning as you think about how you tell you brand story. Edgar Dale was an American educationist who developed the Cone of Learning. He made several contributions to audio and visual instruction, including a methodology for analyzing the content of motion pictures. Figure 8.5 is an illustration of Edgar Dale's Cone of Learning.

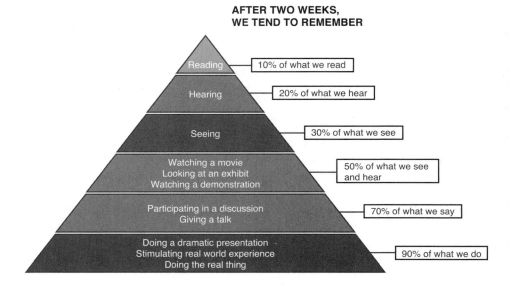

**AFTER TWO WEEKS,
WE TEND TO REMEMBER**

Reading — 10% of what we read

Hearing — 20% of what we hear

Seeing — 30% of what we see

Watching a movie
Looking at an exhibit
Watching a demonstration — 50% of what we see and hear

Participating in a discussion
Giving a talk — 70% of what we say

Doing a dramatic presentation
Stimulating real world experience
Doing the real thing — 90% of what we do

Figure 8.5   *Edgar Dale's Cone of Learning*

In this model, Dale builds a hierarchy of various learning experiences. The percentages given relate to how much of the content that people retain. Essentially, the model shows the progression of experiences from the most concrete (at the bottom of the cone) to the most abstract (at the top of the cone). It is important to note that Dale never intended the Cone to depict the way consumers interact with content. It was developed for the classroom environment. Nonetheless, the model clearly illustrates that after two weeks most people tend to remember 10% of what they read, 20% of what they hear, 30% of what they see, 50% of they see and hear, 70% of what they say, and 90% of what they do.

So the question is, how we can take the Cone of Learning and apply it to the content you create for your audiences? Table 8.1 breaks down how you can apply the Cone model to diversify your content.

Table 8.1   Diversifying Content Using the Cone of Learning

Cone of Learning	Content Opportunities
We remember 10% of what we read.	Blog posts, Tweets, Status updates
We remember 20% of what we hear.	Podcasts, Webinars
We remember 30% of what we see.	Videos, Infographics, Photos, Slideshare
We remember 50% of what we see and hear.	Videos, Webinars with visuals
We remember 70% of what we say.	Online focus groups, Two-way discussion
We remember 90% of what we do.	Production, Co-creation, Enabling advocates to create content

The Importance of Visual Storytelling

Sara Quinn, Professor of Visual Journalism at The Poynter Institute, recently said during a presentation at Arizona State University that alternative story forms attract a lot of attention and more attention than traditional text. And when something is different, it stands out. Makes sense, right?

If you spend any time on your Facebook news feed, you'll probably agree. Even your Facebook friends are catching on that photos and videos drive more engagement and "Likes." It's the only thing we notice as we scroll through our feeds.

If you look closely at the Cone of Learning, the importance of visual content plays a significant role in content retention. I am sure you can remember a funny photo that one of your friends posted on Facebook, but can you remember the last post that didn't have a photo or some type of visual element? Unless it was a relationship status change, which there are a lot of, you probably don't.

In a 2012 *CNET* article, Jay Parikh, Facebook's Vice-President of Infrastructure Engineering, said that there are 300 million photos posted to Facebook every single day. The number of photos on Instagram aren't quite as high, but 40 million uploads per day isn't all that bad. And, of course, visual sites such as Tumblr and Pinterest have surged in usage, with 23 million unique visitors per month. And that number will surely grow, especially with Yahoo's acquisition of Tumblr in May 2013.

Consumers aren't just visiting visual sites like Pinterest and Instagram, they are interacting more with its content. Isn't that how it is in your own personal network too? According to analytics and measurement vendor Simply Measured, visual content generates five times more engagement than non-visual content on Facebook. Since the launch of the Timeline in 2012, engagement with visual content has increased 52%.

And certainly brands are taking note. According to a white paper written by Monte Lutz, Executive President at Edelman Digital, when Johnnie Walker launched on Instagram, they handed the reins of their new channel to three established Instagram influencers who posted their own Johnnie Walker inspired photos for the first month.

Simultaneously, Johnnie Walker evolved its Facebook presence to tell a more visual story; featuring fan-generated Instagram photos in its cover photo and posts. Interactions on Facebook surged, and fans flocked to Instagram. Recognizing the innovative campaign, Instagram featured Johnnie Walker in its own feed and on the Instagram blog, too.

Visual storytelling is also driving a surge in consumption of mobile video, with significant increases in mobile video views. According to the U.S. Digital Video Benchmark 2012 Review from Adobe, over the last two years, the audience for mobile video in the U.S. jumped 300% in 2012, accounting for 10.4% of video starts, up from just 3% in 2011. This will continue to increase as the smartphones and tablet sales explode.

It's clear today that your brand must learn to master the art of short-form and visual storytelling. Technology today enables it, and consumer attention spans demand it. Whether it be a 6–15 second video, a photo, or 140 characters, you must learn how to tell your brand story quickly and efficiently.

The Importance of Long-Form Content When Telling Stories

With all the hype about short-form storytelling, too many of us often forget about the longer brand narrative, and we are making a big mistake by doing so. Search engine visibility and thought leadership are two reasons why your brand must not abandon long-form content.

Search Engine Visibility

Even with the rise in social media, people still use Google. It's a fact. It's the home page for millions of people globally. It is for me, and probably for you too. When is the last time you saw a tweet or Vine video in the search results? I would guess never, unless of course you are searching for a specific account or person.

And I can almost guarantee that you'll *never* see a Facebook status update or Instagram photo/video in the search results for obvious reasons. Facebook purposely blocks Google from indexing all their content. We can only assume that they are building their own search engine.

The truth is that we use search daily, and when we do, we are on a mission. We are looking for information that's important to us at that specific moment in time. It's not like Twitter or Facebook where we scroll through our feeds casually; check our @replies, messages, and follower counts; and then mosey on over to LinkedIn to see who's been stalking our profiles.

When we use search, it's because we want something and want it now. It could be movie tickets, information about a vacation destination, or research in the latest data center technology.

With short-from storytelling and social media in general, we are trying to interrupt customers with our brand message, and the question you have to ask yourself is whether or not your content is actually surfacing in the search results when customers are looking for you or something you can offer to them.

If your focus and financial investment is purely on short-form storytelling, you are missing out on a huge opportunity to reach new people, sell additional products, and demonstrate thought leadership.

Thought Leadership

One advantage of using social media, specifically in the B2B space, is to demonstrate thought leadership. Hopefully, you have some really smart engineers, scientists, and product managers that work for your company. And they most likely have a very specific point of view about technology, which can be used to start conversations and influence people.

As mentioned in Chapter 1, "Understanding the Social Customer and the Chaotic World We Live In," data tells us from the 2013 Edelman Trust Barometer that when it comes to trust and credibility, "people like yourself," "subject matter experts," and "employees of a company" always rank high when people are seeking information about a company.

But isn't it possible to demonstrate thought leadership in a tweet? By using a series of tweets or videos, yes. But that's assuming that you have an audience and that they are actually paying attention to you. But what about the CIO of a company that's interested in investing in new data center technology? Yeah, they might go to Twitter and browse their feed. But I guarantee you this: They will go to a search engine because they know, just like you know, that Google knows best. They want information and they want it now.

Striking a Balance Between Long-Form and Short-Form Storytelling

I have repeated this phrase several times already in this book—there is a content surplus in the market place today and also an attention deficit in the minds of consumers. This makes it extremely difficult for you to reach them with your brand message.

Short-form storytelling is important. It's your attempt at breaking through the clutter with compelling, creative, and visual content.

But I ask you this: Why not try to make their lives easier by allowing them to reach you? You can do so by spending a little more of your time and resources telling a complete story that's more than just 140 characters long.

Two brands in the B2B space do this extremely well. Visage, an enterprise mobility management software company, uses long-form storytelling to reach their customers. Their blog Chief Mobility Officer (http://visagemobile.com/mobilityblog/) uses creative titles and quality content to add value to the "enterprise mobility" conversation. Very rarely do they even talk about their products.

The American Express Open Forum (https://www.openforum.com/) is a small business community that uses third party influencers and contributors to create content about a variety of topics including leadership, marketing, and technology. All that rich content and thought leadership is finding its way into the search engines, driving traffic back to Open Forum, and maybe even influencing people to sign up for an American Express credit card for their small business.

Best Practices for Writing Long-Form Content—It All Starts with the Title

What would a book about content strategy be without sharing some best practices when writing long-form content? There are already several books in the market today that go into great detail about each social media channel and the best practices for driving engagement. But I believe your long-form content is what is going to help tell your story most effectively, differentiate your story from your competitors, and capitalize on search at the same time.

Outbrain, a content discovery platform, can give your brand the ability to reach a highly engaged audience with your content. Outbrain uses personalized links to recommend content across a network of more than 200 premium publishers, including CNN, Fox News, Hearst, *Rolling Stone*, *US Weekly*, and MSNBC. I go into greater detail about Outbrain's capabilities in Chapter 9, "The Role of Converged Media in Your Content Strategy."

In 2012, Outbrain analyzed their data stack to uncover insights about effective title writing for blogs. They did this by looking at click-through rates (CTR) gathered from 65,000 paid link titles that ran on Outbrain's content discovery platform between April and July of 2012. Although this content was distributed within their network of advertisers, the report provides excellent insights because your content might also be distributed in their network at some point (if that's what you choose). And hopefully your long-form content will also be distributed, shared, and retweeted in social media channels such as Facebook and Twitter.

Outbrain's white paper gives specific examples on what kinds of blog titles attract people based on the number of clicks to that specific piece of content:

Titles that contain negative extremes ("worst" or "never") performed 30% better than titles that did not contain either of these words. Likewise, titles that contain the word "lie(s)" outperformed titles without this word by 10%.

Titles that contain the word "don't" generated a 15% higher CTR than titles without this word. It appears that accentuating what the audience does not know or should not do in your headlines is an effective way of enticing readers.

Titles that contain the word "surprise(s)" generated a 35% higher CTR than titles without this word. The human urge to satisfy feelings of curiosity is incredibly powerful. We see countless attempts by marketers to evoke curiosity among consumers for this very reason. This result suggests that the word "surprise" is effective in activating such feelings and getting readers to click through.

Titles containing a dollar sign performed 20% better than titles without dollar signs. Research has shown that the human brain perceives the reward value of money to be on par with that of primary resources like food and sex. It certainly seems wise for content marketers to capitalize on this with dollar signs in headlines.

Titles that contain the word "hot" achieved a 25% higher CTR than titles that do not contain this word. The word "cool," however, had no significant effect on CTR. When it comes to attracting readers, it appears that "hot" is the way to go.

Titles that contain the word "photo(s)" performed 15% better than titles without this word. This is consistent with our previous finding that paid links perform better in Outbrain's thumbnail image widgets than in our text only widgets.

Titles that include the word "who" generated a 35% higher CTR than titles that do not contain the word "who." The words "why," "where," and "which" did not have any effect on performance, implying that the "w" in "who" is the "w" that counts when it comes to intriguing readers with your titles.

Titles that contain a hyphen performed 10% better than titles without a hyphen, suggesting readers tend to be attracted to titles that are broken up by a hyphen (for example, headlines with subtitles).

Outbrain also gives us insight on the titles that actually repel consumers.

Titles that make references to the reader by including the word, "you," "your," or "you're" performed 24% worse than titles that did not contain any of these words. The attempt to make readers feel as though they're being spoken to directly appears to do more harm than good. Readers are aware that they are part of a vast audience and may be showing reactance by avoiding these headlines.

Titles containing an imperative ("must" or "need") generated a 20% lower CTR than titles that did not contain either of these words. Readers appear to be resistant to words that demand action or attention. It may be that these words are more reminiscent of advertorial calls to action than editorial language or that their overuse in headlines over time has weakened their ability to convey a true sense of urgency.

Titles that contained positive extremes ("always" or "best") performed 29% worse than titles that did not contain either of these words. Contrary to popular belief and their widespread use in headlines, these words do not appear to be compelling to readers. In fact, our data shows just the opposite. This may simply be a product of overuse, or it could be because readers are skeptical of sources' motives for endorsement. On the flip side, sources of negative information may be more likely to be perceived as impartial and authentic.

Titles that contain the word "watch" performed 35% worse than titles that do not contain this word. "Watch" is often used in titles to designate video content. The negative impact of this word suggests that there may be constraints (for example, time, environmental, device-specific) on readiness to consume video content that are not factors (or less of a factor) for article consumption.

Titles containing the phrase "how to" performed 43% worse than titles without this phrase. This finding is consistent with the distinction between search mode and content consumption mode that we've long emphasized in our definition of "content discovery." How-to's can be highly desirable to consumers entering their present goal into a search engine, but they may be less timely and appealing to readers in content consumption mode.

Titles that contain the word "easy" generated a 45% lower CTR than titles without this word. Readers are constantly bombarded with "easy ways" and "easy steps" to an end and our results suggest that they are not convinced. Or, following from the above finding, readers in content consumption mode may be less likely to be pursuing a specific goal at that moment.

Titles that include a colon performed 10% worse than titles without a colon. It seems that marketers would be better off turning to hyphens than colons when looking to break up headlines or create subtitles.

Remember that this data is only analyzing titles and click-through rates. Not only should you create compelling titles that tell your story effectively and encourage sharing, but the content itself must be game-changing and add value. And as difficult as this may sound, you brand must strive to create long-form content consistently. As I mentioned in Chapter 4, you can leverage your employees as brand journalists and customers as advocates to help if you don't have the resources to do it yourself (you should be leveraging these two groups regardless). You may also consider platforms like eByline, Skyword, or Contently that have large networks of journalists, writers, and bloggers that can also help supplement your content efforts.

Vendor Spotlight—Contently

Contently is a NYC-based technology company whose mission is to help brands and journalists tell engaging, original stories. The company is really at the center of three converging trends: the shift in the creative economy to a freelance market, the idea that brands must think like publishers, and the rise of content marketing (or what some call *native advertising*). If you are unsure of the definition of native advertising, Wikipedia's definition is pretty clear:

> Native advertising is a web advertising method in which the advertiser attempts to gain attention by providing valuable content in the context of the user's experience; it is similar in concept to an advertorial, which is a paid placement attempting to look like an article. A native ad tends to be more obviously an ad than most advertorials while still providing interesting or useful information. The advertiser's intent is to make the paid advertising feel less intrusive and thus increase the likelihood users will click on it.

It's clear that your brand must create engaging content that tells a specific story across the entire digital ecosystem. And unfortunately, you might lack the resources needed internally to deliver such content day in and day out. The Contently platform can connect your brand to a network of journalists, writers, and bloggers and provides the technology needed to quickly and seamlessly manage the complicated workflow from content ideation to creation and all the way to distribution.

Contently's Storytelling Platform (see Figure 8.6) allows you to quickly and seamlessly manage both staff and freelance contributors and their work. You can build custom teams of contributors (writers, photographers, editors, and so on) and communicate with groups, source story ideas from teams, create assignments, manage permissions for individual team members, and more.

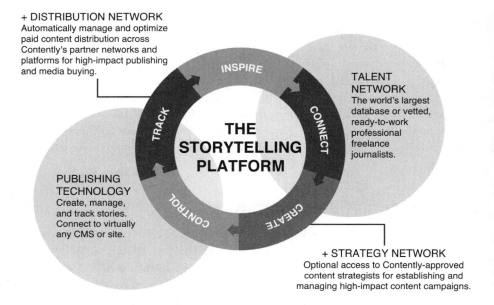

+ DISTRIBUTION NETWORK
Automatically manage and optimize paid content distribution across Contently's partner networks and platforms for high-impact publishing and media buying.

INSPIRE

THE STORYTELLING PLATFORM

TRACK

CONNECT

CONTROL

CREATE

TALENT NETWORK
The world's largest database or vetted, ready-to-work professional freelance journalists.

PUBLISHING TECHNOLOGY
Create, manage, and track stories. Connect to virtually any CMS or site.

+ STRATEGY NETWORK
Optional access to Contently-approved content strategists for establishing and managing high-impact content campaigns.

Figure 8.6 *Contently's Storytelling Platform*

The platform allows all deliverables and approval workflows to live in the cloud, and you can drag and drop an editorial calendar, which is customizable to the scale and frequency of any size of branded content campaign.

Contently's platform can also help you streamline the tedious process of legal signoff and internal content approvals. Instead of passing content back and forth via email, Contently allows you to create custom approval chains, so when an assignment is ready for review by your team of lawyers, managers, or clients, the appropriate parties get emails with special links to review and approve the work (or sent back for revision). When stories are complete, they can be easily published to an existing CMS, such as Wordpress.

The platform also includes content marketing analytics, which measures the reach, engagement, and influence of every individual story your brand publishes (whether it's on your owned properties or published elsewhere). Additionally, you can break down their metrics by topic, author, and channel.

9

The Role of Converged Media in Your Content Strategy

Tweetable Moment: *Your content strategy must include paid, earned and owned media in order to reach your target customers.—#nextmediaco*

In 2008, I was working for Intel as a social media strategist. My role was primarily focused on all of the social media initiatives that the company was doing on Intel. com, meaning all of our blogs and communities were my responsibility. There was another team responsible for all of the social media activations within social networks such as Facebook, Twitter, YouTube, and so on. And a completely different team was responsible for all the paid media activations that were happening in the market— display advertising, paid search marketing, sponsorships, out of home, and so on. Intel was and still is a massive marketing engine.

As a part of the Centrino 2 (Intel's chipset) product launch, we decided to go to market a little differently by integrating some of the amazing work we were doing within our Intel communities and combining it with paid media, specifically display advertising. The goal was to highlight long-form blog content written by Intel subject matter experts—mostly product managers and engineers—into a 300 x 250 pixel banner unit via an RSS feed.

We handpicked and tagged compelling content tagged with #centrino2 and dynamically pulled those specific blog titles into the banner unit. The results were amazing, but only lasted a day or two. The banners had such a high click-through rate that the ad had to be pulled because our servers couldn't handle all the traffic.

This was well over five years ago and is one example of converged media— integrating paid and owned media in the market place.

More recently, a brand doing extremely well integrating paid, earned, and owned media is Pepsi. Pepsi converges its media types in a variety of different ways. If you head over to Pepsi.com, you will notice a Pinterest-like page full of branded and unbranded content about Pepsi. The site is powered by Mass Relevance, a social engagement platform that can curate paid, earned, and owned media in visually appealing ways. Pepsi has integrated several of its in-market contests and promotions on the page, most notably the "Beyoncé's Mrs. Carter Show World Tour." Pepsi also uses Newscred, a content marketing platform to pull in licensed content and highlight the top five trending music-related stories from notable sources like the *Guardian*, *ABC News Radio*, and *Bang Showbiz*. And it aggregates tweets and Instagram photos using the #Pepsi and #LiveForNow hashtags.

Another example is a mom-focused community called Social Moms. It is an independent social network of more than 30,000 moms who are influential and highly active across all social media channels: Facebook, Google+, Twitter, blogs, mobile social networks, and more. They work with large and small brands to create word-of-mouth programs that drive "earned media" for the companies they work with. They also use Outbrain to syndicate their blog content on to high-traffic sites such as CNN and others, which drives mass amounts of traffic back to their online properties.

These are examples of what's being referred to today as *converged media*. This chapter discusses the role of converged media in your content strategy and gives you actionable recommendations on how to bring this to life for your brand.

Defining Converged Media

As you read the rest of this chapter and try to make sense of the previous examples, it's important to define what paid, owned, and earned media actually means for your brand. There are a lot of different examples floating around on the Internet, so I will be as clear as possible. Figure 9.1 shows the relationship of each media and who the target stakeholder is.

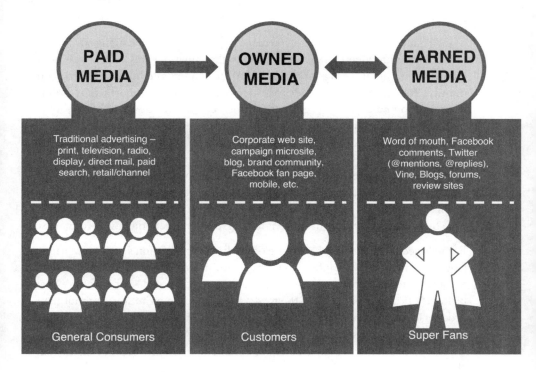

Figure 9.1   *Paid, earned, and owned media and their target stakeholders*

Paid media is often considered "traditional advertising" and includes banner ads, paid search marketing, sponsorships, and content syndication (or native advertising as mentioned in the last chapter). Paid media initiatives usually target prospects in an effort to create brand awareness or new customer acquisition.

The advantage of using paid media is that it can scale quickly and easily. If you have a message you want the masses to see today, paid media is the right channel through which to do that. Although paid media is more expensive than the others, your brand has complete control of the content, creative, and marketing spend.

The disadvantage with paid media is that it's often ignored by consumers because they are inundated with advertising messages daily and not just from your competitors, but from every other large brand with a marketing message and a significant budget.

Owned media is the content that your brand has complete control over, such as the corporate website, blogs, communities, email newsletters, and social media channels such as Facebook, Twitter, YouTube, and Instagram. Owned media initiatives typically target to your brand's existing community and current customers.

Many believe and say that owned media is free, specifically managing social media accounts. And though there is some truth to that, the time and labor investment are worth noting. It takes a lot of time to create content and build a thriving community. You also have to consider working with customer support teams, building escalation models, and preparing for crisis communications. This takes a lot of time planning and collaborating with other internal stakeholders—and time is money. There are other challenges you should be aware of as you think about your owned media. First, most consumers don't trust pure "marketing messages," whether in an advertising campaign or on a Facebook page, so it's important to establish a content narrative that adds value to the conversation, as discussed in detail in Chapter 7, "Defining Your Brand Story and Content Narrative." Spend time building trust with your current fans first. Then figure out a way to monetize.

Earned media is the natural response of public/media relation's efforts, ad campaigns, events, and the content you create within your owned media channels. It is not a revolutionary concept either. For the last several decades, brands have been hiring PR firms to reach out to the media to get them to write stories about their products and services. Today, that has expanded to influencers who have popular blogs as well. When someone not associated with your brand mentions you on Twitter or Facebook, within a YouTube comment, or on any other social media channel, it's earned media.

Other types of earned media include consumers' social media posts, tweets, product reviews, videos, photos, and general dialog within online communities.

If you study the digital ecosystem closely, it should be clear to you that consumers have become the "news outlet" and are spreading brand messages through word of mouth. Third-party recommendations from friends, family, and colleagues are so much more credible and transparent than what your brand says about itself. Of course, your brand has little or no control over what consumers will say through social and news media channels, so not all earned media is guaranteed to be positive.

Although each of these channels plays a critical role in your content strategy, the real power is when you can integrate two or more of the channels into one campaign or initiative. This is referred to as converged media. The same thinking has led to the recent surge in "native advertising" as discussed in Chapter 8, "Building Your Content Channel Strategy." Sites such as Buzzfeed, Crave, and Forbes are capitalizing on the opportunity to mobilize their lean but hungry editorial teams to create paid content for brands that live alongside the site's original content.

In some cases, native advertising is backfiring. In January 2013, the *Atlantic* published a sponsored post titled, "David Miscavige Leads Scientology to Milestone Year," which explained that the Scientology religion had expanded more in 2012 than in any other year since its inception. The article has since been deleted. The post itself caused a stir among journalists, ad folks, and random readers of the Atlantic because many felt that readers don't come to the *Atlantic* to read content about Scientology.

Charlie Warzelm, staff writer for Adweek wrote a post a few days later called "The Real Problem With The Atlantic's Sponsored Post." He argued that the promoted post from an incendiary organization such as the Church of Scientology from a publication like the *Atlantic*—whose reputation rests on thought-provoking journalism—rankled a subset of readers unfamiliar with the world of native advertising as well as those who felt that the paid religious content bordered on "blatant propaganda."

Why Converged Media Is Important to Your Content Strategy

According to the Altimeter Group, Converged Media utilizes two or more channels of paid, earned, and owned media. It is characterized by a consistent storyline, look, and feel. All channels work in concert, enabling brands to reach customers exactly where, how, and when they want, regardless of channel, medium, or device—online or offline. With the customer journey between devices, channels, and media becoming increasingly complex and new forms of technology only making it more so, this strategy of paid/owned/earned confluence makes marketers impervious to the disruption caused by emerging technologies (see Figure 9.2).

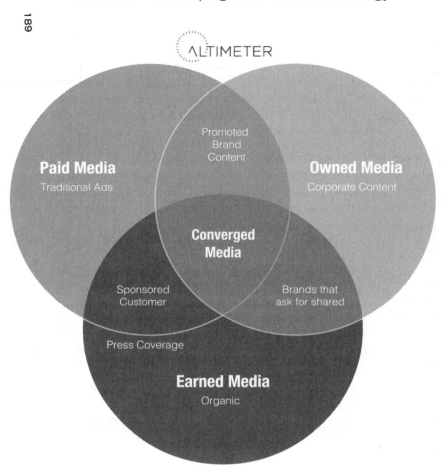

ALTIMETER

Paid Media
Traditional Ads

Owned Media
Corporate Content

Promoted
Brand
Content

Converged
Media

Sponsored
Customer

Brands that
ask for shared

Press Coverage

Earned Media
Organic

Figure 9.2 *The convergence of paid, earned, and owned media by the Altimeter Group*

As mentioned in Chapter 1, "Understanding the Social Customer and the Chaotic World We Live In," customers are unpredictable, and their daily lives are dynamic. And when you combine that with the fact that there is a content surplus and customer's suffer from attention deficit, it makes it that much more difficult for you to reach them. This is why converged media is important to your brand's content strategy.

What you do within your owned media channels alone cannot scale or allow you to grow your communities effectively. Of course, it's good to optimize your corporate website, blog, and online community for search and provide compelling content to your existing fans. That's a given. But without integrating your owned media initiatives with paid media, for example, you cannot reach the mass market with your content.

The same thing can be said with paid media. Traditionally (before social media was born), paid media was pretty much the only channel for brands to communicate with customers outside of public relations. With the rise of social networking and the increase in general content proliferation, it's difficult to reach them with just paid media. Plus, they normally reject, filter out, or flat out ignore traditional advertising alone.

Although earned media, assuming it's positive, is always good for your brand, you cannot just hope that it sustains long term without nurturing it. In addition to general community engagement, you must focus heavily on building customer advocacy. And there is no better way to do this than to integrate earned media conversations into both paid and owned media. Imagine a situation where you are leveraging the power and reach of paid media to highlight customers who are saying great things about your brand. It can be done with converged media, and that content is trusted.

There are many reasons why building converged media into your content strategy is a smart thing to do:

- Consumers need to see, hear, or interact with your message three to five times before they will start to believe in it. The only way to do this is to use various forms of converged media.

- Paid media has reach. In minutes, you can get your content in front of millions of people. And when the content itself becomes the ad that delivers value—like highlighting user stories (earned media)—your traffic and engagement numbers will explode, and consumers will start to trust your messages.

- Whenever you post a status update on your Facebook page, you only reach between 8 and 10% of your current fan base. So by promoting your organic status updates, you can reach a higher percentage of your community.

- By amplifying your earned media and displaying it within your owned channels, you will build brand advocacy by showcasing those consumers who already love your brand to inspire others to love your brand as well.

The truth is, if you fail to integrate and align paid, earned, and owned media, you will be at a disadvantage at getting your content in front of customers and prospects. You should be less concerned about what your competitors are doing in the space and more concerned with the billions of tweets, status updates, and text messages, as well as the 3,000 or so marketing messages that interrupt consumers' lives every day. Delivering a converged media strategy can help break through a lot of this madness.

According to the Altimeter Group, marketers who fail to learn how to reconcile paid, owned, and earned media today will be at a distinct disadvantage in the future when, in less than 10 years, most media will encompass elements of paid, earned, and owned. To arrive at this state, you must change the way you think about marketing and take this transition from brand to media company seriously.

Converged Media Models

There are several ways to integrate paid, earned, and owned media. I focus on three of them here: Facebook promoted posts, content syndication, and earned media amplification.

Facebook Promoted Posts (News Feed Marketing)

Fifty years ago, David Ogilvy asked: "Are your ads looking more like magazine spreads yet?" He challenged the status quo and asked his teams to design magazine spreads that looked like an editorial because he understood that people read good content, not advertisements. The ad world listened and has since given birth to infomercials, advertorials, product placement, sponsored programming, and brand journalism as manifestations of his original idea. If you're a night owl like me, you may have seen some of this on late night television—Chuck Norris and the Total Gym.

Converged media has blurred the differences between paid, earned, and owned media, making it extremely difficult to tell the difference between an advertisement and plain content. The *Atlantic* article mentioned earlier is a clear example of this. The reality is that you don't need to design ads that look like editorial content. It won't work because people don't "like" (literally and figuratively) ads. The converged media model emphasizes that the content itself can and should be the ad.

Instead of investing your entire budget to buy ads within Facebook's Marketplace (located in the right column of Facebook), sponsored posts can boost the reach of your brand's content within the news feed, where all users spend their time anyway. Content developed by your community manager—who knows the community better than anyone else—can boost an organic piece of content at a moment's notice.

I call this *news feed marketing*, and it works.

According to a February 2013 *eMarketer* report, sponsored content displayed in the news feed has 46 times the click-through rate of ads in the right-hand column (Marketplace ads). I am not against using Marketplace ads, but rather, use them in conjunction with sponsored posts. Because the mobile Facebook experience is only the news feed for now, sponsored posts are even more important for mobile.

Engagement on mobile news feed ads is twice that of news feeds on a laptop computer. Figure 9.3 shows the process by which to promote organic Facebook status updates into a promoted post.

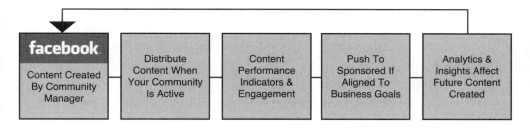

Figure 9.3   *Pushing Facebook page status updates into promoted posts*

To capitalize on Facebook promoted posts, you must first be focused on creating compelling content daily. This means that the content should be visual, relevant, tailored, actionable and in some cases, real-time. It's important to note that not all of your posts will be promoted. If you recall from Chapter 7, the content itself should align with your business goals or to a specific theme or pillar that you have already predefined. For example, it may not make complete business sense to promote a post that links off to a third-party article. It might be smarter to promote a post announcing a new product or better yet, one that keeps your fans within the Facebook ecosystem. In either case, your content narrative should have editorial guidelines that you can use to determine whether or not a post should be promoted.

The promoted post can be content that's planned or unplanned (using real-time monitoring of trends). Platforms such as SocialFlow, Trendspottr, and Rt.ly can help you capture and identify trends. Aligning your content, community management practices, and real-time analytics gives you the ability to deliver actionable insights based on the content performance and behaviors of your existing communities. After your content hits a certain engagement threshold, you can then turn your organic content into a promoted post. Following is an example of how this might play out.

Let's assume that you have analyzed your last 10 highest performing Facebook posts and the average number of engaged users for each post is 200. An engaged user equals a Like, comment, or a share. This is the most basic way to do this. If you are more sophisticated with Facebook or analytics in general, you might weight a share more so than just a Like or comment mainly because it takes more effort from a fan to share content on to their feed.

The 200 average engaged user number could be your threshold and performance metric that would trigger you to push all future organic posts into a sponsored post, assuming that content falls within your editorial guidelines. The key here is that you will have to monitor the content performance closely for the first three hours, as this is usually the timeframe for when a particular post reaches the 8 to 10% critical mass. The analytics and insights will feed back into your engagement threshold and content performance indicators and will influence all future content—theme, creative elements, time, day, and so on. It's also worthy to note that SocialFlow's Crescendo product, mentioned at the end of Chapter 1, can automate this process for you.

Although this is an example of pushing owned content into paid media within the Facebook ecosystem, there is still a pretty big world outside of Facebook as well.

Content Syndication

Certainly Facebook is the social network of choice for many large brands. Not only are there over a billion users who spend a lot of time on the site, but the network itself is slowly becoming the social layer of all Internet activity. However, there is still a very large world outside of the Facebook ecosystem where users spend a great deal of time as well. In fact, Nielsen reported that Facebook lost 10 million users in 2012 (note: data didn't include mobile users), so it's wise to think holistically about converged media and diversify your media budget accordingly.

Another option for implementing a converged media strategy is to use the power and reach of paid media to amplify your owned media content; also known as content syndication. Figure 9.4 illustrates how this would work.

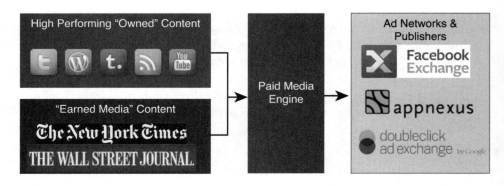

Figure 9.4   *Using paid media to increase the reach of owned media content*

This model can work several different ways. Similar to the Facebook example, you can identify a high performing Facebook update and not only push it to a sponsored post, but also turn the post into a display ad and serve it within a targeted ad network outside of the Facebook ecosystem. You can do the same with other forms of owned media content as well: long-form content, white papers, product spec sheets, tweets, and so on. One vendor in the marketplace today has built an engine that can help you do this quickly and at scale—OneSpot.

Austin-based company, OneSpot, can utilize any type of content, either owned content or earned media content, and turn it into ad creative for display, social, and mobile environments. It automates the complete process of ad creation, which can turn your entire content portfolio into a library of display ads.

OneSpot uses machine learning algorithms and big data to analyze both the content and the ads created in the system. It then analyzes the ad inventory available within their ad exchange network, targeting thousands of sites whose users it predicts would engage with your content. It places your ad using RTB (real-time bidding). The algorithms consistently improve their bidding efficiency, allowing you to garner more high quality impressions with the same budget.

The OneSpot platform actively uses your ads and content to move viewers through your purchase funnel or customer journey. By retargeting viewers, their platform serves up your content (ads) based on user behaviors and increases your ability to convert customers wherever they are in the purchase funnel. Based on sites visited and content consumed, content you created can be sequenced—a viewer reading content about "big screen TVs" today can later be retargeted with a content ad with a review of a specific TV model and ultimately content about a specific promotion.

While platforms like OneSpot can turn any piece of content into a display ad, other platforms are syndicating long-form content on to third-party media sites. Many believe that this is a more effective approach, as it aligns more naturally to the way web users browse through and click on content. Have you ever noticed after reading an article on CNN or AOL, a group of links at the bottom with titles that say "We recommend" or "From around the web?" This is what I am talking about.

Outbrain is a content discovery and syndication platform that distributes branded content to third-party media sites using a widget that can be integrated on any site to match its look and feel. Outbrain has two core products that can help you engage your audience with compelling content and also amplify the reach of your existing content. Outbrain Engage is for publishers (such as CNN and AOL) and makes targeted recommendations of other content that reflects their interests, which is based on past behavior and predictions of future behavior. As illustrated in Figure 9.5, content is recommended to your readers based on their content consumption habits.

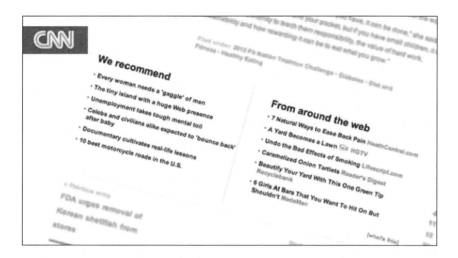

Figure 9.5   *Targeted content recommendations based on users interests*

Outbrain Engage uses a complex series of algorithms to understand your audience's browsing habits while they are on your site. The platform is able to recommend personalized links based on each individual's content preferences.

The key differentiator from other content syndication platforms is that Outbrain's algorithm measures reader engagement with a site after the click through on a link and classifies its content recommendation algorithms into four major buckets:

- **Popularity:** The content that is trending up in popularity on the site
- **Contextual:** The content related to the page the person is currently on
- **Behavioral:** Audience dynamics (that is, what people with similar reading habits have read or have not read before)
- **Personal:** Broad categories the person reads but are not necessarily related to the page she is on

Outbrain's other product, Amplify, is for brands that want to increase the reach and visibility of their owned media content. If you aren't familiar with Outbrain, chances are you have probably come across its platform without even knowing it. The company counts publishers like CNN, the *Wall Street Journal*, Fast Company, and Slate, and brands like General Electric, among those using its widget to suggest links for further reading alongside content on the site. The platform offers one column of stories from the site itself and other stories from third-party content sources. Outbrain is currently embedded across 90,000 sites, generating more than 6.5 billion page views per month.

Assuming you abide by their content guidelines, Outbrain gives you the flexibility to choose which content you want syndicated, and there is also the option to use an RSS feed so that new articles are automatically included for distribution. Their platform works best for brands that are able to produce high quality content consistently. They use a Cost-Per-Click (CPC) model to determine the prominence and reach of content across their network of publishers. You have complete control as you decide what you are willing to pay for others to view your content, similar to Google Adwords. You can start as low as 10 cents per click, although Outbrain recommends starting at around 15 cents and then lowering it over time after your content becomes more popular. This ensures you get more clicks for your daily budget while maintaining your reach, to optimize ROI.

Earned Media Amplification

In 2012, San Francisco-based company, InPowered, launched their Earned Advertising Platform, a self-service platform that allows you to take influential, third-party content written by experts (influencers, analysts, bloggers) and amplify that content using paid media. Peyman Nilforoush, CEO and Cofounder of the platform, explained in a 2012 Techcrunch article that his platform creates a new way of influencing people. He said that when a company releases a new product, positive reviews are going to be much more influential than any form of banner advertising.

When you use InPowered, you are basically paying for advertising, but it doesn't really look like an ad. Rather, it's a collection of stories and articles aggregated together that you have already predefined as the "earned media" you want to promote using paid media. If a user clicks the ad, he gets directed to the article but within an iFrame where other earned media content about your brand can be consumed, emailed, or shared within social media channels (see Figure 9.6 on the left column).

Figure 9.6   *InPowered aggregated earned media content that can be shared into social media*

On the back end, InPowered provides you with a dashboard that displays how many people have been "influenced" by the specific content (that is, read the content) and how many of those who read the content have become "influencers" (shared the content). The goal, then of course, is to increase those numbers. You can also browse a list of articles, which are classified as positive, negative, or neutral, based on InPowered sentiment engine. When you find three third-party pieces of content you want to promote, you can bundle them into a single ad, which then runs as a custom unit on InPowered partner sites and which is also distributed through ad exchanges that more closely resemble traditional banners.

The Promise of Real-Time Marketing

Real-time marketing has become a topic of conversation among marketers today thanks to Oreo. Several other brands are trying to capitalize on this growing trend. For example, shoe manufacturer Adidas is taking insights from their London 2012 Games sponsorship to react more quickly to news events. According to a 2013 article published by *Marketing Week*, Adidas's new strategy aims to accelerate its shift to real-time marketing by having social media teams in place to react within minutes of key sporting moments. All decisions are made in real time during the events with marketers, artists, and agency members all working together to create content around sports fans' conversations. Adidas is hoping the combination of speed and cultural relevance can propel its social media messages to the forefront of online conversations in a similar way to Oreo's reaction to the Super Bowl blackout.

General Electric is attempting to do the same thing with its content strategy. It firsts builds a robust long-term editorial calendar and then brainstorms a production schedule that is specifically for "unplanned" or "real-time" content creation. According to Digiday article, "GE's Take on Real-Time Marketing," the company assembles the right internal resources: a strategist, producer, designer, and a lawyer and they all sit in the same room during an event to ensure fast decision making for real-time content marketing.

In the article Linda Boff, Executive Director of Global Brand Marketing at GE, told Digiday that real-time marketing is the ability to produce a response through content, experiences, or service to a live event or customer event that delights your audience or customer into engaging with your brand around a shared moment.

And GE has delivered.

On February 11, 2013, which is both Inventor's Day and Thomas Edison's birthday, GE launched a real-time campaign that made a significant impact. GE asked their followers on Twitter to share what they'd like to invent using #IWantToInvent hashtag. GE then picked the most interesting ideas and sent them to a design studio that it had partnered with for the day to draft digital blueprints and sent them back to the people who had tweeted them—all within an hour. GE ended up producing 70 digital blueprints over the course of seven hours, ranging from a "Horse Scuba Suit" to a "Doorbell ID" to Boff's favorite, an "Invisible Suit."

There's good reason why some brands are activating real-time marketing programs. Data from Edelman's clients who are executing real-time marketing programs are seeing 400 to 600% increases in engagement.

Sometimes your brand has to go outside the natural boundaries of your content narrative to break through the clutter—and you have to be comfortable with that. Real-time marketing is needed to reach consumers with low attention spans and that are also inundated with content, media, a multitude of devices, and so on. If your brand can't act fast and capitalize on the news cycle, you might never get a second chance to get your content in front of them again.

Choosing themes that are relevant for your brand, resonate with audience interests, *and* are timely helps ensure that real-time content has a long-term benefit instead of just a short-term burst of Likes that amount to nothing more than an increase in data points. There are three descriptors you must consider when evaluating real-time content marketing opportunities:

- **Relevant:** Align with brand values, orientation, and priorities online.
- **Resonates:** Map to audience affinities and fan interests beyond your brand.
- **Timely:** Drive interest and conversation online now.

Ideally, the content you produce in real-time must fall within each of the characteristics if you truly want to reach consumers with game-changing content.

Real-Time Marketing Is More Than Just Being in Real Time

Content must be more than just real-time, visual, and timely to succeed. It must also be prominent—appearing in the communities where your fans spend the majority of their time. It should be relevant to the audience and appear at the peak of conversation when they are thinking, talking, and commenting about a particular topic (such as the Super Bowl). Real-time content must also be immediately recognizable at a glance in the news feed so that fans are more likely to read it, remember it, and credit your brand for the time they spend with it.

This is where the effective blend of real-time and planned content is key.

There's a difference between real-time marketing and relevant editorial content. True real-time marketing, where an opportunity is identified and content is created in the same conversation cycle, should only represent a small, but important, percentage of your content strategy. In fact, I would say that real-time content should comprise between 10 and 15% of your overall content portfolio. You can't just sit around and wait for the news cycle before you create game-changing content. You should already be doing this day in and day out.

The rest of your planned content should be timely, but it doesn't have to be created on the fly. In fact, it shouldn't be. You can plan for most content through a proper editorial strategy, as discussed in detail in Chapter 8. For example, you know that Valentine's Day is on February 14 every year. You also know two years in advance when the Super Bowl is scheduled. However, you'll never know for sure when a random video will break a million views overnight or when the lights will go out at a major sporting event.

Real-time content marketing works best when you can anticipate the unexpected and react quickly when you cannot. Ninety percent of editorial content can be planned in advance, with a strong editorial calendar that aligns with brand strategy, key announcements, industry-related developments, and audience interests. But the remaining 10% of real-time content provides breakthrough opportunities that can shape perceptions of increased brand relevance and reach consumers who might not know you are.

All content, whether planned or real-time, should be aligned with your broader content strategy that tells the same brand story across all social media channels. Additionally, the execution of a content strategy not only involves a set of editorial guidelines that outline what the brand is or isn't comfortable talking about online, but it should also help identify teams, assign roles and responsibilities, build workflows for the content supply chain, and determine the right technology to make it all happen, all of which is needed to build your real-time creative newsroom.

The Creative Newsroom

A traditional newsroom is the central place where journalists, writers, reporters, editors, producers, photographers, along with other staffers work together to report on news stories that will be published in some form of media.

Edelman's Creative Newsroom is similar in concept, but different in operations and content. It is a central place where copywriters, community managers, analysts, creative producers and brand journalists use technology to monitor trending topics within the news cycle in order to create real-time content that's relevant to your brand's audience.

The Creative Newsroom has the potential to transform a trending conversation into a brand-relevant visual masterpiece that resonates with your audience in hours instead of days. It's a radical shift in marketing and communications if you think about it. This idea of helping brands spot a trend, map it to an opportunity, develop and approve a creative concept, post it, measure performance in real-time, and amplify it with paid media—all within a two-hour cycle—has never been possible before now. Figure 9.7 illustrates this process.

Real-time marketing is not for the faint of heart. It's a hyper-accelerated environment that requires agility, laser focus, and lightning fast decision-making. But fast doesn't have to be the enemy of good. News organizations today are accustomed to making high-pressure, high-quality decisions on the fly. To succeed, they need the right people, processes, and tools in place to bring a story from ideation to distribution quickly. This is one reason why your brand must think like a media company. Traditional marketing silos, organizational models and thought processes need to be adapted.

Figure 9.7   *Edelman's Creative Newsroom Model*

The Creative Newsroom works well because it integrates the four critical disciplines needed to deliver smart and effective content—community management, creative, analytics, and paid media. Together, these four disciplines, which traditionally live in silos, can provide real-time content performance data, audience insights, design excellence, and immediate amplification across the digital ecosystem. Each layer of integration increases the efficiency of the creative newsroom process, ensuring that real-time marketing can be executed efficiently and effectively several times over.

The combination of content, brand, and creative strategists with community managers, designers, analysts, paid media experts, brand planners, and a chief editor of the newsroom is a powerful mix.

Creative Newsroom 5-Step Activation Process

It's relatively easy to jump into real-time marketing: pick a story, write a quip, create a visual, and post it. But it's hard to get it right—developing timely content that is relevant to your fans and adds value to your brand.

At Edelman, Executive Vice President Monte Lutz has operationalized the Creative Newsroom, providing real-time marketing opportunities for Edelman clients and including a critical enrollment process that ensures the brand strategists, community managers, and creative teams are aligned on the best style, approach, editorial focus, and goals for the program:

1. **Define the Social Persona:** The first part of this process is to clearly articulate your brand's traits into a social persona. In addition to true brand personality traits, this also involves developing filters for tone, including linguistics, attitude, enthusiasm, humor, and cadence. With the persona defined, the next step is to translate your brand's style guide, assets, ad campaigns, and key art into social-specific guidelines, templates, and creative assets. These will serve as visual markers to ensure that Creative Newsroom content for your brand is easily identifiable in the feed.

2. **Determine Audience Affinities:** After defining the voice, tone, and persona for Creative Newsroom content, the next focus is understanding the interests and affinities of your current and target social audience to craft an editorial approach that inspires maximum engagement. Using native Facebook and YouTube insights, as well as third-party tools such as Demographics Pro, the Wisdom App, and Simply Measured, the development of demographic, geographic, and psychographic profiles are created for your audience segments.

3. **Develop Content Themes:** Applying the insights from the audience analysis, the next step is to develop content themes for your Creative Newsroom. This provides a critical filter for evaluating whether news, events, trends, or memes are relevant for your brand and customers. With time a critical factor for success, the framework is essential to maximize efficiency, audience interest, and brand consistency. This framework gives you the license to talk about things that are beyond the brand itself but are still of interest to the community. Creating real-time content about these topics would engage and excite the community in a manner that's consistent with your brand narrative.

4. **Determine Topics to Avoid:** It's equally important to identify the topics that should never be used for your Creative Newsroom content or that should be handled with extreme care. Although most brands are

anchored in social or political causes, you should proceed cautiously when creating content about religious figures, politics, natural disasters (unless focused on support), celebrity scandals, or negative stories about another brand or competitor. There are plenty of other memes to jump into without getting your brand into deep water.

5. **Setting Performance Goals:** Establishing performance goals and KPIs to ensure the investment in Creative Newsroom delivers a commensurate return on engagement and acquisition, as well as brand affinity. From the studies we have done at Edelman, we have found that real-time content typically generates four to six times higher engagement than planned content because of higher relevance and resonance with the audience. It also provides signals to help identify which content is worthy of incremental, paid promotion (that is, converged media as discussed earlier in this chapter).

This enrollment process can be your brand's playbook for activating the Creative Newsroom.

Creative Newsroom Models

If you are thinking about launching a Creative Newsroom for your brand, there are three different models to consider:

- *Trendspotter* programs are designed to help your brand become more interesting and relevant in the news feed. In this model, a team actively monitors the online conversation for stories and trends that have reached a tipping point and are relevant to the brand's audience. The top stories are selected, and original, real-time content is created, distributed, and promoted to keep your community engaged with your brand being top of mind.

- *Newsroom Campaign* is your opportunity to turn a launch into a cultural milestone. This approach helps ensure that conversation about product launches, milestones, and brand activations don't end with your announcement. This model extends the conversation about your brand by demonstrating relevance to the trends and topics that people are already talking about online and develops a regular cadence of real-time content for the extent of the campaign, be it a week, a month, or the holiday season. For example, Oreo's Daily Twist turned the 100th anniversary of the brand into a 100-day celebration, where they made real-time content for 100 days straight and also made news headlines daily.

- *The Daily Desk* is the most ambitious model, yet the most powerful. It is designed to ensure your brand isn't just catching trends, but defining them. As the conversation changes every day, the Daily Desk can help your brand spot and jump on new stories, trends, and ideas quickly and strategically. Each morning, a Newsroom team meets to match real-time opportunities with audience affinities to engage and excite fans in ways that further your long-term brand narrative.

  Within a two-hour creative cycle, the team develops, posts, and optimizes visual content that connects with audiences at the peak of interest for the things they are talking about today, as well as the fascinating things they have yet to discover. The Daily Desk is designed to help your brand spot a trend, create a meme in real-time, and be the most relevant brand in the news feed all the time.

Vendor Spotlight—Newscred

A significant percentage of your content strategy must include curating third-party content, specifically from trusted sources. Newscred is a content marketing platform that can give you access to high quality, licensed content to use on your owned media channels. It's more than just curating.

NewsCred sources and licenses trusted content across a broad range of subjects and perspectives, providing you with the tools necessary to drive traffic, engagement, and revenue for your business. With third-party, licensed content from high-quality, premium publishers, such as the *New York Times, Wall Street Journal, Forbes, Bloomberg, The Economist, Chicago Tribune, Huffington Post*, you can develop niche editorial sections, scale email marketing campaigns, power social media channels, and build mobile applications and products.

NewsCred can offer you a selection of products to license, syndicate, curate, and publish content across multiple platforms. From their Syndication Suite, publishers can track, manage, and analyze their content as it flows to third-party sites. The SmartPress platform allows you to publish and manage content, while the tool's design capabilities provide you with the opportunity to design your own layout to meet the look and feel of your brand. All pages are optimized for natural search, and articles are sorted by relevance and popularity across social channels. NewsCred's SmartWire technology is the company's licensing tool, organized article content via filtered news feeds, while editors go one step further by manually curating topical content tailored to your audience interests, content strategy, and brand goals. Following are two quick case studies that show Newscred in action.

When looking to augment their social media following, Pepsi turned to NewsCred to develop its first-ever global online marketing campaign, "Live For Now." As illustrated in Figure 9.8, the campaign was centered around Pepsi's homepage (Pepsi.com), specifically the "Pepsi Pulse" platform, the brand's unique content hub focused exclusively on music and entertainment news. The goal was for fans to turn to Pepsi when searching for the latest track or video in addition to following the industry's best new artists, musicians, and performers. The NewsCred team built the Pulse multimedia platform, aggregating content from across the Web, curated with real-time entertainment news and social media content. In turn, Pepsi.com gained an 87% increase in traffic and 2,700% increase in social referrals just one month after launch.

Figure 9.8   *NewsCred powers third-party licensed content on Pepsi.com.*

As mentioned several times in this book, brands are now turning to content marketing as a viable solution to drumming up user engagement and brand loyalty. The insurance industry especially, keen on attracting customers via thought leadership and education, has become a major player in the content marketing space, leveraging content as a means to draw users to their websites and position themselves as experts in their field.

International insurance and financial services firm AIG turned to NewsCred when looking to develop an integrated marketing campaign with content at its core. The result is CyberEdge, an insurance product and iPad app from AIG intended to help clients prevent security breaches in internal data, hacking, and information and identity theft. The iPad app, powered with licensed, third-party content from NewsCred, includes the latest cyber and security news from leading publishers, information on data breaches, resources including how AIG handles security breaches, a liability cost calculator, information on how to best protect yourself and your company, as well as details on the CyberEdge product itself.

10

How Content Governance Will Facilitate Media Company Transformation

Tweetable Moment: *Content governance ensures that there are controls in place so that consistent brand storytelling is told across all channels.*
—*#nextmediaco*

Red Bull is a media company. They produce compelling content because they are creative, they understand their audience, and they have a well-oiled machine that facilitates the content supply chain within their company—from content ideation, to creation, to approval, and finally to distribution. Because of this, Red Bull has built its brand using social media and has been extremely successful at engaging with customers day in and day out and across all the major social networks. This has made it the model that many brands turn to when looking to become a media company. Red Bull has built a combined social audience of more than 42 million users on Facebook, Twitter, YouTube, Google+, and Instagram, and as you finish reading this sentence, the number has most likely already increased dramatically.

Facebook is Red Bull's largest audience segment with more than 37 million fans and makes up nearly 90% of its community. This has been a key network for Red Bull, which now currently ranks among Facebook's top 10 fan pages.

Visually stunning content has contributed to Red Bull's success on YouTube, where it has cultivated a subscriber audience of two million, and on Instagram, the brand's smallest but most engaged audience. Twitter is the brand's most active channel and serves as a vehicle for distributing content from each network to an audience of nearly one million followers.

Red Bull's network of highly engaged audiences are valuable channels for content distribution, and it is growing each one by providing a stellar customer experience coupled with compelling content. Figure 10.1 shows Red Bull's growth from March to April 2013.

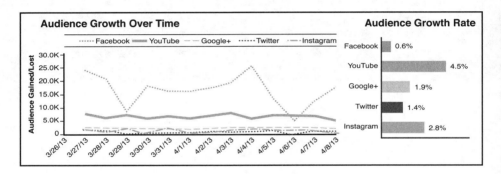

Figure 10.1   *Red Bull's audience growth rate*

On Facebook, Red Bull added more than 200,000 fans in the same reporting period, according to Kevin Shively, Marketing Analyst for Simply Measured, a leading social media measurement and analytics vendor. Although Facebook accounted for the most new fans, YouTube has been Red Bull's fastest growing channel, with a 4.5% subscriber growth rate month to month. Red Bull's YouTube channel was established in 2006, but the brand's steady stream of professional, highly produced video continues to build its subscriber audience.

Red Bull's Instagram channel is also growing quickly; during the reporting period, it was the second fastest growing channel with a community growth rate of 2.8%, outpacing longer established channels Twitter and Google+ (see Figure 10.2).

It's clear that visual content is a major contributor to Red Bull's success in social media and continues to serve as a model for other brands that want to engage with customers using visual storytelling. Visual content captures our attention, and it's often what comes to mind when we think about Red Bull and what they do in the marketplace.

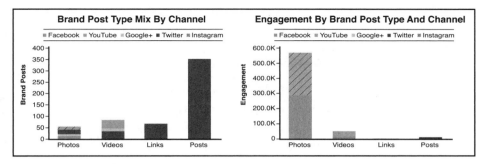

Figure 10.2   *Red Bull's Instagram growth rate is 2.8%.*

What makes Red Bull successful is more than just their brand story or the epic content the company creates each day for the community. Their ability to make this happen is largely because of a content governance plan that controls what type of content is created and when it's shared within each channel.

Defining Content Governance

Content governance is a strategic imperative when deploying an enterprise-wide content strategy for the purposes of the following:

- establishing content and workflow accountability
- auditing content engagements
- managing risk
- setting content permissions

Every contributor to your brand's storytelling initiatives, whether employee or customer, has a specific role when it comes to managing the content supply chain. The content workflows that facilitate ideation, creation, approval, and distribution must be built to ensure consistent storytelling across paid, earned, and owned media.

By implementing a content governance framework layered across the entire organization, teams are enabled to collaborate through an approval process with distinct workflow and established audit trails, ensuring the right content is being utilized in the right channel. Audit trails through all processes and actions are an overall best practice for all large and small brands and must be a requirement regardless of what industry you work in. These audit trails should always be referenced for the purposes of displaying content and user action history with corresponding approvals. Documenting a governance hierarchy reduces risks during a crisis and can be used to "lock down" publishing access across all social accounts if certain situations arise.

Content governance can also be defined as a detailed framework of content delivery and management that ensures there are documented controls in place that facilitate consistent brand storytelling across paid, earned, and owned media. A content governance model should include

- Collaboration models for internal teams complete with audit trails
- An approval workflow for proactive content (unplanned and planned content)
- An escalation workflow for reactive content (crisis, customer support)
- Workflows that mitigate risks, such as access to social properties, employees leaving the company, accidental messages being sent, and so on
- Processes to handle rogue accounts and the creation of new branded accounts
- Enterprise-wide, single-point password control systems
- Establishing user roles within a content strategy (contributor, approver, publisher, administrator), which is discussed in Chapter 11, "Structuring Your Teams to Become a Content Driven Organization"

It might be easy to confuse content governance with a social media policy. Usually, content governance is a subset of a larger policy but it can certainly stand alone within an editorial team or department. A *social media policy* (sometimes referred to as social media guidelines) is a corporate code of conduct that provides guidance for employees who post content on the Internet or engage with external customers either as part of their specific job functions or just as employees. My book *Smart Business, Social Business* walks readers through the process of creating a policy, step by step.

Content governance is just as important as it ensures that there are controls in place that govern when, what, and why content is being created, approved, and distributed. It's a strategic imperative that enables a brand to tell a consistent story across all forms of media.

The first step at deploying content governance is to build a collaboration model that helps facilitate internal communications, integration, and best practice sharing between all of your internal stakeholders.

Building a collaboration infrastructure is important to ensure consistency and that everyone involved in the content supply chain understands the business and marketing goals and proactively shares knowledge. This is more than just a conference call. It must be a collaborative, ongoing working session and a place where new ideas are welcomed with open arms.

Building an Effective Collaboration Model

Collaboration is a working practice whereby teams and individuals work together for a common purpose to achieve positive business outcomes—in this case, the journey to become a media company. Collaboration is based on the concept that sharing knowledge through cooperation helps solve business or marketing problems more efficiently. In the enterprise, this principle couldn't be truer; especially as more and more employees engage with one another through asynchronous, real-time technology platforms such as Yammer or Chatter.

Charles Darwin, an English Naturalist in the 1800s said, "In the long history of humankind, those who learned to collaborate and improvise most effectively have prevailed." And if you think about this and apply it to your content strategy, it makes perfect sense. If you can tap into the collective knowledge and brainpower of others on your team, the positive business outcome will be the production of better content, smarter marketing, and more effective customer relationships. Figure 10.3 is one way to look at a collaboration framework.

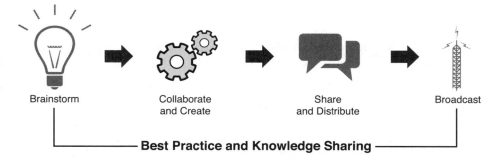

Figure 10.3   *Internal collaboration framework*

Collaboration models can be complex and detailed. It is simplified here so that you can easily adapt it to make it work in your organization. The elements that make up this framework are

- **Brainstorming:** All stakeholders meet periodically (daily, weekly, monthly) to discuss content with high engagement numbers, as well as content that might integrate with current marketing campaigns or other initiatives. This meeting can also serve as the daily gathering of the creative newsroom team to identify trending topics in the news cycle and determine whether or not there is an opportunity to capitalize on it.

- **Collaborating and Creating:** Stakeholders work together to create, co-create, aggregate, and curate content from third-party sites. Again, this could be a situation where the team is creating content in real-time or be more of a longer-term content planning cycle.

- **Sharing and Distributing:** Content and editorial teams share content direction, assets, and general strategy with brand, product, or regional teams. Content can be housed in a content library for easy consumption and sharing or placed into a content platform such as Sprinklr, Spredfast, or Kapost for dynamic delivery to stakeholders.

- **Broadcasting:** Content teams publish content and provide strategic counsel to regional teams. Regional teams localize and publish content within their social media channels.

There are also several technologies in the market place that can help facilitate collaboration whether you work for a large organization or small business. If you work for a large company, most likely you may have access to some of these tools. If not, you will have to invest in a platform that can help you achieve better collaboration with your teams.

Yammer is probably the most well-known internal collaboration platform for small to medium-sized businesses. With Microsoft's recent acquisition of its platform, Yammer now stands to compete with other enterprise-level collaboration systems.

At a high level, Yammer is a social network that's entirely focused on your business. For you to join the Yammer network, you must have a working email address from your company's domain. You can also create external networks to allow for non-employees, such as suppliers and customers, to communicate with your company. Yammer allows you to share and discuss documents, images, videos, and presentations with your coworkers. It also enables you to upload new versions of files to ensure everyone sees the latest draft and maintain older versions as well.

You can also work with a team to create, edit, and publish content; you can display team goals, compile notes, and draft documents together online, viewing character-by-character changes in real time as others make edits. Finally, you can stay on top of activity from across your company as it happens—discover newly created documents, new members of your groups, recently shared images, active discussions, and activity taking place in other business applications. Other platforms that offer similar capabilities to Yammer are VMware's Social Cast, Jive, IBM Connections, and Salesforce's Chatter. Following are a few other collaboration platforms that you might not have heard of:

- Co-op is a free application with a simple user interface similar to Twitter. The features allow you to post updates, ask questions, share links, and track time. Co-op also enables you share your daily agenda with your coworkers so everyone knows what projects that you are currently working on. Their web application automatically stores records of you and your team's activity, allowing you to review what your team has accomplished each day.

- Cynapse's Cyn is an open source community and has a complete collection of enterprise-grade collaboration tools. Three versions of their platform are available:

  - The free community edition includes Active Directory integration, application source code, web-based appliance management console, and more.

  - The other editions sell for several thousand dollars a year and have features such as wikis, blogs, file repositories, event calendars, discussion boards, image galleries, collaboration spaces, status logs, people directory, crowd rating and voting, and more.

- CubeTree, recently acquired by SuccessFactors, is an on-demand enterprise collaboration suite available in free and premium versions. The free version includes user profiles, micro-blogging, file sharing, wikis, and 10MB of storage per user. Their standard features include the above as well as status updates of 140 characters; a commenting feature (similar to that of Facebook's); feed filtering, which lets you choose who to follow and what feed items you'd like to receive; direct addressing (similar to Twitter's @name function); and open APIs that allow for the integration with several third-party systems and applications.

- Hashwork is a simple internal social network for small- to medium-sized businesses. It doesn't require a company administrator, and it's as easy as entering a company email address to sign up and get access. The user interface and functionality is similar to Twitter with features like 140-character posts, direct addressing, groups, hashtags, and so on. You can get more robust features with paid versions of their application.

The second step for building a content governance framework is creating workflows for planned and unplanned content, which is discussed in the next section.

Proactive Content Workflows for Planned and Unplanned Content

The ability to control content is imperative to becoming a media company. Having controls in place helps deliver content that's integrated, and it also ensures that the content shared externally is aligned with your brand's storytelling narrative. There are two sets of workflows you should consider as you build your content governance model: proactive workflows and reactive workflows. The good news is that many of the Content Management Systems (CMS) mentioned in this book allow you to build and customize these workflows. Figure 10.4 is an example workflow for proactive (planned) content creation.

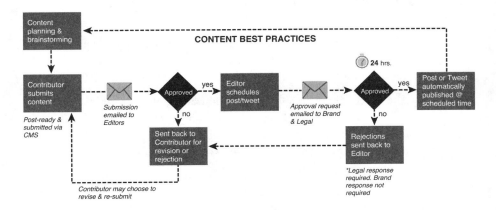

Figure 10.4 *Example proactive workflow for planned content*

The foundation of this workflow starts at the beginning with content planning. As discussed in Chapter 3, "Establishing a Centralized 'Editorial' Social Business Center of Excellence," your Social Business CoE (or centralized editorial team) is responsible for driving the content strategy and facilitating your content planning sessions. This can be done daily, weekly, biweekly, or monthly. It depends on how far out you are building your editorial calendars. Many of the topics discussed at these meetings include brainstorming content topics or themes, assigning content to various contributors, discussing historical content performance, sharing best practices, and trendspotting.

The next phase in the workflow is when the contributor submits the content for approval. This can be done via email or a CMS that has this built-in capability. After the editor is notified that there is content submitted, he or she approves the content or sends it back for revision. If approved, the editor can schedule it to be published or add it directly to the editorial calendar for the next round of approval. If not approved, the editor sends it back for revision or rejection. At that point, the contributor can choose to revise the content and resubmit it for approval.

The next phase of this workflow comes after the editor approves the content. The editor then sends the content to be approved by your brand or legal team. If approved, the content will go live at the day and time the editor scheduled it. If not approved, the content gets sent back to the editor for revision.

There are a couple of things you should remember when designing your content workflows. First, content approvals can be sequential or simultaneous. With a simultaneous approval workflow, when the content is submitted for approval, it goes to all the approvers at the same time. Each approver can "approve" or "reject" the content, and then it is sent back to the contributor. With the sequential approval workflow, the content goes through each approver in order: editor, brand, legal. In this case, for example, the legal team would not be notified that they need to approve the content until after it's approved by the editor and the brand team.

What you find in this process is that there will always be bottlenecks in the content approval process. And based on my experience, that usually happens with the legal team. What you might want to do is build a workflow that gives each approver a certain amount of time (say, 24 hours) to approve content *before* it goes live. In other words, if legal does not approve the content within the allocated time, the content goes live automatically. This approach ensures that any and all approvers are held accountable in this workflow.

Having a 24-hour approval process is "nice to have" especially if you work for a large organization, but 24 hours is way too long to take to capitalize on real-time marketing. Chapter 9, "The Role of Converged Media in Your Content Strategy," discussed Edelman's Creative Newsroom, which is a real-time content marketing approach that can help you transform a trending conversation into a brand-relevant piece of content that resonates with your audience in hours instead of days. Figure 10.5 is an example workflow in the Creative Newsroom.

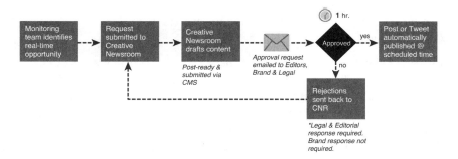

Figure 10.5   *Example of a proactive workflow in the Creative Newsroom (unplanned content)*

In this workflow, a community manager or monitoring team identifies a real-time opportunity to insert your brand into a trending conversation. As discussed in the last chapter, there are several tools in the marketplace today that can surface real-time trending data: the Dachis Group's Real-time Marketing Dashboard,

SocialFlow, Trendspotter, and Rt.ly. When the content is spotted, you must determine whether your brand has license to actually talk about it (that is, it's somewhat relevant to your brand and what it stands for).

After the trend is spotted, it then kicks the Creative Newsroom operation in gear to start creating the content. Copywriters and designers are then deployed to create a piece of visual content and then submit it to the approvers. In this case, it can be the editor and brand and legal team, sequentially or simultaneously. The main difference between this workflow and the previous one is the approval time. For real-time marketing to actually be in real time, approval cycles should be no more than one hour. This is certainly much easier said than done, but if you can establish a level of trust with the approvers, specifically brand and legal, eventually you can work your way to under an hour approval time.

As much as proactive content workflows are important to your media company transformation, you must also be prepared to be reactive and respond to issues when they arise.

Reactive Escalation Workflows and Risk Assessment

As with most content marketing and community management initiatives, there is always the possibility of running into disgruntled customers or even a potential crisis. It will happen, and these issues cannot be ignored. Having a crisis escalation plan is important to ensure that all content contributors, community managers, and customer support teams understand the process if they have to escalate conversations and to whom they should escalate them.

Escalation workflows are nothing new. Back in 2008 (yes, five years ago), the United States Air Force created and made public their Web Posting Response Assessment. It's a 12-point plan developed by the Emerging Technology Division of the U.S. Air Force's Affairs Agency that illustrates how U.S. Airmen should respond to social media conversations online. The plan provided a specific workflow that Airmen should use when responding and engaging with the public. It was created in response to negative opinions about the U.S. government and also to bolster support and credibility for content that was positive about the Air Force.

Figure 10.6 is an example of escalation workflow that takes into consideration when you should respond to a compliment, complaint, or potential crisis.

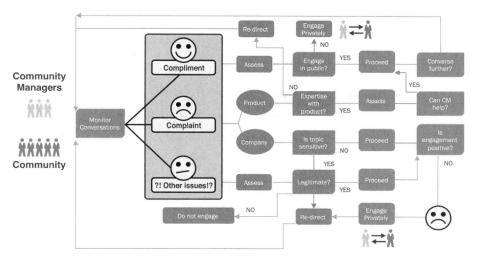

Figure 10.6   *An example of reactive escalation workflow*

This might seem complicated at first glance, but after you go through the process of putting the workflow together and identify the right teams to be involved, it will become second nature when it's time to put it into action.

As you are building these workflows, it's important to also create a risk assessment guide so when your team members are engaging externally, they can be smart when they identify and flag potential risks. The simplest way to do this is to create a green, yellow, and red flag assessment guide.

Similar to traffic stop lights, green symbolizes that the conversation is good to go and that community managers can respond without escalation. Yellow means to "proceed with caution," and careful consideration should be made when responding and/or escalating. Red means to stop what you are doing and force teams to meet and decide what the appropriate next steps will be. Following is a break down of potential topics that would fall into each of these flag categories.

Green flag issues include questions about

- New account setup
- Account management
- Positive brand experiences and praise
- Career opportunities
- Company information
- Partner information
- Innovation requests and ideas

Yellow flag issues include

Potential Crisis

- Negative blog/media mentions about your brand
- Negative mentions from celebrities of influencers
- Negative mentions from employees (previous or current)
- Critical feedback about products and/or services
- Negative feedback or criticism about a current marketing campaign

Customer Support

- Product or transaction requests
- Dispute resolution regarding customer orders
- IT-related issues or website errors

Last red flag issues include

Potential Crisis

- Hacking claims or account security-related issues
- Legal threats
- Suicide or criminal threats
- Negative news articles mentioning your brand
- Key sensitive topics

Customer Support

- Customer service complaints
- Major account issues (shipping, transaction, order not received)
- Fraud complaints

Although some of these issues might not be relevant to your brand, you should go through this exercise and categorize each of these issues accordingly. This helps you train your team to be able to engage with customers, identify potential issues, and escalate accordingly.

Governing New "Brand" Account Creation

As mentioned in Chapter 2, "Defining Social Business Strategy and Planning," the "bright and shiny" object of social media has caused a craze in many companies today and quite possibly yours, whereby hundreds of siloed teams create social media channels resulting in poor integration, disjointed content, and lackluster community management practices. And if you are the person who is driving this organizational change, you have to audit and potentially close down certain social media channels for a variety of reasons:

- Community is abandoned; no one is posting content.
- Content strategy doesn't align with the brand.
- Community was created around a product that does not exist anymore.

Hundreds of other reasons for consolidating or shutting down existing social media channels can exist, so you must create a process that prevents these things from happening in the future. Figure 10.7 is an example of a process that governs new brand account creation.

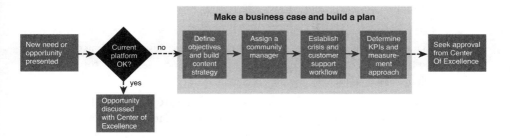

Figure 10.7   *Process for creating new social media accounts*

Usually in a situation like this, a specific marketing (or regional) team identifies a need to create a new social media channel. There could be a variety of reasons for this request. Perhaps the company is launching a new product. Perhaps the company is expanding into new geographical territories, or maybe there is a huge event happening that you are sponsoring.

The first step in this process is to evaluate whether or not an existing channel can be used to support the initiative. In some cases, it will, and in other cases, it won't. When you evaluate specific requests, each one should be carefully considered before making a decision. The good news about using Facebook as a part of your content strategy is the launch of Global Pages, which helps address this issue head on.

Instead of a single Facebook page in the specific language that it was originally created, Global Pages now have the benefit of both global and regional content. In essence, it's one page with one URL, for example, Facebook.com/YourBrand. Instead of users searching for your brand by country and in the language they prefer to read, they will only have one option to Like your page.

With the new Global Pages structure, you can create localized versions of your cover and profile photos, apps, milestones, and "about" info and provide locally relevant and regionally specific content to your community in the their news feeds. An English version's cover photo might say "Hello," but users visiting from Italy would see a different version welcoming them with a "Ciao!"

Your Facebook administrators can set up local versions for different single or multi-country language regions, plus a default for everyone else. A single, global URL dynamically directs users to the appropriate local version. This can help consolidate workflow, content creation, and analytics and at the same time, provide a seamless experience for your customers. So in the case of launching a new Facebook page for a region, you can potentially leverage the new Global Pages feature. In some cases, there is certainly an opportunity to create a new channel. However, you must ensure that the teams that want a new channel have the following documented and well planned out before they move forward to create one:

- **Content narrative:** What are the goals, and do they have a content narrative that is consistent with the brand's storytelling objectives? Do they have content themes/categories and a documented editorial calendar?

- **Community manager:** To prevent communities from going stale and customers from falling "out of love" with your brand, there must be community managers who are not only responsible for creating content, but also responding to the community when necessary. They are the face of the brand, and they should advocate on behalf of them.

- **Moderation and escalation policy:** This chapter is all about governance, so it's possible that new teams requesting a new channel will adopt many of the governance models you create as a part of the CoE. However, part of that model should include identifying the proper "regional" resources for escalating customer support issues or handling crises.

- **Measurement framework:** Before launching a new channel, the teams should have a solid understanding of how they are going to measure success and determine KPIs.

When the internal teams have their plans of action documented, the final step in this process is to seek approval for the Center of Excellence.

Managing the Security of Social Media Passwords

2013 has certainly been the year of "social media password" challenges. And although this is amusing to watch and read about from the outside looking in, it can cost you your job if it happens to your company. Two significant incidents happened this year, one at HMV and one at Burger King, each making it clear why carefully managing your passwords is a huge deal.

HMV is a British entertainment retail company located in the United Kingdom. In January, employees fired by HMV decided to get even by live tweeting their "mass execution" on the company's official Twitter account, which at the time, had almost 64,000 followers. According to the *Independent*, HMV attempted to delete the posts from the @hmvtweets account, but it was too late. The tweets had already been copied on screen shots and widely distributed across the social web via retweets and blog posts.

One rogue employee tweeted: "We're tweeting live from HR where we're all being fired! Exciting!!" Another tweet, apparently from an iPhone, reported "60 of us being fired at once." A subsequent posting read: "Just overheard our Marketing Director (he's staying, folks) ask 'How do I shut down Twitter?'" The fiasco lasted about 20 minutes before the company removed the tweets, which began trending with the hashtag, #HMVXFactorFiring. Later on, more tweets appeared, apparently from a different member of HMV personnel, referring to the earlier comments.

In this situation, several HMV employees had access to post directly to the brand's social media channel. Unfortunately, they didn't have a content governance model to prevent this from happening.

In Burger King's case, they faced an entirely different challenge.

In February, the Huffington Post reported that someone apparently hacked Burger King's Twitter account and changed its photo to the McDonald's logo and name to "McDonalds." During a series of tweets rife with poor grammar, the hacker claimed Burger King was sold to McDonald's and then posted a host of other raunchy messages. The account's bio was also changed to:

"Just got sold to McDonalds because the whopper flopped =[FREDOM IS FAILURE."

The perpetrator referenced several Internet hacker groups, including LulzSec, Anonymous, and DFNTSC. About an hour after the unruly tweets began, the fast food chain's Twitter account was suspended. It was reported that Burger King reached out to Twitter to have the account frozen.

What happened to Burger King, and then a day later to Jeep, is every marketer's nightmare. Bu they weren't alone. Other prominent accounts have fallen victim to hacking, including those for *NBC News*, *USA Today*, Donald J. Trump, the Westboro Baptist Church, and even the "hacktivist" group Anonymous.

So what does this mean for you?

These specific situations should raise question marks about the security of your social media passwords and the ease of gaining access to your branded accounts. The good news is that Twitter launched a new login verification feature in May 2013. The new login verification levels-up the account security, preventing the possibility of email phishing schemes, as well as breaching of passwords. With the login verification enabled, your existing applications continue to work without disruption.

Both Twitter and Facebook have begun introducing a number of paid advertising options, raising the stakes for advertisers. Brands that pay to advertise on Twitter are assigned a sales representative to help them manage their accounts, but they are not given any more layers of security than those for a typical user.

One way to minimize your risk is to deploy the content workflows mentioned previously. Doing so provides two layers of security. If you have invested in a content publishing platform, users are given login credentials to the system, not the social network itself. Second, if you build your workflows correctly, content has to go through a series of approvals before it becomes public.

Of course, if your community manager is terminated for some reason, that's a completely different story. In that case, you need to ensure that you are in constant communication with Human Resources. You might even consider them to be a member of the CoE.

You should also look into investing in password management software. This type of software can help you create unhackable passwords, secure them, and log in to your accounts automatically without having to memorize them or write them down. Every single day in the media, we hear of a large number of accounts being hacked, from online banking to social media and email accounts. Password management software can help you avoid the risk of people stealing your login info, accessing your accounts, and posting objectionable content. Not only is this bad for your brand but if hackers can get into your Twitter account, what's stopping them from accessing your work email account or bank information?

The way password software works is simple. You basically secure your login information into a platform and automatically log in to any of your accounts through the software or a browser button add-on. With a portable version of your software installed on a USB drive, you can use it to view and log in to your accounts on other computers. Many of these platforms also provide sync-able versions for smartphones.

One of the reasons accounts are easily hacked is that many people have a hard time remembering their passwords, so they use common words like their last name, family name, kid's date of birth, their own date of birth, Social Security numbers, or sometimes they even use "password" as their password. To escalate the problem, they might also use the same password for numerous accounts. Password software can help you create complex passwords, store them in a database for you and use them to log you in to your accounts quickly and easily. All passwords are encrypted and locked behind a single master password that only you know.

Beyond the security benefits of using this type of software, it also helps you stay organized by storing all of you password details in one, secure place. Many applications also provide mobile tools so that you can take your secure passwords with you, especially if you are mobile worker or use multiple computers.

Here are some basic criteria you can use when you are evaluating password management software:

- **Basic management:** The best password software platforms can automatically create accounts as you log in to websites and automatically log you into a group of your favorite accounts simultaneously. Other tools include auto-filling long forms and templates for popular account types.

- **Security:** Because password software can store your login information and account numbers all in one place, security is critical in this situation. The best applications encrypt your files using 256-bit (or higher) encryption protocols, generate complex passwords, and protect you from keylogging and phishing attempts. Keylogging is the practice of using a software program to record all keystrokes on a computer keyboard. Phishing is a scam to try and obtain financial or other confidential information by sending an e-mail that looks as if it is from a legitimate company, usually a bank, but contains a link to a fake website that looks just like the real one.

- **Mobile capabilities:** Many employees use smartphones and tablets to log in to their online and social media accounts. Some password programs have mobile versions of their software that operate independently, or in conjunction with the PC or Mac.

Most password management tools offer many of the same features. Useful features to look out for include

- Centralized deployment where one administrator has complete control over accessibility to specific social media channels such as a blog, Twitter or Facebook accounts, and for how long. Easy to update when someone joins the company, leaves the company, or is assigned to a new role.

- Shared password data on a person-by-person basis or for teams, departments, or regions within a company.

- Options to hide a password from an employee while still allowing access to a brand's social media channels via auto-fill functions.

- Generation of secure, unhackable passwords and an option to replace old passwords with unique, randomly generated ones.

- Password data stored and encrypted online, allowing secure access to passwords when on the go via mobile devices.

- One-time passwords are useful if using an untrusted shared computer.

Vendor Spotlight—Spredfast

Governing your brand's social activity requires a great deal of organization across people, accounts and content, as well as the need to uphold your company brand standards. Spredfast, a social media management system provider, helps brands organize and orchestrate social media, specifically content, to facilitate the ideal interactions between brands and their communities.

Each company has its own unique structure and guidelines. As shown in Figure 10.8, Spredfast can adapt to organizations of all sizes and structures by managing all groups and social accounts in a single location. Each department can be self-sufficient in governing its own social programs and accounts by authenticating social accounts across networks such as Facebook, Twitter, LinkedIn, Google+, and blogs from one centralized location. Content contributors can be assigned roles and manage complex user permissions so the right people have access to create content and engage with the right audiences.

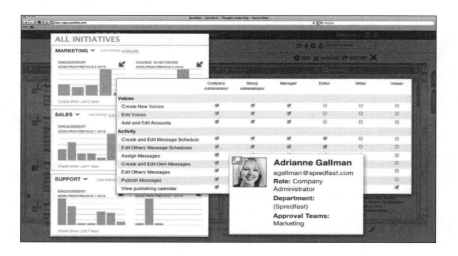

Figure 10.8   *Spredfast has built-in controls to manage content governance.*

Spredfast can also help you collaborate so that workflows and approvals help teams engage productively. As shown in Figure 10.9, teams can highlight activity proactively to share with contributors for reference or assign activity reactively to entire teams based on response needs. This collaboration replaces long email threads with system notifications and workflow automation within Spredfast to provide visibility across the team of what's been assigned, what needs prioritized attention, and what actions have been taken with visible audit trails.

Figure 10.9 *Spredfast has built-in collaboration that increases productivity.*

Planned content can be organized and created across a team editorial calendar, with contributors having the ability to use preapproved content from the Spredfast Content Library. Content types and accounts with specific approval needs can be auto-routed based on user, account, or content type to ensure the proper oversight and approvals are in place before being publically published. All content published within Spredfast is archived so that teams can reference all historic activity, conversation histories, approvals, and audit trails at any point in time.

Spredfast protects the security and safety of brands by equipping administrators with the power to manage accounts, passwords, and user roles from within the platform. Content contributors are given access to engage directly within Spredfast rather than have direct access to the many passwords needed to access company social media accounts. For companies in regulated industries or those with additional security needs, Spredfast offers enhanced password management functionality, Single Sign-On, and IP restrictions.

Following are two Spredfast customers who use their tool for varying levels of governance:

- **Whole Foods Market** (Workflow, Processes, and Orchestration): In addition to maintaining globally managed presences on Facebook, Twitter, and Pinterest (among other social networks), Whole Foods enables over 2,500 employees at its 340+ stores to provide relevant, local, and timely content to their communities. This allows each region to share its own local flavor while preserving brand integrity (see Figure 10.10).

Figure 10.10   *Whole Foods Market uses Spredfast to manage global content.*

- **AARP** (Organization and Structure): There is no one right way to organize your social presence. A few common configurations include organizing by business unit, geographical location, or product offering. AARP blends corporate, business objective-focused accounts with state-level accounts to provide relevant local information to members of the nonprofit organization geared toward serving people 50+ (see Figure 10.11).

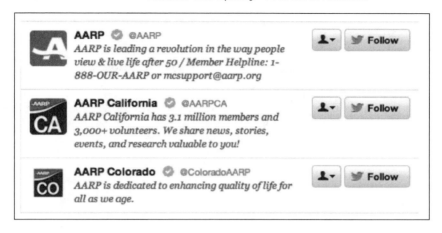

Figure 10.11   *AARP uses Spredfast to manage corporate, business, and objective-based accounts.*

Structuring Your Teams to Become a Content-Driven Organization

Tweetable Moment: *How you align and build your team is one of the most important factors of your content strategy.—#nextmediaco*

There isn't a right way or wrong way to structure your content organization. Every company is different. Culture, leadership, and business objectives vary and are often dynamic. This usually results in you having to shift roles and responsibilities, the general team structure, or your content strategy to adapt to the current business climate.

The holistic view of this book is that you have to change the way you think, communicate, and operate to transform your brand into a media company. Although this is easy to say or write in a book, it's much more difficult to make happen. A shift like this requires radical thinking. It requires a change in behavior and organizational dynamics. Why? The answer is that most organizations today operate in narrow silos when it comes to job function. So as you create your Center of Excellence, build your content strategy, and assign editorial roles and responsibilities, you have to prepare for an uphill battle.

The good news is that company leadership is realizing the importance of social media, even though these silos still do exist. According to a 2013 Altimeter study "The Evolution of Social Business: Six Stages of Social Media Transformation" by Charlene Li and Brian Solis, 60% of organizations have identified the right roles, responsibilities, and governance for the execution and resourcing of social media efforts (see Figure 11.1).

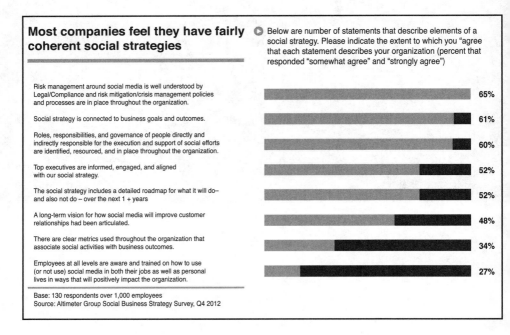

Figure 11.1 *Most companies have coherent social media strategies.*

If you look closely at this data, only 27% of employees are actually trained on how to use social media, both professionally and personally. This number must go up if you are looking to transition your brand to a media company. This type of change cannot happen in a silo and it can't be forced from the top down either. It must be a collaborative effort.

Additionally, we have to remember that the transformation from brand to media company is much bigger than just social media. All forms of communication need to contribute to the brand story and be distributed like a well-oiled machine—paid, earned, and owned media; customer support; employee and customer advocacy; and so on. This requires even more radical thinking because it will require you to collaborate with your internal teams—not always an easy task.

Unfortunately, it's not like we can turn on the "media company" button and change operations and behavior overnight. It requires a change in attitude, behavior, and thinking that is coupled with processes, governance models, and technology that can facilitate the transformation. In this chapter, I discuss organizational structure and roles and responsibilities.

A Quick Lesson in Change Management

Organizational change occurs when a company changes its business strategy, merges with another company, acquires a company, or is acquired by a larger company. Sometimes, and in the context of this book, organizations are forced to change they way they communicate externally in order to reach customers with valuable content that meets and exceeds their expectations and ultimately changes their behavior.

Traditional change management initiatives are usually based on a *push model*. This means that business leaders attempt to change the organization (process, organizational structure, behaviors, culture, values, and so on) and expect the employees to follow their lead.

The push model of change management is often referred to the *crisis-oriented approach* or *burning platform model*, where sudden movement (crisis) in the external market requires a quick pivot in business operations or culture. The burning platform model is actually based on a true story of a huge fire on an oil-drilling platform, which killed nearly 200 men. The handful that survived did so by jumping 15 stories from the platform to the ocean—they understood that they had to jump or burn to death. It is a graphic illustration on what pushing change in an organization truly means.

In this model, change is forced, almost with a command and control type of behavior, by trying to convince your internal stakeholders that the pain of doing nothing is greater than the change being proposed. This type of change management is used when people are unwilling to change their behavior or have a "this too will pass" type of attitude. This model is most often used when companies are experiencing difficult times, when change is a matter of survival, whether for internal (executive turnover) or external factors (struggling economy.)

Resistance to this type of change is normal. Your employees will undoubtedly rush to defend the status quo if they feel their security, job status, or function is threatened. Organizational change naturally generates skepticism and resistance by employees and, in some cases, senior management, making it difficult or impossible to move an organization forward.

This *pull change* management model is based on the concept that this change is viewed as an opportunity. It assumes that your employees are willing to change their behavior and that there is something "in it" for them if they do. This is based on a participatory style of management, where there is a shared vision rather than one dictated and forced by company leadership. The pull method of change management is most often used when times are good (increasing profits and margins and revenues are up.)

This organizational change might focus on repositioning your company in the marketplace, launching a new product or service, or expanding into new markets that would allow you to dominate a new category. But to succeed with this model, your company needs the agility, flexibility, and a culture of continuous content and marketing innovation. It must be responsive enough to pivot when threats happen in the marketplace, which will undoubtedly put the company through difficult times.

Many organizations today that have adopted Enterprise 2.0 technologies (collaboration tools for internal social networks as discussed in Chapter 10, "How Content Governance Will Facilitate Media Company Transformation") are more likely to embrace a pull approach or at least more of a balance between push and pull change management models. The great news is that these social tools are already becoming a driving force to this change. The challenge arises in certain organizations when employees aren't using these tools, or even worse, when they are prohibited to use these tools because they are against corporate or IT policy.

Regardless of where your company is financially or what your market share looks like compared to your competitors, it's imperative that you think about how you can implement change in your organization. What's in it for your internal stakeholders is the ability to increase your relevance to your customers. The end result is you selling more products, increases in revenue, salary bonuses, and happy employees.

Tearing Down the Organizational Silos

As President Ronald Reagan challenged Soviet leader Mikhail Gorbachev to "tear down this wall!" referring to the Berlin wall that separated East and West Germany, so should organizations tear down their silos. The challenge with this is that leadership usually cycles in and out of companies every three to five years. When new leaders come into your organization, they bring new theories, processes, and even new employees with them. So in this case, your efforts might take a few steps back in some cases.

Wikipedia's loose and somewhat candy-coated definition of organizational silos is the following:

...is a management system incapable of reciprocal operation with other, related management systems. With department specialization came a silo operational culture for many large organizations. The silo effect is characterized by a lack of communication or common goals between departments in an organization.

Many organizations today are not only incapable of communicating with each other, but they are also unwilling and often refuse purposely to share knowledge. It's a form of job protection, ego, or just ignorance because that's the way the organization has always operated. Many employees are just afraid of change.

It's not always the human factor either. Today, there are still isolated systems and processes that keep valuable information, workflows, and transactions from moving freely throughout an organization. If you think about it, it kind of makes sense. Organizations gave birth to silos to accomplish various tasks: sell products, provide customer support, advertise their products, and so on. The problem arises when there is no governance, guidance, or proper organization for how each of these functions can work together to increase efficiency, save money, and more importantly, provide a more positive customer experience.

The first step in driving organizational change is to create and identify roles and responsibilities of your internal/external stakeholders.

Identifying Roles and Responsibilities

As you are building your content organization, it's important that you document and evangelize the job functions and roles and responsibilities that you need for you to transition your brand into media company. Here are several job roles and functions to consider:

- **Chief Content Officer:** There has been a lot of talk about whether or not there should be a Chief Content Officer. My stance is that every company is different, and if you feel like having this role in your organization will add value, more power to you. So whether it's a Chief Content Officer or a Vice President of Marketing, you need a strong leader who has a vision and executional experience to actually move the needle.

  This role requires a significant amount of leadership experience, obviously. He or she should have a significant amount of expertise in marketing (paid, earned, owned media), journalism, and the content production process. He or she will ultimately be responsible for the content strategy and be the primary interface with the rest of the company, evangelizing the vision of taking the brand and shifting it to a media company. This person could very well be the "lead" of your Social Business Center or Excellence. The Chief Content Officer should also be accountable for the performance of the brand's content marketing efforts, measuring relevant data points such as links, traffic, leads, and general content performance within social media channels (Likes, comments, shares, tweets, and so on). In smaller companies, the Chief Content Officer might very well be the editor in chief, editor of content operations, or a director of marketing.

- **Managing Editor:** This person must be a veteran of traditional media and have a proven ability to run an editorial operation. The managing editor is responsible for all content to include content ideation, creation, approval workflows, and distribution and optimization of the content after it's posted—essentially, the entire content supply chain operation. In a global company, the managing editor might be responsible for ensuring that the content strategy is coordinated across all the brand's regional content operations. They might also be responsible for recruiting regional (U.S., Canada, Latin America) or channel editors (Facebook, Twitter, blogs) as the organization scales its content operations. Last, the managing editor is responsible for all the content performance metrics and feeding the insights back to contributors and editors.

- **Editors:** Depending on how the company is structured and as just mentioned, editors could be in charge of regions, specific products/ brands, or channels. They also play a pivotal role in editing and approving content that's submitted by contributors. They also are responsible for finding and training new contributors. Additionally, if a brand has a real-time Creative Newsroom, editors will be the one giving editorial approval to create content based on what's trending in the news cycle.

- **Community Managers:** The days of hiring an intern and paying them almost nothing to manage your social media channels is over. Community managers do more than just manage content calendars and tweet all day long. The truth is, many community managers today are already driving fully robust social CRM programs. They are engaging day to day with customers. They are working with technology platforms and sometimes making critical business decisions. They are gathering and reporting analytics. They are creating workflows and feedback loops with other, internal teams (which almost always requires change management initiatives and cross functional/geographic collaboration). And a strategic community manager advocates

on behalf of the social customer back to the business and on behalf of
employees back to management for internal community initiatives.

The new role of the community manager is changing dramatically.
Today's community managers must have specific experience in content
creation and production and must understand the fundamentals of
paid media. For smaller brands with the Creative Newsroom model as
well as a converged media strategy, the community manager might be
the only one spotting the trends, writing the copy, building a piece of
creative, and then making the strategic decision to promote it, all by
herself.

- **Brand Journalists:** For your brand's content marketing to provide the
  highest level of value, it's imperative that subject matter experts contribute articles, posts, presentations, and any other thought leadership
  material that will help add value to customers. As discussed in Chapter
  4, "Empowering Employees, Customers, and Partners to Feed the
  Content Engine," employees can be your biggest brand advocates. They
  just need to be trained, empowered, and enabled to do so.

- **External Contributors:** Successful content marketing operations often
  use external content contributors, specifically influencers or brand
  advocates. Also discussed in Chapter 4, your customers can play a significant role in your journey to become a media company. You will just
  have to operationalize your brand advocate programs and enable them
  to help you tell the brand story.

- **Analysts:** For large companies, having a dedicated analyst is a neces-
  sity. Not only for reporting and measurement purposes, but also for
  making real-time decisions on pushing organic content to sponsored
  or promoted as well. A good analyst has more than superb Excel skills
  and the ability to make fancy graphs when reporting back numbers. He
  should also be able to extract insights so that the editorial teams can
  iterate specific content to improve its performance.

It doesn't necessarily matter what you call these roles specifically. But the important thing to remember is that someone should be responsible for your content
operations. And if you have made a strategic investment in a content marketing
platform such as Kapost, Compendium, or a social CRM platform such as Sprinkr
or Spredfast, you should also consider outlining and documenting the following
user roles and responsibilities as they relate to the platform as well as the controls
they have to create, edit, approve, and distribute content:

- **Administrators:** This person is responsible for creating and deleting accounts within the content management system. They assign user roles and responsibilities within the system as well as assign platform-specific controls (that is, the ability to publish directly to the brand's Facebook page). The administrator can be a project manager, someone in IT, a community manager, or someone from your supporting agency.

- **Editors:** In the last chapter, I showcased several examples of content workflows for planned and unplanned content. In this case, editors are the ones responsible for approving content submitted by contributors. It's likely that they also give feedback and editorial direction to the content contributors. They might also be responsible for adding approved content to the master editorial calendar or submitting approved content to the next level of approvers: brand or legal review.

- **Contributors:** Anyone in your company can be a content contributor, and hopefully you have a lot of them. You can think of them as brand journalists. The important thing to remember is that as you scale and add additional contributors, you simultaneously have to add additional editors as well. It's pretty self-explanatory what contributors are responsible for: contributing content. Of course, each contributor should have a different editorial focus, especially if you work for a large brand with multiple products or specific verticals.

- **Community Managers:** Specific user roles need to be created that allow for this role to monitor specific social media channels and interact directly with customers or escalate specific conversations to customer support teams. And in many cases, community managers might also be editors of specific channels, like Twitter, Facebook, or the company blog.

- **Customer Support:** Additionally, specific user roles should be created for customer support staff. This role is vital and should have the capability to create tickets as well as respond directly to customers when they have specific issues with the company's products or services.

Rebecca Lieb, analyst from the Altimeter Group, identified the following enterprise models for governing the orchestration of content within organizations. The model a company selects is determined by several factors, ranging from culture, structure, budget, business goals, and the types of volume of content produced (see Figure 11.2).

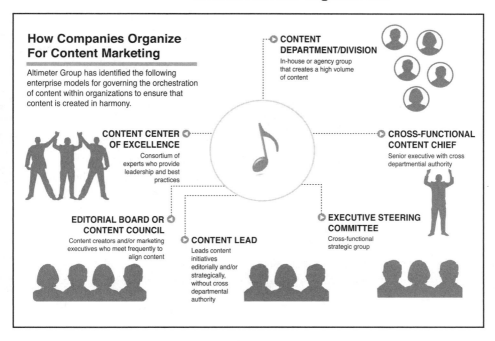

Figure 11.2   *How companies organize for content marketing*

Although this specific model is focused solely on content marketing as a specific
job function with your company, you can also look at it through the strategic
lens as you take your brand to a media company. Here is a quick summary of
Altimeter's models:

- **Content Center of Excellence:** This is similar to what I described
  in Chapter 3, "Establishing a Centralized 'Editorial' Social Business
  Center of Excellence," where I discussed the Social Business Center of
  Excellence and how you will involve team members from various job
  functions and expertise to be a part of the centralized team. Topics
  other than content are also discussed and managed by this team—
  governance, training, measurement, global expansion, and so on.

- **Editorial Board or Content Council:** In this model, internal teams
  meet to align content, editorial calendars, workflow and try to avoid
  duplication of effort. They examine content performance metrics and
  use those insights to drive future content. This is a tactical model that
  essentially "keeps the train running" according to Altimeter.

- **Content Lead:** This model is where one executive is responsible and oversees the brand's content initiatives. The content lead is also responsible for putting together strategy documentation—tone, voice, and copy guidelines. In this case, a supporting agency might have the responsibility to execute.

- **Executive Steering Committee:** This model is a cross-functional group of senior executives responsible for approving general content direction, ensuring it lives to the overall brand voice and personality.

- **Cross-functional Content Chief:** This model is where one person is responsible for the brand's content strategy, also referred to as the head of digital strategy. Usually this person has more than just content that she is responsible for. This role would oversee paid media, analytics, channel marketing, and so on.

- **Content Department:** This model can almost be compared to an internal agency. They are usually responsible for creating high-end and highly produced content—videos and technical whitepapers.

As you think about building and structuring your content organization, there are several approaches you can use. In the following sections, I identify three— structuring by channel, by brand, or by region.

Structuring Your Content Organization by Channel

If you work for a large organization, chances are you have several Facebook pages, Twitter accounts, and blogs. Perhaps you have consolidated many of these channels to a size that's much more manageable. Figure 11.3 illustrates how you can align your content organization by specific channel. It's important to note that this model only takes into consideration the creation of owned media content. There still has to be collaboration between paid media teams and others in the organization to ensure consistent brand storytelling. Additionally, these models are meant to document structure for branded accounts, not employee owned and managed accounts.

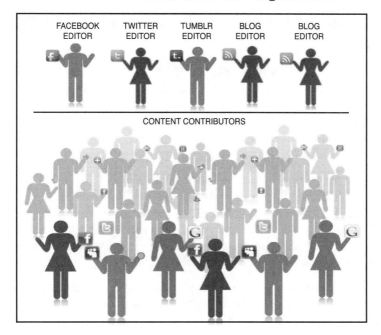

Figure 11.3 *Content organization by channel*

In this model, you see that there are several hundred content contributors, which could be employees (brand journalists), customers, partners in the supply chain, or a combination of all three. At the top, there is a specific editor for Facebook, Twitter, Tumblr, and a few blogs. This is probably the most basic model for a company with one Facebook page, one Twitter account, and so on. It can get extremely complicated with companies that have Global Facebook pages or multiple pages for specific events, product launches, or regions. If you recall, Chapter 10 helps you create governance models to ensure that you can manage the proliferation of several accounts and take the appropriate action to prevent the creation of channels if they aren't needed.

Additionally, if you have a company blog with multiple categories, it's good practice to have one editor per category that can manage all the content and content contributors.

If you work for a smaller company, it's likely that a one or two person team is responsible for the entire content and marketing operation. In this case, you may consider identifying customers to contribute content or use platforms such as eByline, Contently, or Skyword to help you feed the content engine from third-party influencers and freelance journalists.

Structuring Your Content Organization by Brand or Product

If you are a fan of Google like I am, you already know that they have several products in the market—Chrome, Android, Search, Ad Words, Toolbar, YouTube, Picasa, Gmail, Books, Drive, Blogger, Google+, and the list goes on. And though many of Google's products are developed to work together, each one has different teams working on the product internally, different external audiences, various revenue models, and different marketing objectives.

If you work for a company like Google, there are a few ways you can structure your content organization. You can simply take the previous model and replicate it at the product level. This means you would have several content contributors and one editor for each specific channel for that product. So Google's Facebook page would have its own set of contributors and editor who would differ from Google Chrome's Facebook page.

There must be one level above the editor to ensure there is a cohesive relationship among the editors of each of the products channels. It could be the Chief Content Officer mentioned previously, a Vice President of Marketing, or simply a managing editor who is responsible for the integration and storytelling initiatives of each of these brands.

Structuring Your Content Organization by Region

If you work for a large multinational organization, managing content can be difficult. In this example, you can take the first model (structuring your content organization by channel) and replicate it at the regional level. Figure 11.4 illustrates how this would work.

In this model, you see that there is an editor who is responsible for all the content in the given regions—North America, Latin America, EMEA, and Asia Pacific. Again, there would have to be an additional level of editors who would be responsible for integration with each of the countries.

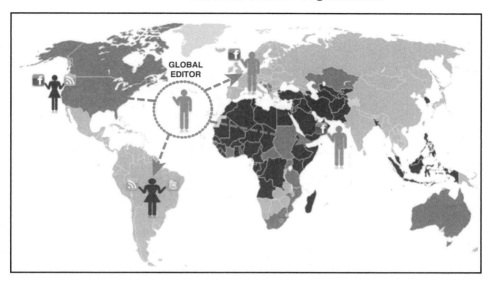

Figure 11.4   *Content organization by region*

Structuring for Converged Media and Real-Time Marketing

In Chapter 9, "The Role of Converged Media in Your Content Strategy," I went into great detail about converged media and the promise of real-time marketing. As you are building your content organization, you must consider all of your stakeholders (teams and agencies) when you develop your converged media strategy. If you currently work on a social media or corporate communications team, then most likely, your team doesn't have responsibility for paid media initiatives or have creative (or designer) type of resources. However, I am seeing a shift with many brands where these teams are now taking on the responsibility of paid media, specifically within social media channels.

Because of this, you have to ensure that you are building the right relationships, structures, and workflows internally that bring community managers, marketing managers, paid media specialists, analysts, and designers together to help you achieve earned media at scale. This is even more important if you are implementing a Creative Newsroom.

In the "Converged Media Imperative: How Brands Must Combine Paid, Owned, and Earned Media" report, Jeremiah Owyang and Rebecca Lieb from the Altimeter Group showcase success criteria for successfully launching a converged media strategy in a company (see Figure 11.5).

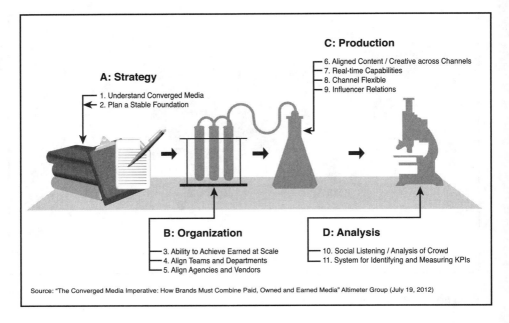

Figure 11.5   *The success criteria for launching a converged media model*

At the beginning of this model in the strategy section, you will notice that planning for a stable foundation is mentioned. This is about collaborating with internal teams to ensure the right content is being amplified and that it aligns with your company's business goals.

The next section is about organization and is the foundation of this chapter. As mentioned in Chapter 3, one of the members listed in the inner circle of the Social Business Center of Excellence is the Digital Marketing team. Having this team at the table is imperative to ensure that converged media is a part of your content strategy. Also if you work with several agencies, you should make it crystal clear that each agency works together and collaborates with each other. The last thing you want is for your content strategy to suffer because your agencies aren't playing nice together.

The last two pieces of this model—production and analysis—not only play a significant role in your converged media strategy, but they are both imperative to your media company transformation.

Choosing the Right Technology Platforms

There are several technology platforms you must consider that help you scale your content creation; facilitate process workflows; and build controls for content distribution, listening, and measurement. Although this book highlights several technology vendors in the market, you must do your own due diligence and make sure you ask all the right questions and communicate with your IT teams before making your decision. Also it's important to remember that you should never compromise your technical requirements based on the limitations of a specific vendor. What you should do is let them know what your requirements are first and then see if they can match it with their capabilities. For example, one requirement may be the need for a sequential approval workflow, where content approvals go through a series of approvers in sequence before the content gets published. If a particular vendor cannot deliver on that requirement, you should look to a different one.

Content Marketing Platforms

Most content marketing platforms have built-in workflows that can manage an entire content marketing operation—content ideation, creation, approval, distribution, as well as report on content performance metrics. Following are a few vendors that provide this service (in no specific order); some have been featured quite extensively in this book:

- Kapost—built in workflows, content planning, and can also publish to Wordpress and other content platforms.

- Compendium—hosted content marketing platform that has built in workflows, research tools, and content performance metrics.

- Cadence9—several products for CMOs, smaller marketing teams, and agencies with workflow and publishing capabilities.

- Relaborate—mainly for small business or agencies with built-in technology that will help you identify trending topics.

- Percolate—built-in workflows, access to licensed stock photography, and also surfaces third-party curated content that you can publish on your channels.

- Skyword—more focused on writing long-form content emphasizing keyword optimization. They also have access to third-party writers who can write content for your brand.

- Contently—also focused on long-form content creation, planning, workflows, and has a network of journalists that can feed into your content engine.

- Ebyline—also focused on long-form content creation, built-in workflows, and has a network of freelance writers that can feed into your content engine. They also have their own "newsroom" service in case you don't have the internal resources.

Social CRM/Content Publishing Platforms

These platforms also have outbound content publishing capabilities and workflows that allow you to respond, escalate conversation, and fully manage social networks such as Facebook, Twitter, YouTube, and many others. Many of them also have built-in listening services so that community managers can monitor brand related conversations, assign tickets, and respond directly to customers through the platform. They also have reporting and measurement capabiltiies. They are typically more expensive than the content marketing platforms:

- Spredfast
- Sprinklr
- HootSuite Enterpise
- Adobe Social
- Expion
- Falcon Social
- Raven Tools
- Hubspot

Online Monitoring Vendors

These platforms give you the ability to monitor brand and industry-related conversations, report on share of voice, sentiment, and total brand mentions. Some of these platforms also give you the ability to monitor owned media analytics and compare the data with external brand mentions, share of voice, and so on. Some platforms have a built-in engagement dashboard so that you can respond directly when someone mentions your brand. Some also report on specific content performance, general engagement, and community growth:

- Simply Measured
- Adobe Social
- Radian6
- Sysmos
- Tracx
- Mutual Mind
- HootSuite Command Center
- Tickr
- Brantology
- Brandwatch
- Ubervu

Vendor Spotlight—Skyword

Skyword has a content marketing platform and services that can help your company reach and engage customers with original content that is designed to succeed in search engines and on the social web. In addition to its technology platform, Skyword provides many of its customers with access to its community of thousands of professional writers for content creation and helps them plan, execute, and manage their content marketing programs with their teams of content strategists and editorial staff.

The Skyword Platform has a flexible, automated content production workflow that can be tailored to your specific organizational requirements. Its platform streamlines and tracks every aspect of the content production process, including third-party writer recruitment and management, automated writer payments and tax administration, content assignments and creation, the ability to optimize your long-form content for search, topic recommendations, editorial review, social media distribution, promotion, and measurement.

Skyword has a seven-step process that can you help you achieve your content goals efficiently and effectively. Each step is outlined in the following sections.

Step 1—Recruit and Manage Your Writers

Skyword allows you to recruit freelance writers from their searchable database of third-party journalists, with expertise in online writing, past experience, writing samples, and performance metrics. Their platform also allows you to manage your existing writers on the platform, specifically managing content creation workflows, writer payments, and tax administration.

Step 2—Plan Your Content Strategy

In addition to managing and recruiting writers, their platform also allows you to execute your content strategy and plan your web content on a daily, weekly, monthly, or annual basis with their online editorial calendar. You can manage your content by category or topic, schedule automatic publishing, and manage for editorial deadlines. You an also schedule assignments and publishing, plan for upcoming events and programs; and gain visibility for budgeting and forecasting. Figure 11.6 is an example of their editorial calendar.

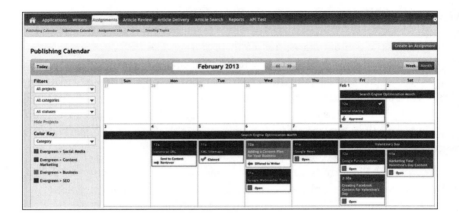

Figure 11.6   *Skyword helps you optimize your long-form content to maximize search engine visibility.*

Step 4—Create and Optimize Your Content

Skyword allows you to create and optimize writing assignments and review articles and article proposals from your contributing writers. You can help your contributors identify what news stories are trending with the platform's breaking news module and set program guidelines and SEO optimization requirements to ensure that editorial content is ready for web publication. Figure 11.7 shows what content is trending based on the keywords your brand is optimizing content for.

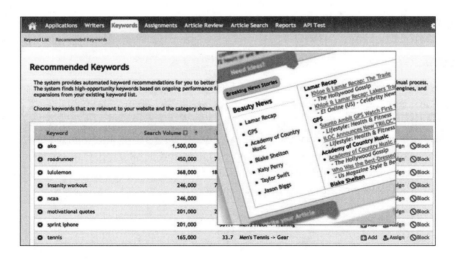

Figure 11.7   *Skyword surfaces trending content based on relevant keywords.*

Step 5—Edit and Review Your Content

The next step is to edit and review content that flows automatically into the queues of program managers, your own editors, or Skyword copyeditors. The Skyword Platform lets you track who changed a piece of content, why they changed it, and where it is in the approval process. You can also check to see if any content submitted is duplicated or lacking proper attribution. Finally, you can customize your editorial and review workflow to match your organizational needs and requirements.

Step 6—Promote Your Content Socially

Skyword has the capability to promote your online content via social media platforms. They have built-in tools that allow your contributors to quickly share articles with their social networks. Skyword tracks social sharing activity on each article published and allows you to easily see which content is making a significant impact on your content performance metrics.

Step 7—Measure and Analyze the Performance of Your Content

Skyword has robust measurement and analytics capabilities. The platform enables you to measure program results quickly and make adjustments on the fly. It has extensive tracking and analytics capabilities including article marketing and writer performance, social media metrics, and keyword search engine rankings. You also can easily make assignments to writers based on what is most impactful.

Index

Foreword by Jeremiah Owyang
Partner, Altimeter Group

YOUR BRAND
THE NEXT MEDIA COMPANY

How a Social Business Strategy Enables Better Content,
Smarter Marketing, and Deeper Customer Relationships

MICHAEL BRITO

Safari
Books Online

FREE
Online Edition

Your purchase of *Your Brand, The Next Media Company* includes access to a free online edition for 45 days through the **Safari Books Online** subscription service. Nearly every Que book is available online through **Safari Books Online**, along with thousands of books and videos from publishers such as Addison-Wesley Professional, Cisco Press, Exam Cram, IBM Press, O'Reilly Media, Prentice Hall, and Sams.

Safari Books Online is a digital library providing searchable, on-demand access to thousands of technology, digital media, and professional development books and videos from leading publishers. With one monthly or yearly subscription price, you get unlimited access to learning tools and information on topics including mobile app and software development, tips and tricks on using your favorite gadgets, networking, project management, graphic design, and much more.

Activate your FREE Online Edition at
informit.com/safarifree

STEP 1: Enter the coupon code: GQHMPEH.

STEP 2: New Safari users, complete the brief registration form.
Safari subscribers, just log in.

If you have difficulty registering on Safari or accessing the online edition,
please e-mail customer-service@safaribooksonline.com